Just Beyond Dreams: A True Life Odyssey

Copyright © 2018 by Jasmine Jibrael

All rights reserved. No part of this publication may be used, transmitted, stored in a retrieval system, or reproduced, in any form or by any means (electronic, mechanical, photocopying, recording, information storage, or otherwise) without prior permission in writing from the publisher. The only exception is for "fair use" as brief passages embodied in critical articles and reviews. The opinions and statements in this book are intended for the general spiritual welfare of the reader, and are not substitutes for professional and/or medical advice and should not be used as treatment for physical, emotional, or medical problems without the consultation of a licensed professional. In the event that you use any of the provided information for yourself, the author and publisher do not assume any responsibility for your actions.

All the names of the people involved in the experiences presented herein have been changed to protect their privacy.

Just Beyond Dreams Publishing
www.justbeyonddreams.com

ISBN: 9781719853880

Cover Lower Image courtesy of © Mark A. Garlick / markgarlick.com
Cover Water Ripple Image & Text © Catherine McManus
Moon Flower photo credit Lisa Gonzalez
Contributing Author & Microcosmic Mirror photo credit © Aimee' Jordan
With the deepest gratitude, Thank You to all Contributing Editors

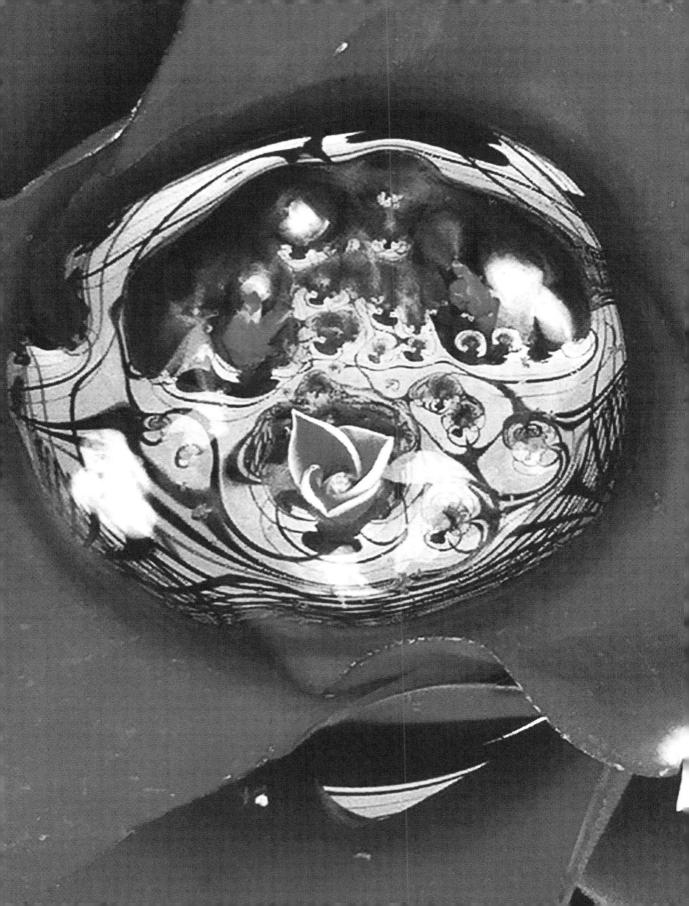

Table of Contents

Entrance..6-7
   {1} The Flower of Damascus..............................8-11
   {2} Sacred Rebellion and Allegiance..................12-19
   {3} Dream: Three Black Birds............................20-27
   {4} Tangible Jewels of Fruition..........................28-35
   {5} Trojan City...36-45
   {6} An Intruder in the Name of Truth..............46-61
   {7} Petals of Timely Connections......................62-73
   {8} Union with Halos and Horns.......................74-79
   {9} Eclipse of the Sun and Moon....................80-101
   {10} Unleashing of Medusa's Rumors............102-119
   {11} Dream: The Key and the Jewel...............120-127
   {12} The Chaos of Isis......................................128-137
   {13} Ascendency of the Queen........................138-149
   {14} Descent into Valley of Shadows..............150-159
   {15} The Forty Days and Forty Nights...........160-167
   {16} "My People"...168-177
   {17} Zenobia's Illustrious Golden Chains.......178-191
   {18} The Chariot of Revelation.......................192-205
   {19} The Telling of the Sacred Rose...............206-215
   {20} Dream: Old Friend...................................216-221
   {21} Sanctuary of Dreams...............................222-227
   {22} Shattered Palace......................................228-245
   {23} Surrender?...246-251
   {24} Ultimate Offering of Reality...................252-267
   {25} Truth's Miracle and Resurrection...........268-281
   {26} Wounded Healer.....................................282-287
   {27} The Legacy of the Soul............................288-295
Exit...296-297

Entrance

Something came knocking at the door, requesting four things: sacrifice, understanding, love for truth, and faith in something beyond the five senses. Upon opening the door, I discovered things I never believed. I am inviting you to take this journey, as every word was written just for you. An odyssey is a "long wandering voyage usually marked by many changes of fortune," and this story most definitely became that.

I will begin at the point of conception. I had no thoughts, interest, or desire to write a book of any sort. Life had other plans, as it does for so many of us. It all started with encouragement from someone to record certain foretelling dreams and their fine details. At first, I resisted even the notion, but then figured, "Why not? What is there to lose by simply writing down a few dreams?" I had no idea what this one small decision would entail, let alone the amount of time it would take. I surged forward, answering the call, knowing that others would find refuge within the pages.

The experiences shared in this odyssey transpired over a time span of twenty-five years. No matter if they appear dim or brightly shimmering, they are jewels. The course taken to inscribe these gems brought a roller coaster of exploration, unlocked numerous doors of greater knowledge, and swung the clockwork of time.

I am opening the door for you now. I want this narrative to pave the way for you to discover who and what you truly are. Trust in the process of life, be inspired by it, and transcend the suffering. Above all, my hope is you will gain a different perspective of what we call "reality."

Our mind is programmed to utilize the five senses that have been masked in fear and doubt. Our soul is forgotten, even when we are trying to connect to it. You will begin to understand, as our souls evolve, we ascend to our divinity. This is the key to the magic and true fulfillment of life.

The Flower of Damascus

The lens looked through is crystal clear and free of bias. I am not here to judge. I am not here to point fingers. Nor am I here for sympathy. These are simply truths retold in humility and understanding, with respect for all individuals involved. Everything you read here is true. There is no exaggeration or fabrication of personalities or events. The names of the people connected to the experiences have been changed to protect their privacy, including the person narrating it. The name Jasmine has always resonated, so I chose it as the first part of the pen name. The roots of the last name came from my grandfather, and when I saw it I immediately chose it without a second thought. I came to find the capital city of Syria, the country of my birth, is known for the jasmine flower. The name Jibrael (Jibra'il) is an Arabic form of archangel Gabriel, the messenger. These are the first of many synchronicities, and you will see more reveal themselves.

The vortex of chaos enveloped the soul. The truth of this world came to find me, both in the light and the dark. Nothing in my background prepared me for the path my journey would take. Without awareness or recognition, life accumulated into a series of testaments. Not until much later, did I connect the dots. **I realized the purpose was to reveal and share with others what is just beyond our dreams.**

This book had a snowball effect, taking over eight years to complete. It was painstaking and involved multiple sacrifices. Many people who know me personally, would describe me as a transparent yet private person in the same breath. Therefore, I wrestled deeply and was terribly uncomfortable with having to expose so much. I cannot express to you how much I did not want to write this book. However, I had no choice. My hands were pressed to the keyboard and I literally could not move them away. I went beyond personal comfort to serve a higher purpose, to serve you.

Everyone possesses the commonality of an internal compass, pointing us in the right direction. This is part of the true source, which we cannot see, but is both outside of us and within us. This is where things come to life, rather than lingering in the dream world. The true source allows us to transcend the ugliness, to find the beauty and grace in even the most bitter and difficult circumstances.

Within our beings are a soul and a mind. They are two aspects that typically have opposing views and responses to reality. In this book, we see their roles. They engage in debates that resemble how a person's conscious operates. The mind follows a wavelength of logic, whose reasoning is based on past experiences combined with the present reality being

faced. On the other hand, the soul searches for the truth to add to its growth from a collection of knowledge and wisdom gained from the beginning of time.

The soul wants to evolve, while the mind wants to stay in comfort. If the mind and soul could engage in actual dialogue, it would be something along the lines of...

The Mind asked the Soul, *"Why do you do this to me?"*

The Soul replied, "Why do you ask a question you already know the answer to? But to satisfy your desire for the mystery of life, I will let you in on a secret to its true meaning."

With a pause, the Soul continued, "There comes a time in one's life, when one needs to return to the basics—to the fundamental foundation of their being. You can question me for the rest of your existence, but you will never comprehend this true essence of life, or love for that matter. I come to you with an open heart. You come to me with closed doors. I have treasures for you to behold. I come to you with locked gates. You come to me with no key. But you cannot perceive what is beyond your limited senses. At times, you come close to me, but fear resides in your memory bank. The fear instilled in your cognition holds an unrelenting impulse to run, hide, and escape my grasp. But again, I will try to place your inabilities aside to unravel what you declined to follow..."

Sacred Rebellion and Allegiance

The soul can be described as an eternal aspect of one's being. The first alignment with the soul's yearning for evolution turned into a four-year venture. Something I knew little of, took the steering wheel of my life. Yet, it was the same thing that continued to carry me through this turbulent time. It acted as a north star in the night sky. I came to recognize it as **an inner knowing, that gut feeling we all have and experience. I discovered this to be the soul's voice.** It was always present, and kept getting stronger.

At the age of twenty-three, I began to feel as if I was physically shifting back and forth in time. It was a surreal and confusing experience. The days were filled with numerous moments, as though I lived them before. I came across people I thought I had seen previously, but was meeting for the first time. Somehow places that were new, seemed so familiar. I could not understand why these moments were happening routinely with such intensity. I started to collect, examine, and dissect the occurrences to make sense of them.

These déjà vus provided reassurance I was following the right path during the hardships of those four years. **Déjà vu is the sense of having already experienced something, which in reality is being encountered for the first time.** I learned any person, place, or object I connected to set off the unforgettable phenomena. As time went on, they became less powerful and visible. Despite this, living through things twice eventually caused frustration to be a dominant feeling. I wondered why nothing else in life was moving forward, and if these déjà vus were leading to something more.

As this déjà vu passageway opened, I also began to realize I had the life and future of someone else in my hands. This young Palestinian woman was a childhood neighbor named Fatima. After nine years, my parents returned to the states from Syria, moving back into a suburb of Cleveland. This is where I met Fatima, a relationship that became the first testament in this book, and cascaded into a greater awareness of the inner knowing.

Fatima lived one house over, on the top level of her uncle's house. You would think being the same age and living one house away from each other, Fatima and I would have formed a strong friendship. That was not the case. Somehow, we were kept apart, and the reason revealed itself many years later. Fatima was friends with my older sister who did not appreciate me around anyone she liked. The few times I did play with Fatima, it was not a positive experience. She introduced me to the word "jinn" which means evil spirit in Arabic. Fatima retold elaborate tales she heard from the many women who came over to visit, drink coffee, and gossip with her mother. One involved a jinn jumping into her cousin when she was in the shower. According to the women, the jinn was attracted to her body and decided to step in. Fatima was completely surrounded by and consumed with immense amounts of serious superstition. This was one of the differences in our upbringing.

Both ten years old at the time, Fatima brought me down to her basement and got me to watch my first horror movie. This was the last one I would see for over twenty years. It was her favorite genre and she spent hours viewing them. I observed her entranced by dark scenes, and her laughing at violent ones.

We had a chance to grow close around the age of eleven when my older sister started high school. However, Fatima entered a new phase in her life. She became infatuated with her Muslim religion. Instead of being the Syrian neighbor, I became the Christian-Syrian neighbor. Her anger grew for no apparent reason. One day I was walking through our neighborhood when Fatima caught sight of me. She immediately began yelling. I continued to stroll down the sidewalk, watching her erratic behavior. Fatima ran across the street and approached me. She saw no fear, and proceeded to shove me on the ground. I had not provoked her in any way, but the mere sight of me enraged her.

She slowly came out of this phase when we were in high school. At that time, her uncle moved to Florida, forcing her mother to move them to the other side of town. Her mother did not let her hang out with anyone who was not of the same culture, which were most of her high school friends. I was introverted, did not go out and party, and was Middle Eastern. Because of these factors, her mother trusted me. Therefore, I became the only person she could spend a lot of time with. We started forming a deeper bond, where she felt full acceptance of who she was.

As time progressed, both of our families moved away from the old neighborhood. By chance, our parents' new homes were a straight shot and less than fifteen minutes away from each other. The close relationship we developed in high school did not continue when I went away to college. We would connect sporadically during holidays when I returned to Cleveland, but on a superficial level. One morning, during the last winter break of college years, I woke up with a definite sense something was in the air. The impression lingered and strengthened throughout the day.

Later on that evening, I received a phone call from Fatima. Her chattering, smoky voice dramatically narrated stories about the numerous Palestinian weddings she attended. She spoke of the outlandish fights that broke out during receptions, which usually had over five-hundred attendees.

Fatima exclaimed, "All of a sudden, I saw a guy flying across the room, crashing into the tables! The old ladies started screaming! Some of the wives joined the fight too!"

I attentively listened on, as these visuals grew increasingly comical. One story of the wedding disasters included a man that caught her eye. When she described his big, sparkling blue eyes, the air shifted around me like the wind was changing course. Baffled by what I felt, I asked her to tell me more about him. As she went into greater detail about the encounter, I was trying to figure out why he seemed so familiar. I asked Fatima if something unique had taken place before she attended this particular wedding.

Amazed, she replied, "Yes, how did you know that?"

Fatima went on to tell me the full story about this wedding and how she did not want to go. She explained the aggravations that ran through her head a few hours before the wedding was to start. Thoughts about being a distantly related guest, the repetitive motions of the event, and the judgmental people that would be there, discouraged her. The requirement of having to pick out a dress, and to look a certain way that fit and appealed to her culture was another aspect she disliked. All of this contributed to her resistance in attending this wedding. An extraordinary experience changed her mind.

Fatima was cleaning her house, thinking about yet another wedding she was obligated to go to. She was distracted by these thoughts when she walked into the kitchen. Fatima reached for the cabinet handle to grab a metal pan. When Fatima closed the cabinet door, golden particles surrounded and encircled her entire head. These sparks followed her down the hall as she waved her hands, attempting to swat them away. The lights continued to follow her around, finally vanishing after several minutes. Without her awareness, these glimmering lights distracted Fatima long enough to forget the negative thoughts she had about attending the wedding. In addition, they lifted her out of the mood she was in. She decided to attend but was still unsure why.

The illuminations Fatima described are forms of angelic energy. These shimmering lights present themselves in shades of gold. The closest resemblance is a collection of glowing fireflies. It is almost as if you have to blink, because you are not sure if they are really there. **The golden sparks serve as comforting reminders of the angels' existence, validation, and, in this case, divine intervention.**

During the wedding, Fatima's cousin dragged her on the dance floor. Fatima described "something" telling her to glance to the left. As she turned, her eyes met the man with the big blue eyes. This was when an activation transpired. Nothing came of the encounter, but Fatima could not stop thinking about this stranger for several days and wondered if she would ever see him again.

The story of the blue-eyed man would be forgotten until this chilly winter evening, when she called to tell me about the numerous Palestinian weddings. As I listened to Fatima finish, my intuition and perception sharpened. I unexpectedly saw visions of each person she was sitting with at the wedding. I described their physical features and behaviors. She confirmed everything I revealed.

In astonishment, she spoke, "I can't believe you know all of this, when you weren't even there."

I had no clue how I did this, it just came so naturally. Too excited to understand how or why I could vividly picture everything as if I was present, Fatima returned to the subject of the man with the big blue eyes. I strongly sensed this was a special character in her life. I shared that with her, and this became the marker of our four-year venture.

What was an ordinary conversation with a unique occurrence, winded up producing spiritual, emotional, and mental challenges. For Fatima, it became a path of shedding environmental influences and discovering true confidence in herself. It became a balancing act of keeping Fatima afloat and myself centered with my career search. Her issues surfaced, and she could no longer hide from them. She felt unworthy of a good man and had very low standards of what she thought she deserved in life. Fatima's uncle was the only father figure she came to know. Her father had an affair, left, and later divorced her mother. He abandoned Fatima and her brother before she was four years old. Because of their culture, and due to her father leaving, Fatima fell under different, and ultimately lower expectations. Without a firm male father figure, a woman is thought to be more prone to becoming promiscuous. The chastity of females is the most defining status symbol of Middle Eastern women. Her low self-esteem led to self-destructive behaviors.

As Fatima and I became more interconnected, she trusted me beyond a shadow of a doubt. She took a trip to visit her uncle in Florida, which turned into an event where she feared for her life. During her stay, the uncle confiscated her phone when he found texts he did not approve of. Fatima's behavior was not just viewed as her own, but as a reflection of the entire family's reputation. Trapping her in a bedroom, he threatened to show her mother and brother the texts. Revealing this to her family would have extreme consequences, and possibly put her life in danger.

Fatima's cousin slipped a cell phone into the bedroom, so she could call me. She spoke nervously and quietly in fear of being caught using the phone. With utter dread, she explained what happened, and the dire situation she was in. As she was talking, I saw a vision of angels surrounding and protecting her. Along with seeing this, I had a strong feeling she was going to be home-free.

I took a deep breath and deciphered if what I saw was real, or if it was just what I wanted for Fatima. I was well aware of how emotionally charged and reactive her family was. Their beliefs controlled them, and they were perceived as the only right way. The circumstances were overwhelming, my mind could not deny that. However, I knew her uncle would not tell her mother and brother. Ultimately, she would return home safely. I shared the vision and feelings with Fatima. I reassured her she would be out of danger, even though it seemed like there was no way out. To my deep relief, this came to pass.

The angels were the shoulders I leaned on, and trusted. Even though we cannot see them or hear them with our five senses, they are a true-life form. They have existed since the beginning of time and transcend all religion. Angels are found under different names and personas but have the same characteristics. These spiritual beings have been consistently described as trustworthy and aiding.

Angels do not always appear with wings and harps as portrayed in paintings or figurines. Instead they take on many appearances and can be in many places at the same time. We each have assigned angels, who communicate at the soul level. Because of no physical evidence, we often shut them out. If we pay attention, they can communicate with us by means such as numbers or songs.

How could we think everything created in this world, is visible to our eyes? Before electricity was discovered, did we realize it existed? It took multiple people to learn separate pieces of the puzzle to develop the present day understanding of electricity. Prior to this profound discovery, it would have been thought of as make believe or even magic. **Both electricity and angels are energy, just different forms.**

The angels' vision and the strong feeling I had, guided and eased Fatima. When she arrived home safely, it reinforced this inner knowing was not imaginative, and confirmed it was concrete. With Fatima's hardships in hand, my own conditions worsened. It took me to new depths. The experience was like being on a boat out at sea. Suddenly, the waves would intensify and crash against the vessel. All I could do was let go of the wheel, hold on internally, and let the wind guide us. Throughout this journey, I would tear up from frustration and fear we would both drown. In all this, I relied on an inner knowing that had no tangibility, but felt solid as a rock.

Dream: Three Black Birds

This path to Fatima's love would take many winding roads. It felt like we were riding tidal waves at times, the boat was rocking, and I was being pulled in so many directions. I was a sounding board for Fatima's doubts, fears, and hardships. At this point, I had known Fatima for over fifteen years, but now found myself in a different role. While still a peer, I became a teacher. There was a strong sense of responsibility to help her as she struggled to navigate through the barriers of her upbringing.

Fatima described her mother as always teaching by fear. Her mother scared her about life, things she should be weary of, and how she should behave. In addition, Fatima became the outlet for her mother's overreactions and self-created stress. Her mother did not mean any intentional harm. It was in accordance with the behaviors she saw and went by for years and years. This mentality of Fatima's mother caused so much damage and continued the cycle of feeding into negativity. It became a place of comfort, what her mind recognized as normal, no matter how miserable it made her and her children.

There was one similar belief shared in both Fatima's culture and mine: the likelihood of marriage for a woman decreased after the age of twenty-four. Many of our family members often told us we were getting old, and time was running out to have children. Rooted in our cultures, these expectations placed pressure on Fatima and me. However, this was much more severe and real for Fatima. Her Palestinian background, and the extensively large community in the Cleveland area, tied her to their old way of thinking. Fatima's mother continually threatened to take her overseas to Palestine to arrange her marriage. The badgering about getting married was not limited to her mother. Numerous relatives constantly reminded her if she kept ignoring men's offers, they would stop asking for her hand in marriage. The fact that she was past her culture's age deadline made their predictions seem all the more likely.

It is essential to understand in Fatima's upbringing, marriage was everything for a girl. Thoughts of future proposals were in perspective even as a young child. Her perceived value, present and future, was based on this lifestyle. The judgment about marriage and her increasing age, was no longer limited to the elders. It started to include her age group. This persistent tension would ensue through the years of this journey, adding to its complexity.

Watching her much younger cousins getting married, Fatima ran to me with questions. Over and over, she asked, "How much longer, Jasmine? When is it going to happen? Did I delay it? Why is it taking so long?"

Anything can happen in a moments time. We can get in a car, drive the same route, and have a different experience. Something causes a delay or changes the timing, to intricately place you in line to meet someone. Your perception influences how you receive what is transpiring. A resistant or closed mind, prevents the natural flow of life.

The questions turned into disbelief of the inner knowing she was following. Doubtingly, Fatima stated, "I have to face the reality and stop living in this dream he will come. I have made myself believe I'm going to meet the blue-eyed man again. I'm going crazy from this. I can't do it anymore."

Fatima was getting marriage proposals from many men. Most of them older, some contemporary, but none seemed to be "the one." If I walked away from this role, she would accept one of the proposals to someone she simply tolerated. How could I keep encouraging Fatima to stay on course when I was fully aware, her chances for marriage were decreasing with each passing year? In addition, the ticking of time brought more complexities. After twenty-one years of separation, Fatima's mother decided to remarry her biological father. He was still married to the woman he left Fatima's mother for. It opened a can of worms. A family member slammed a chair on Fatima, threatening to kill her over his false belief she was sleeping with a man. I had no evidence, no proof her love would materialize, or that it even existed. It was only an inner knowing flowing through my being which reinforced this to be true.

Foretelling dreams replenished Fatima and I along the way, playing out like movies of mystery. Certain dreams are simply the mind reducing clutter, or subconscious material filtering through. Some other types of dreams can predict a future time. These dreams have a higher purpose and focus on soul related work. Called prophetic dreams, they involve a little extra dazzle. I found some contain pictures of places that exist, which the physical eye has not seen yet. By sharing a few of them in this book, you will see what I mean.

The first prophetic dream occurred on an ordinary day when Fatima and I decided to go to the gym, her place of employment. We met at my parent's house and as I waited in the driveway, she pulled up, parked on the street, and walked toward my car. I watched her shoulder-length brown hair, framing her heart-shaped face and square jawline, float in the wind. Something was shifting in the air again. Driving down a main road debating which gym location to go to, we approached a streetlight. One direction would lead us to a nearby branch, and the other would lead us to the location she worked at, which was further away.

Fatima pipped up and suddenly turned to me, saying, "Something is telling me we need to go to the gym where I work at."

I agreed, acknowledging, "Then we should follow that feeling."

I questioned each instruction she gave of this alternate route, but still went along with her directions. Local bars, grills, and small businesses lined the street where the gym was located. We passed a restaurant directly across from Fatima's work, which neither of us noticed before taking this unexplained, guided route.

With a mystified expression, I asked, "Fatima, what is that place over there with the iron gates?"

She answered, "I don't know. I've driven past here a hundred times, but I have never seen it before."

"Neither have I…Why don't we stop and take a look, before we work out?" I asked.

Nodding her head, she replied, "Why not?"

At the end of the restaurant strip, I turned left on a small one-way street, catching sight of a connecting parking lot behind the buildings. The air had been changing density ever since we stumbled upon this mysterious location. I pulled into the narrow drive and parked my car in the vacant lot. We walked around to the front entrance. There was an iron fence lining the perimeter of the restaurant. When we approached the gates, they were locked. I peeked through the heavy, metal bars and discovered something unexpected. There was a red brick pathway, surrounded by lush green trees and plants. The brick lined trail led to a Mediterranean-style ivory patio. The place felt secluded, hiding behind the wrought iron bars, like a secret garden. I ran my fingers over the cold gate, trying to feel the essence of this beautiful space. It was hard to believe a place like this existed here.

As I was entranced with the familiarity of the restaurant, Fatima was getting antsy. Though she agreed the restaurant was attractive, Fatima was uninterested in it. "Come on, let's go Jasmine."

I ignored her impatient words and responded, "No, I think I have seen this place before."

I thought to myself, *"But where?"*

I heard an inner response to my question saying, *"Dream."*

In a staggered manner, I said, "Fatima…I dreamt of this restaurant before…You were in it. The blue-eyed man from the wedding was also present…"

The moment I heard the word dream, it brought flashbacks, and the reason why this place was so familiar became clear.

In the dream, I appeared in front of the same iron gates. My eyes were drawn upward to a sign post painted with three, simple, jet-black birds.

The image sparked curiosity and I pondered, *"Where am I?"* and, *"What is this place?"*

The scene fast-forwarded to the gates opening wide, and a dark-haired young woman walking beside me. I later realized it was Fatima. While she kept moving down the brick path, I stopped in my tracks, pausing to take notice of a valet attendant.

A soft voice murmured, "He needs your words of wisdom and testament."

I took heed to the words, sensed he was struggling with life, and walked over to him. I reassured the valet attendant this was a temporary place, it will pass, and the sacrifices will be worth the end result. I could see from the expression on his face, he was puzzled as to why I was telling him this, but he carefully considered the message. Fatima's demanding voice drew my attention away from the valet attendant. She stood at the bottom of the steps which took one to the balcony area.

Again, I looked at him. "I have to go, but don't forget my words."

Hurrying to Fatima's side, we walked up the short staircase to find two men sitting uncomfortably across from one another. They both stood up, pulling out metal chairs for Fatima and me. My mind saw them as unfamiliar, while my soul recognized them.

I gazed at Fatima embracing one of the men who had big blue eyes. As I kept trying to remember where I had seen him, a touch from the other man curtailed these thoughts. I turned in the direction of his touch. He was tall with dark hair, olive skin, and chocolate-brown eyes, waiting patiently for my eyes to meet his.

After recalling the vivid dream, I told Fatima the details of the story. The blue-eyed gentleman was the same man from the wedding.

Amazed by the description I gave, Fatima questioned how I remembered everything so clearly and intensely.

I replied, "I don't know. I have always been able to do that with people, places, and dreams."

This uncanny ability to recall memories began at an early age. However, if you ask me to remember a person's name, forget it. With the dream in mind, I peered through the iron gates again to compare the reality in front of me to that of the dream.

I stated, "There should be a valet attendant here."

"What are you talking about, Jasmine?" She examined the entire area, "I don't see anyone."

"I know, I don't see any signs of anyone either, but I'm telling you, they have valet service."

Fatima shrugged off the whole experience and she briskly said, "Umm…Okay. Well, we need to go work out."

That was that. We did not linger or discuss it any further. Three weeks later, Fatima called me ecstatic. She went back to the restaurant and saw the valet attendant standing at the gate. Her phone call was confirmation the dream matched reality. I too was curious about the place. I discovered the grand opening of the restaurant was the exact same month and year I had the dream. I frequented, not only for the scenery, but in hopes of a conclusion to this journey with Fatima. I thought the swirling of the fiery-colored leaves at the end of the dream meant she would meet him in autumn. I visited the restaurant many times, until no leaves were left to fall. While the visits gave us a sense of light at the end of the tunnel, the falling of the last leaf crushed me. It sent me to new depths of disappointment. With a fading glimmer in my eyes, I looked at the empty, grey branches and dark shadows of the trees. I shook my head side to side, as my inner light dimmed further. I grasped the cold iron gates one last time, looking in the direction of the three black birds sign.

Even though the gym Fatima worked at was further away from my parent's house, I kept going there. One winter day, with the wind whistling through the naked branches of the trees, I was stopped at the intersection between the gym and restaurant. I had every intention of turning left but felt a strong urge to return to the parking lot behind the restaurant. All I wanted to do was work out, and before I knew it, I was parked across the street. Realistically, I could not figure out how I ended up there. Not only was it cold and windy, the temperature was frigid. My mind was confused, but I somehow knew this was the last fateful visit to the iron gates for the year, and there was no way around it. Approaching the entrance, I finally saw the valet attendant from the dream with my own eyes. At that moment, I knew the significance and purpose for this place passed. I recognized the dream held accuracy, just not in the way perceived. The valet was the beginning and the ending. The dream instilled a level of patience I never thought I could achieve, and gave Fatima proof. I stopped counting the months since the onset of these trials, keeping the inner knowing close and the ultimate goal of Fatima aligning with her love even closer.

I recalled three dreams between the ages of sixteen and twenty-one, which held the tall dark-featured stranger, and the blue-eyed man. The prophetic dreams kept us going during this time period, which turned from months to years. I never wrote anything down, however, these dreams were so realistic and profound I inscribed a few remarks about them. I placed the thoughts in an untouched journal purchased seven years prior. On a regular trip to a large store chain, I found it in a picked over, dusty section. The journal was unlike any other. The cover was a light midnight blue, with touches of purple and magenta, resembling a picture of the universe. On top of this beautiful background were patterns of different star constellations. After I scribbled down a paragraph, I closed the flap and to my surprise, noticed the binding stated it was a dream journal. It was not a coincidence.

Through dream experiences, I found there are different types of prophetic dreams. Prophetic dreams of reality are about seeing the future. The Three Birds dream just described is a clear example of this type. Having this dream and eventually seeing the place in reality, revived Fatima's confidence in the inner knowing we were following. Many of you have also had dreams in which you experienced or saw a glimpse into the future. In these dreams, you see a person, place, or event that eventually comes into fruition. Sometimes you meet someone and have a feeling of déjà vu. This could have been someone you were meant to meet and saw previously in a dream, and now the encounter manifested.

Dreams of reconciliation may come in two different forms. The first is when a person, who passed, comes to you in your dream to provide closure, or healing to an unresolved issue. Maybe you were unable to say goodbye before they left their body. Perhaps there was a disagreement with a parent, or a childhood event where they may simply come to ask, or offer forgiveness. You may also have a vivid dream that will provide you comfort, knowing your loved one is at peace, or still existing on an ethereal plane.

The second form of reconciliation dreams contain a person who is still alive. They visit you when their subconscious bypasses their conscious ego. The subconscious involves more of what someone is truly experiencing. Often times, the person's conscious ego simply cannot express the things they know they should. Even the simplest of words, such as an apology, are too much for some people to share. **These dreams help heal connections, draw people together, and open doorways of communication in the present moment.**

The last prophetic dream type are dreams of manifestation. These dreams entail hopes we have for the future regarding our careers, relationships, families, and/or desires. This could include places you wish to travel. Perhaps, many times you dreamt about being in a certain place. There is a reason for that. In reality, you may be meant to visit and have a transforming experience. This is the product of your soul guiding you. Eventually, these manifestation dreams conjure our desires and wishes into reality.

Prophetic dreams have a different essence to them: A realness, and a distinct clarity. **They leave you feeling as though you have gained something from them. They are indicators, subconscious navigators of our soul's calling. Discerning the morsels of truth within these dreams provide you with validation of your gut feelings. Prophetic dreams pave the way to discovering who you really are. Live with your dreams, not in your dreams.**

Tangible Jewels of Fruition

The pomegranate, an autumn delicacy, is considered the fruit of the mythological Greek gods. The outer shell of this fruit conceals the beauty of the core. Once opened, the interior exposes shimmering red seeds, which bear a resemblance to rubies. What makes pomegranates even more satisfying is the process it takes to unravel the red jewels. You carefully slice through the thickness of the skin and with just the right amount of pressure you crack it open, delicately remove the jewels, avoiding the staining of the tangy juice. **This tedious, but satisfying process of preparing to enjoy this delicious fruit is symbolic of truth. The truth does not always come in a beautiful box. It must be searched for and once found, one must peel off the outer layers to reveal the true core.**

After the winter break in Cleveland, I returned to Columbus to finish the last quarter of college. While Cleveland has a tremendous amount of diversity, the cultures are segregated. In the city of Columbus, the cultural diversity is much more interlaced. Through acquaintances including Indians, Turks, Latinos, Greeks, South Pacific Islanders, and other Arab nationalities, I experienced different backgrounds. Each ethnic group taught me about their culture, and confirmed my knowing, we are all basically the same. Columbus is home to one of the largest universities in the nation and many would say it is a place of testing. This was true for me. I arrived with no close friendships and came from a disadvantaged household. Personal support was scarce and responsibility for my own finances, education, and living expenses laid solely in my hands.

Working lengthy, demanding shifts, I still partook in the journey with Fatima. Two months had passed since the unraveling of Fatima's encounter with the blue-eyed man at the wedding. One night, Fatima called. During the conversation, she had an abrupt inner insight I saw the second gentleman from the Three Birds dream in reality. Much to my amazement, she began to accurately describe the bar setting of where he appeared and how I felt about being there. Without any effort, I was suddenly able to fill in the rest of the story. At this moment while Fatima was talking, I accessed a past memory where Grace, my cousin and roommate was present. Reliving a previous night out with her at a lounge, I remembered meeting a man's gaze. I automatically scanned him with my eyes, from head to toe. He had dark-brown hair with a light wave, and medium toned skin. Wearing a navy-blue sweater, he stood with his hands in his pockets. This was the only portion of the memory I recalled. When Grace arrived home, I shared with her the flashback of this event. We both could not remember where we were that night. For some reason the location was blocked from us.

A few months passed, and Grace called me to excitedly explain her morning. She decided to take a different route to work that day. Driving down a busy one-way street, she came to a red light which took much longer than usual. Grace went on to tell how she suddenly had a strong urge to turn her head to the left, where she caught sight of the corner lounge. She recalled the time her and I met up with a group of Persian men there. It was the only time we were at this particular lounge.

The memories began to rush back to me. The conversation with Grace solidified the location and setting where I saw that navy sweater man. Flashes of that unusual night returned, and the rest of the details came together. My irritation with the environment at the lounge hastened my departure. I turned the corner at the end of a dimly lit hallway with Grace following right behind me. I entered a narrow pathway created by a wall to my right and a large, oak bar to my left. I quickened my steps to be halted by a familiar face standing next to the bar. It was a friend of Grace. Although I was on a mission to leave, this friend and I spoke for about thirty minutes. Ready to go again, I nudged Grace's arm with mine to give her the signal to leave. She nodded in agreement and started to walk behind me once more.

Moving forward through the crowd, I suddenly felt Grace was not near me. I turned to look back for her, and found her speaking with that same friend. I knew she was safe in his company and swung back around to continue my mission to the door. I took three steps forward, and was abruptly stopped by something. I hit an invisible wall. Next, two strong unseen hands grabbed my shoulders, propelling my entire body to spin in the opposite direction. I was thrown off-balance in my heels but regained my footing. Directly in line was the dark-haired man, standing hands in his pockets. A long-legged, blonde woman stood in front of him. I thought to myself how lucky this woman was, and how it would be a dream to be with someone like that.

This real-life man was the exact dark-featured male who appeared in all of those prophetic dreams. When I spoke to Fatima again, we revisited those moments with the blue-eyed man at the wedding, along with the memories at the lounge with Grace. This was tangible evidence. We were amazed, and unbeknownst to me, this would begin a journey where inner knowing guided the way.

I returned to Cleveland after hitting a dead end in my Columbus job search. Throughout the four-year time period, I asked myself many times what we stumbled into. I questioned whether it was wrong for me to usher Fatima to this path. As time went on, the few prophetic dreams and angelic golden lights seemed further and further away. Staring out the bedroom window, I called out for a sign, a whisper, but received only silence. Yet in this stillness, I knew deep inside everything would be okay, it would somehow all work out. This knowing became my sign and my whisper.

Each and every time we hit a roadblock, I pulled Fatima out of the darkness of fear, and back to the light. However, my foundations shook as I recognized a life was in my hands. This was unknown territory for the both of us. Fatima aligning with her love seemed out of reach. We had to continue forward. There was someone destined out there for Fatima and we both knew it.

As this was going on, I encouraged Fatima to enroll back in college courses, finish her degree, and make something more of her life than marriage. As much as she wanted more than what her culture imposed on her, she wanted the easy way out, and that was through getting engaged. I explained to Fatima, whether you get married today or five years from now, your relatives and cultural community will move on to something new to trouble you about. Fatima could not deny this as fact. From the numerous Palestinian marriages, she saw with her own eyes this happen repeatedly. The cycle would go from marriage to when are you going to have children. There was no need to rush, or settle on this significant part of her life.

We unpacked the years of trauma Fatima experienced, and rewired her negative way of thinking. There were countless hard days, with very few days of inspiration. With each passing year, Fatima would reminisce about the foretelling dreams, the many challenges we went through, and were still experiencing.

Fatima would always say, "And we still have our sanity."

I would laugh and nod my head in agreement at such an accurate statement. Laughter was the precious remedy to those weighed-down moments. So instead of taking Fatima's dramatic freak-outs seriously, I just laughed at her antics which in turn, made her laugh.

"Oh my God, Jasmine! We are turning twenty-five in less than thirty days!" I watched Fatima place two of her fingers on her neck.

With a questioning look, I asked, "Fatima, what are you doing?"

"I am checking my pulse!"

Expecting a sympathetic response from me, she received laughter instead. With a smile, she remarked, "I know I'm crazy."

The gym Fatima worked at was undergoing major renovations and was relocated to a temporary site. It was such a small space that she was often scheduled to close alone. I sometimes would keep her company for the last two hours. As she went to clean equipment in a separate room, I sat behind the front desk and watched over everything. On one of these nights, something drew my attention away from reading a magazine and up toward the wall which held a doorway connecting the two rooms. I watched a six-foot-two-man step in the room, swinging his shoulder-length, wavy brown hair off his face, like some breeze existed around him. He strolled through with his broad shoulders and huge chest puffed up, ready for a photo shoot. I wondered to myself who he reminded me of. Suddenly, Fatima came from behind him, greeted him with a friendly smile, and that was when it hit me.

I exclaimed out loud, "Palestinian Fabio!"

Surprised by my outburst, Fatima turned to see my lit-up face. She then looked at the gigantic statue of a man next to her, brushing his hair off his face again.

"OH MY GOD, Jasmine!!! He does look like a Palestinian Fabio! Man, you always come up with the best stuff!"

Fatima, the Fabio man himself, and I were in tears from laughter.

When his friend came into the room, he asked, "What are you guys laughing about??"

None of us could stop laughing to give him an answer. **Laughter is a universal language for everyone, from all cultures.**

While the laughter eased the stress and discomfort through the years, no man appeared for Fatima. I listened to my intuition, it never led me astray. However, after almost three years, intuition was not enough. This is when faith takes over. When faith is spoken of in this book, it is not of religious belief. It embodies a confidence and trust in the inner knowing which is emitted from the soul. **A knowing, everything works out as it is meant to be. Everyone is born with a certain amount of faith. It either develops or diminishes throughout life.** In the midst of these trying times, faith was the weapon for defeating fears. Many times, this faith involved persuading the mind to agree to what the soul declared. The mind rationalized taking the journey with Fatima was an illogical venture. The harsh reality and obstacles proved it accordingly. Nevertheless, the soul affirmed the genuineness of the task in the form of an inner knowing.

Some days I reached out to a higher place. Other days I blocked out the whole matter, and saw only a bleak future ahead for the both of us. Maybe the numerous times I came close to surrendering, were the times I grew? I do not know. All I knew was Fatima was going to somehow, someway meet her love, and that was enough for me to survive and continue. Fatima, on the other hand, was not so easily sustained in the quest. This situation caused a reaction in her. She called me one day to confess she had gone to visit a "psychic."

Fatima requested, "Promise me you won't judge me if I tell you something."

I answered, "Have I ever judged you on anything you have told me?"

"No, but you might be disappointed in me. I ignored everything you taught me. Three days ago, I went shopping because I ran out of perfume. When I was walking through the mall, this random lady approached me. She started telling me about my future husband and what he looked like. It matched everything you told me. Then she told me I had a curse over me and she could remove it."

My voice rang of disappointment for a childhood friend who would take three steps forward, only to move five steps back. "Fatima…"

"I know Jasmine, but this challenge or whatever you call it, has made me go crazy. She gave me proof of something real."

"I understand why you went to the psychic. It has been three years since I started us on this. I can't expect you not to break down."

If I knew it was going to take so long, I would have never begun this testing voyage.

Fatima asked, "So can you tell me the truth and make me feel better!? I don't have a curse over me, right??"

"Of course not, Fatima. She just picked up on a couple of true things, saw your belief, and took advantage of you. It happens to many people. Will you please do me a favor?"

"Sure," she responded.

With a sincere voice, I pronounced, "Stop believing in those things."

There is something one must understand about a person's ability to predict the future. Except for certain predestined occurrences and people, everything is in a state of limbo. Picture your life as a map. **X marks the spot of your truth, the hidden treasure.** Different paths can be taken to arrive at this destination. One is treacherous, which would take courage to travel. Another may appear to be a short-cut with an easy terrain. The first one offers growth opportunities, self-discovery, and eventual empowerment. The latter provides illusions of comfort, the quicksand of reality, and empty pleasures. While this might seem to be the easier trail to the mind, the soul will be compromised. This comfortable route can eventually develop into a journey of emptiness, where hunger for happiness and fulfillment may never be satisfied. **The desire of the mind creates mirages of truth, a hallucination of what you want to believe.**

Whatever path you choose, things almost change by the minute, depending on your decisions, growth, and state of mind. We have free will, so we have the power to change and influence many things in our lives, even when "psychic" predictions are made. I never blamed Fatima for questioning and doubting the possible outcomes and what we were following. The inner knowing was within and still beyond us, while all around reality was slapping us across the face.

Nevertheless, in all honesty, Fatima created most of her hardships. Even in her mid-twenties, Fatima's mother was strict and treated us like wild teenagers. After convincing her mother to agree to a daytime outing, Fatima would push her buttons. When I would arrive at Fatima's house, her mother would ask, "Where are you going?"

Fatima would reply, "To meet our boyfriends, MOM!"

Those words sent her mom into aberration of deranged yelling.

I would ask Fatima, "Why would you say that, after it took so long for her to say yes? You knew it would infuriate her."

I never got a response. Just a shrug of her shoulders.

The years continued to develop into a series of learning lessons for Fatima. For instance, I warned her to be careful what she wished for, as she could eventually create it. To manifest means to bring into existence, or to make things come to fruition. It is like an antenna, a device that receives radio-frequency signals, and transmits them to electrical signals. It simultaneously reverses this process. An antenna is not just a simple wire, just as we are not solely a body. Both are loops that create. **What we believe, positive or negative, is what will be drawn to us and converted into our life.**

You attract not just what you think about, but what you talk about. Fatima would constantly talk about how she wanted a "real man." She characterized this figure using what she perceived as attractive from her cultural surroundings. She and I grew up with similar types of men. Many of them had fiery tempers, huge egos, and walked around overly macho. In the face of these male role-models whom Fatima referred to as "real men," I found self-worth, while she lost self-worth. I learned on my own not to tolerate any of their chauvinistic behavior, whereas she accepted it as normal and something she must live with. **We can either grow from, or conform to our environmental experiences.** I continued to tell Fatima she deserved better than the image embedded in her mind.

After waiting nearly four years, Fatima met her love. What was the problem? He did not match the blue-eyed man in my dreams or from her wedding encounter. It is difficult when the end result is not exactly what you anticipated. **Just because something does not come in a form we expect, does not mean it should be neglected or bypassed.** I came to understand things such as prophetic dreams, get us where we need to be. The rest is in our hands to mold.

Soon after, this man asked for her hand in marriage, Fatima accepted his proposal. I hoped Fatima would come to see, she always had what she long awaited for. Everything was inside of her. **When we find true love, the fulfillment and gratification depend on us. The only person who has control over your feelings, is you.** They are your internal response, to the world around you. **When you rely on someone else to fill your voids, it is always a temporary fix. For it to be permanent, the key is to find resolution within yourself.**

I thought I would reach some sort of enlightenment when Fatima found her love. Yet, it felt as though I just finished a job. It was bittersweet. How could one be disappointed after devoting so much time and energy? If you take a step back, and look at the bigger picture, you are fulfilling something greater. This experience became the first testament of many to come. I stayed the course of the highs and lows of the four-year journey, and now, I did not know what was next.

The Trojan City

Within our minds, there is usually a hindrance to recognizing the enchantment of life. The wonders are often disguised because we are caught up in the fear, the stress, the heaviness of living. There are thousands of stories which help us escape from our sometimes gloomy reality. They tell of magical tales, infinite possibilities, and remind us of our childhood dreams. They go under different names such as myths and legends. What happens when something out of the ordinary, like you find in these tales, occurs in adulthood? Do we rationalize and just shrug it off? The testaments shared in this book hold what so many of you have experienced, but possibly took little notice of, or thought it was just your imagination.

When attempting to name some of these chapters terms would come to me that represented real legends, myths, and stories. I allowed the soul to determine the name of this chapter, and several of the ones following. As the ideas came, I realized I was not completely familiar with the legendary stories. After researching them, my mind saw the correlation. Connections between the fictional legends and the nonfiction chapters written here were dazzling. This confirmed these stories should be inserted for anyone who might not know them.

The tale of the Trojan War was an engagement between Troy and Greece. During this conflict, the battles lasted more than ten years until the Greek army conjured up an idea to trick the Trojans. They built a huge wooden horse and hollowed it, enabling their soldiers to hide on the inside. The Greeks left the horse outside the gates of Troy, presenting it as a deceiving gift for winning. There was much discussion between the Trojan soldiers, and warning against the entry of the horse from the Trojan king's daughter. Not wanting to displease the Greek goddess Athena, the Trojans pulled the horse into the city. When the sun went down and the sky was completely dark, the Greek soldiers, with Odysseus as their leader, exited the gigantic horse and infiltrated Troy, taking the victory. After the triumph, the Greeks slowly returned home, with Odysseus's venture back taking ten years. The journey about the many delays and tribulations he encountered is retold in classic tale *The Odyssey*. This epic reflects what happened in the city of Cleveland and the nine years it took for this book to come to fruition.

For two years, I attended a liberal arts college smaller than my high school. I enrolled in this college, grateful to be granted an almost full academic scholarship. It is consistently listed as a top ranked college, attracting many students from D.C., Boston, and the east coast. Nevertheless, it fostered isolation. Many of the two-thousand residents drank to excess and retreated to their own private worlds. Far from any major city, many students grew restless.

At the end of the second year, I transferred from this small private school to one of the largest universities in the United States located in Columbus, Ohio. The transition was seamless, but the financial consequence brought challenges. I lost the scholarship that covered nearly the entire tuition. With all of my siblings attending college, the financial strain increased immensely. Daily, my parents worked long hours to support a family of seven. Mindful of their tireless effort, I did not ask for, or accept money offered by them. I did not want to take more from them. Navigating through these circumstances brought me to a financial aid officer at the university.

I asked, "You're telling me with four other siblings in college, you can only give me this much financial aid?"

"Yes," the officer apathetically answered.

I left disheartened and frustrated. I knew there were more resources and actions the financial aid officer could have taken. The weight of uncertainty was on my shoulders, wondering how I was going to survive. I could not fathom becoming a financial burden to my parents. When I got into the elevator, I could no longer hold back. I walked outside in tears and was met with angelic golden sparks. In those very moments, my crying eased, and my heart calmed. At this time, I was employed at two catering companies, one was a temporary agency and the other an event hall. I took action by picking up as many hours as possible. Pushing myself to the limit, I worked an equivalent of full-time at these positions with a full course load. On top of that, I was focused on building my resume, so I took on an unpaid internship. The fourteen-hour shifts, and heavy lifting took a toll on me physically, at times causing shocking pains to flow up and down my lower back. The academic demands at a top-rated business school pushed my ability to concentrate. Life was a juggling act.

My soul found solace in Grace, my cousin and roommate. Her chosen pen name suites her just right, and her doey brown eyes reflect her soft-tempered demeanor. Despite the fact I knew her since childhood, we were not close prior to becoming college roommates. My eldest sister kept a wall between Grace and me. Again, much like Fatima, this prevented a bond from forming until the time was right. Grace grew up with four brothers and was the only girl. I became the sister she never had, and she became the kind of sister I never had. We attended classes separately, but we coordinated schedules to work the same shifts as she was the only one with a car. We cooked for each other and made sure we both had what we needed. Grace and I went out together and both loved to dance. Where you found one of us, you found the other. Our time together was always lighthearted, no matter the heaviness of life. The love we shared made us feel invincible.

Two years into being roommates, Grace moved back to Cleveland. Soon after, she left for a three-month trip to Syria with her mother. She was no longer living with me and the few remaining acquaintances disappeared as well. The circumstances of their lives shifted to romantic relationships or their old network of friends.

After graduation, there were still three months left on the lease. This period of time involved nothing but work, applying for jobs in the Columbus area, and coming home to an empty apartment. I worked very diligently to graduate in those four years, taking summer classes to make up for the credits lost. All this time of hard labor to finally reach the point of getting a career job, and it was not happening. I could not make sense of it. When the lease expired and after hitting dead ends with the job search, the only door left to open led back to Cleveland, my hometown. I was beaten down emotionally and physically, it was like crawling back home.

In college, there was a goal, a finish line. I made it across to meet a bare desert field. In Cleveland, the pressures only increased. Student loans were going to take effect in three months, the expectations of parents were being imposed as I lived under their roof, and there was no longer Grace or anyone else. With less than three-hundred dollars in the bank, my survival options were limited. My degree in Operations Management from one of the top ten business schools in the nation was insignificant. At the end of the day, I did what I had to do. I took the first job offer, which was working at a retail store making half of what I made in college. With my spare time I spent what felt like never-ending hours searching for career opportunities, applying online, and physically taking my resume to prospective employers.

The retail shop was a store for undergarments and placed me in intimate scenarios. I wrapped a tape measure around the bust of women, had to size people's body, and gave opinions on these very personal subjects when asked. I listened tentatively to their body image issues, hearing firsthand the many reasons for breast augmentation. I witnessed several cases that went wrong, and was saddened to see their deep effects. At times while working at this job, I felt the universe was playing a trick on me. It was barley keeping me financially afloat. Nonetheless, I chose to accept, remind myself this is a temporary place, and make the best of the cards dealt. **A job is a paradigm of temporary truth: whether chosen or forced, work circumstances change. Temporary truth resides in the current state, but is in constant motion. It fluctuates with our growth, state of mind, and choices**.

There was a recognition, if I allowed the frustration or disappointment to take hold, it would deprive me of truly feeling alive. So, I looked at the higher purpose of being there as one person helping another feel more confident. **Many times, the mind feels powerless, and unable to influence events and circumstances. Our blinders come on and our view becomes limited. Even when an opportunity presents itself, our perspective is so narrow, we do not see it. Find and return to your purpose.** That divine connection will be the extra charge needed to drive you forward. It keeps the blinders off, allowing opportunities to be perceived. Even though we may justify our feelings because of situations and factors dealt with, we have the power to change and are the architects of our reality. When the soul and the physical mind are unified, the blueprint is clear, and so is the path.

During this retail job, besides a strong will and steady attitude, there was an interesting experience that kept me going. I was rotated from working the floor to the cashier position.

I stood behind the counter, ringing customers out when suddenly I heard a soft whisper-like inner voice communicate, *"Look to your left into the adjacent room."*

My eyes met an older Hispanic woman's presence. She seemed to be staring at nothing but listening to something.

The inner voice gave insight, *"You caught her intently examining you. She had to glance away. She was surprised you knew she was looking at you and that you turned to find her."*

I shrugged off the feeling, rationalized she was just scanning the products, and continued ringing. There was one line in front of the white checkout counter, which split to three cashier stations. The Hispanic woman funneled through, landing at my register. She handed me her items and began to speak in Spanish.

I said, "Ma'am, I can't really understand what you are saying. Can you please speak in English?"

She replied in Spanish, something along the lines of needing help.

"I don't speak Spanish," I replied. "I'm sorry."

After still not getting the English response, I paused for a few moments, and found myself struggling to formulate an answer in Spanish. In my mind, I went back to my high school Spanish class. I knew she was going to continue, so I pushed myself harder to respond in complete Spanish. I was still struggling. She motioned for me to come with her. I left the register and walked with her to the perfume room. In front of the stacked spray bottles, we were suddenly, almost effortlessly, conversing in Spanish. This experience went beyond rudimentary memories of Spanish from the classroom. The words flowed without thought of conjugation. This was proof, we can transcend our own limitations.

After answering her questions about the cost of the different varieties, we went back to the register and I finished ringing her up. When I handed her the bag, she suddenly switched to English saying, "I knew you could speak Spanish!"

Surprised, I replied, "How did you know that?..."

The woman shifted her eyes away from mine, shrugged her shoulders, and walked out of the store. How did the Hispanic woman know something about me that I did not even know about myself? There is more to life than this reality, more than what we may perceive on the surface.

We all have similar abilities; some people are just more in touch with them. For example, let us look at what I call the unspoken word and environmental energy. Imagine you are in a room with a group of five people. You walk out for fifteen minutes. When you return, you somehow know they were talking about you. Even though you were not physically present, and no one showed any real evidence they were speaking about you, how did you know? The answer is the **unspoken word**, a form of sensory beyond the five senses. **Another sensory we have access to is environmental energy.** You walk into an area where to the human eye you are visibly alone. Yet, your body gives you cues such as chills, hair standing up on your neck, or a gut/stomach reaction, that tell you something different. The environmental energy is giving you a definite sense you are not really alone. Both scenarios show **everyone has an extra sensorium of sorts: the quality of being able to perceive and discern other people, things, or situations.**

While working part time at the retail store, months went by with no sign of finding an actual career. I re-evaluated everything possible. Did I start early enough? Does my resume need more revision? Did I send out enough copies of the resume? Do I know anyone else who can help? The analysis and second-guessing went around and around in my head in attempt to see what I could do or change. Even so, the feeling inside told me I had done everything I could, had the right resume format and words, contacted the right people, and spent enough time doing so. Reality showed me otherwise. My mind kept thinking and pushing. My soul weathered the storm with a knowing the right career opportunity would arrive.

In those energy depleting thirteen months, I was back to my early teenager self. The girl who was "simply not good enough." I took my eldest sister's advice to build my college resume with extracurricular activities and sports. I drove myself to try out for the dance, flag corps, basketball, and softball teams. My parents did not have the finances to enroll me in sports or activities. Consequently, I went into tryouts with no experience or acquired skills to apply to any of them. I received one rejection after another.

I would call my mother from the high school office phone to come pick me up. I sat outside the building below the Johnny Appleseed 3D portrait. It pictured a blonde man on his knees planting seeds, surrounded by apple trees. As I waited, thoughts of failure and insignificance took over my mind. I brushed the tears away as I watched my mother's grey van pull up to the curb. On the drive home, tears would surface again. My mother's reaction was like a candle snuffer, putting out a flame. When I walked into the house, my family offered very little support, or comfort.

From these teenage let downs, feelings of inadequacy and unworthiness arose. It affected me on a deeper level, even then, my purpose in life weighed heavy. This led me to think of myself as a person who had nothing of value to provide the world. There was a light inside that could not be extinguished. I needed to change the focus from discouragement to determination. Current challenges ever present, I switched to a true passion, helping and serving others. I began to pour myself into hundreds of volunteer hours. At fifteen years old, I cooked meals for a children's hospital, organized activities for nursing home residents, and participated in fundraisers. This brought a sense of fulfillment and shifted my sentiment. I also joined the newly formed Rugby athletic team, which paved the way for my two younger sisters to be interested and play as well. **Through resilience, you can harness your power, redirect the feelings, and have a better experience.**

You can play one of two roles in creating your reality; a victim or a champion. The script of the victim portrays a person focused on the shortcomings of their life. They ask, "Why me?" "What have I done wrong?" Or "How do I deserve this?" This individual chooses to view their situation as defeating, rather than as an opportunity for development. In contrast, the champion's narrative depicts a person determined to overcome the limitations and/or hardships presented. Their will creates a character of "I can," "There is a way," and "What actions do I need to take?" This person hones in on their desires and assesses the circumstances. Instead of viewing the wall as an obstacle to get past, a champion finds a way to climb over it.

I got through the teenage challenges, but now at the age of twenty-two was somehow brought back to that lower state of being. As a child, we are not worried about what the outcome is going to be. As a teen, we switch gears to an internal survival mode and start losing the liberties of being a child. Our child-like essence, where there is thrill in the unknown or everything is an adventure, fades. Our peers, parents, and/or society has a stronger influence on our perception. Inevitably, when you are connecting more with the soul, you are forced to revisit anything unresolved from the past years.

In the bathroom of my parents' house looking in the mirror, viewing that discouraged fifteen-year-old again, brought back the tears of self-doubt. I tried to tame them, but it was slow coming. Countless days dragged on with complete idleness, while other days brought a glance of greenery to this desolate career search. It felt like I took a major step back, and a wrong turn somewhere, hitting one dead end after another. In the thick of it, the pulsating inner knowing would surface, reminding something would come along.

My parents set off on a job campaign for me as their way of helping. They owned a small grocery store, so they asked nearly every customer where they worked and if they "could get their daughter a job." My parents would return home sharing their stories about potential "real" jobs. I smiled, shook my head, and calmly told them to stop. I explained I would find a career in my field on my own. This tactic did not halt my parent's crusade.

If I was not beating myself up enough, my mother's criticism added to the heavy load. She would say things such as, "Look at your cousin. He went almost a whole year without a job. You don't want that to happen to you! You might have to go back to school. You can't go on like this! What are you going to do?? Maybe you shouldn't have majored in business. Why didn't you just go into the medical field?"

My mother's fear reached a high when she tried to force me to work as an assistant manager at a bar owned by a distant cousin. The idea entailed working under a relative who severely mistreated his employees. No matter what kind of job, I always gave it my all. From washing dishes at a restaurant at the age of fourteen to cleaning up after wedding receptions, my work ethic was the same. This fit the mold for the distant cousin to take advantage. My brother, Nabeel, worked like a dog for him. During a night shift, Nabeel approached him, bringing up a long-standing issue. This relative told him to leave and refused to pay him for the last two weeks of work. After rejecting my mother's proposal, she tried a different angle. She brought up the fact he could pay me more than I was currently making.

I firmly asserted, "I do not care how much he can pay."

Frequently, I would reassure her a career opportunity would be found.

In a dismissive manner, my mother answered back, "You have been saying this to me for over a year. Where is this job you talk of?? I don't see anything!"

I stayed quiet, and walked away. I had no proof to show her. There was only what the inner voice whispered, *"The job will come. It is only a matter of time."*

How much time? I did not know. I simply, with the soul, but not so simply with the mind, trusted the calling from within. The inner knowing.

I had my mother on one front and my father on the other. He made sure to remind me I was not as good as he expected. Even though I volunteered time at my parents' grocery store while working the retail position, I still was not up to his standards. My father was conventional, and held certain expectations of me. His feelings exploded when my car was being repaired. He provided the only transportation to work. The entire ride consisted of him ranting about how frustrating my life was, and how I was not making "good money." I was trapped in the car with no escape from his verbal lashing. I thanked God he did not know I was working at a lingerie store. It would have added fuel to the already blazing fire.

As I looked out the passenger window for some escape, I recalled my six-year-old self barefoot, inside my grandparents' barn in Syria. I stood at a distance in front of their wooden door. Above this door-frame was a semi-circle window, with curled iron bars. As the huge sun beam pierced through the gaps, the little girl stood under its spotlight. She watched the dust particles suspended in the air, intrigued. They seemed magical and reminiscent of something familiar. She lifted her arms wide to the side, imagining she could fly away from this place and return to sanctuary. This child found the closest, next best thing, nature. I retreated into the nearby orchards and woods for comfort, seeing divinity in every tree, rock, and plant. I roamed alone and gave thanks for this green palace.

During the drive to drop me off at the retail job, I was not surprised by my father's harshness. His actions merely echoed the past. He either sat on the couch watching TV, arguing with my mother, or whipping me. His chosen spot for punishment was the area behind the couch. I would stand against the back of the furniture prepared, but not scared. I can still clearly see my father biting his bottom right lip, as he unbuckled his belt and positioned himself for attack. Following procedure, I stretched out my hand. Not taking my eyes off the belt, I watched it fly up in the air and land heavily on my palm. To lessen the physical pain, I alternated hands. Sometimes he would not allow me to do that. My lack of tears and fear infuriated him, making his strokes harder. Even at a young age, I knew there was no justification for such treatment from my father. I saw past him as he was, and loved him anyway. **People rarely choose to change, regardless of what has happened or the number of years gone by.** From a child to now an adult, my father did not change, it just went from physical to verbal.

Working part time, making under nine dollars an hour, and having monthly student loan payments, I was financially tied. The best option was living with my parents, knowing it was where I needed to be at that point in time. However, the strain of it could not be denied. They took turns criticizing and enforcing their ideas of what they thought I should be doing. Sometimes, they teamed up together. I tried to avoid confrontation as much as possible by staying in the bedroom.

The retail position was handled for nearly a year. There were no job prospects in sight, nevertheless an inner knowing came knocking--It was time to leave. I was not better off financially than the day I started, nor did I learn much of anything skill wise. That was the reality of it. In that year, I somehow gained more strength and conviction, as the environment fed me little positive crumbs in a whole cake of challenges.

Baffled and concerned, the supervisor asked me, "Why are you quitting when you don't have another job?"

Confidently, I told them, "It's time to leave. I can't explain why. I just know this is the right decision for me."

At the time, I was not aware of the existence of the inner knowing, nor had any term to describe it. It was an automatic instinct but still took courage to follow through. At its basic level, it is an internal connection we all have to what feels right. No matter the circumstances, place, or time. Sometimes, our minds have a tight grip on reality, and try to talk us out of what we know we should do. We focus on the what ifs, and what could, or could not happen, rather then trusting the instinct of the soul. We try to connect the dots before taking steps. In this experience, I knew I had to let the dots connect themselves.

The validation for doing the right thing unraveled through my father. By quitting the retail job, I was able to fill in more shifts at my parents' grocery store. This freed my father, gave him the opportunity to go to Syria, and see his father for the last time before he passed away. It had been over seventeen years since he last saw him. My father has two natures. One is sweet and kind, the other is cultural-driven ego. Generally, he is removed from life, a coping mechanism for the daily battles with my mother. This conflict between them caused the cultural-ego to take over, as his soul was stifled. Typically guarded and defensive, when he returned from Syria those characteristics seemed to disappear. **When you follow the inner knowing, you gain the ability to let go. This alleviates the stress of major life decisions, because when you follow what is right, you can never be wrong.** I attained a deeper trust, and the voyage continued.

An Intruder in the Name of Truth

After leaving the retail job, I continued to look for a purposeful career opportunity. I applied to jobs I was over and under-qualified for. Jobs that made the most sense with the degree attained, and jobs I had no true interest in taking. In the middle of this quest, I received a phone call from a friend in Columbus who knew about my job search difficulties. She explained a close friend of hers who majored in industrial engineering heard her company updated the requirements to include Operations Management degrees.

I opened my computer and found the job description for the position. I was in no way qualified for the job, but it was worth a try. I applied for it, and to my surprise received a phone call a week later to come in for an interview. I was never provided with an address of where it was to take place. On the day of the interview, after looking online and trying to get a hold of a human resource employee, I could not find it. My mind was convinced I was inexperienced for the position, so I decided to stop searching for the location.

I completely ignored my soul's disagreement with the mind and thought, *"Why walk into a potentially, and most likely, disappointing situation?"*

The mind was the driver, the soul was in the passenger seat reading the map. The mind kept on ignoring the guidance from the soul. Being in the same vehicle, they were now both going in the wrong direction. The soul knew more than the limited perception of the mind. So, it took the wheel and all of a sudden, it felt like an energetic pull to use the only information available, a street name and city, and just start driving. Somehow, I found my way and arrived for the interview on time. I landed the career job three months after quitting the retail job and the day after my father returned from Syria.

My first day was the company's one-hundredth anniversary. I observed a grand celebration filled with festivities and commemoration. Yet, something was amiss. The entire first week, I came home so drained even my mother took notice. She is someone who is rarely aware of emotional states unless extreme and usually I keep to myself not disclosing any details about what is going on. I did not understand why the complete exhaustion from this new employment.

Shortly thereafter it was revealed, this corporation's culture was harsh, negative, and ego-driven. I came in as what they called an "outsider" into the management trainee position. Traditionally, they promoted from within, and it took an average of six to seven years to move up to a full-time supervisor. Ultimately, I found myself in a job environment that proved to be similar to my male dominated upbringing. This never made me feel uncomfortable, I was very much in my power and had clear boundaries. Nonetheless, I was disheartened by the surroundings. **Certain themes have a tendency to spill over into different parts of our lives until all the nuggets of learning are taken from it.**

The blessings offered were not taken for granted. I genuinely felt overpaid for what I was doing and that others, who committed many years to the company, might be more deserving of the position. These feelings were innate but also stemmed from my childhood experiences. I would come home from school to a meal of cereal and tuna fish. When a middle-school friend asked me why I wore the same two shirts every week, I never felt deprived or lacking anything materialistic. My family immigrated to the United States seeking opportunity: The American dream. My mother cleaned houses, worked at my uncle's club, and cooked in his restaurant to support the entire family. I started working at the age of fourteen as a waitress and dishwasher for this same uncle's restaurant. I valued money differently, finding it to be a necessity rather than a luxury. That value did not change in the current management position.

It was three weeks in when the supervisor decided to give me a tour of the operations building. We walked around in full suits, watching the streamlining of packages and bustling of production workers. We were at the top level standing on a black metal walkway. I looked down, making direct eye contact with a silver haired gentleman. In that same instant, flashes of a dream I had many years ago resurfaced.

> I started off seeing myself outside surrounded by grey skies, standing on what looked like an abandoned graveyard with fallen tombstones. I saw myself turn around to find a cream-colored brick structure, deteriorating but you could still make out the engraving above a large doorway. Despite the decrepit scenery, there was a strong urge to enter. I approached the glass front door entrance. They opened automatically. I walked in, and saw a huge space of workers carrying packages and machine production lines. All these people looked up at me. There was a telepathic exchange between them stating they were not going to speak of me being present.

> I paced the floors exploring the building. Suddenly the red alarms went off. I knew I needed to get out. I looked around and found an elevator. I got in and pressed the third level. I walked out and ran into the same dark-featured man from the ending of the three birds dream. In a panic state, I thought, I was found. However, he approached me, placed his hands on my shoulders and reassured me he was on my side. He pointed to the direction of the escalator and said it was the way out. I asked if he was coming with me and with his eyes he told me no. I followed his direction. The higher ups were close behind. I reached those previous glass doors to find them sealed this time. With no other way in sight, I turned around to face the crowd that now arrived. I started to elevate, hovering in the air. Bolts of lightning and electricity emanated from me.

The connecting of eyes led to the recall of this dream which matched the present-day employment setting. It reassured me, no matter how barren this place was, it was exactly where

I was supposed to be. I recognized my view of the bigger picture was lost. **Even if we are not enjoying the current conditions, may it be a job or living situation, there is significance. Wherever we walk, we are contributing, and so are others in the same environment.** It takes a single flame to start a wild fire, and burn down an entire country side. It is our choice how we respond, and if our impact is for the good or the bad. We have a responsibility to change how we view external circumstances, aligning with our life mission.

The career envisioned in business was not quite what I thought it was going to be. Instead of developing my technical and leadership skills, it complimented the retail job left behind. This career job involved monotonous and uninspiring tasks of a different nature. Almost on a daily basis, I underwent one long tedious duty only to go on to an even more mind-numbing project. Traveling to various areas in Ohio for a time-study assignment, the whole day was spent in and out of truck with a parcel-delivery driver. I collected data on their walking distance and number of packages. It was lackluster and physically demanding.

Regardless of how mundane and random this role was, it led me to the necessary events and people, resulting in an influx of spiritual occurrences. I became attuned to my intuition to an elevated degree. One memorable illustration of this was with a driver, named David, who also happened to be a minister. At the time, I wished I was an observer watching us. A six-foot-four-inch Black man and a petite woman, with a twenty-year age gap, jumping off a delivery truck in disagreeable brown matching outfits. As I followed his every footstep like a miniature shadow, I did not doubt the entertainment we brought to the intrigued faces of onlookers. Although we were strangers in every way, we instantly clicked and there was a comfort present between us.

In the beginning of the day, he tried to intimidate me by threatening to leave me behind if I did not keep up with him.

With a witty banter, I replied, "Whatever. Just drive. Do you think I volunteered for this torturous job? No. I was forced to dress in this hideous uniform which, for some reason you all find so attractive on me, and drive to what I consider the south. I am not the management enemy, or here to take time away from your paid day. I'm here to do a job. So, can you please make this easy for the both of us and not pull any driver tricks?"

Shocked by my bluntness and honesty, he was left speechless for a minute, but only for a minute. As the day went on, his guard lessened. I read him like a book and started telling him things about his life.

"Your brother…he's very different from you."

With his deep minister-like voice, David said, "How did you know that?? You are freaking me out again, Jasmine! My brother is kind of the black sheep of the family. He went on a different path, with the wrong people."

I ventured from his brother to the depths of his inner being. I knew he needed to hear this. "I don't know what you did so wrong that you can't forgive yourself. The angels want you to release yourself from the handcuffs you have created. Self-forgiveness is their message. Return to your beliefs and yourself. 'God' forgave you before you even committed what you

perceive to be a sin. Now it's time for you to forgive yourself."

I affirmed, "I know…easier said than done, but it will free you and return you to your rightful path. Do not be afraid to embrace what you think you are undeserving of."

Once more, sensing his thoughts, I said, "God did not forget about you, but you lost sight of the Divine to guilt. Let go of the guilt. Do not let it restrict you any longer. Again, I hear self-forgiveness is the key to unlocking your self-created confinement."

Astonished, David said, "Jasmine, now you're REALLY freaking me out!"

"You know these messages are of truth. You, yourself, preached them to others. Now you must heed the words."

Our roles reversed. There I was "preaching" to a minister. I was the messenger of the higher source and he was the receiver of the wisdom. From there, it was his choice what he did with it. It is all of our personal choice to change. I understood it would take more than angelic words for him to attain self-forgiveness. Going through a similar trial, I learned to see how everything serves a purpose and making mistakes was part of life's process. **While the mind reflects on regrets and passes judgment, the soul desires release from it. You cannot go back in time to change the past, but you can change how you feel about it.** Learn how to accept the wrongs, mistakes, or failures as a way to transform. **When the mind forgives, the soul is set free.** The destructive pattern of the past will cease to influence your present and future.

The day came to a close when the minister spoke of his hobby; photography. I asked David, "Recently, have you had circular shapes of light show up in your photographs? You know when you pour oil in water? They resemble that design."

"Jasmine, you have got to stop freaking me out!…Yes, they just started showing up. How did you know?"

"I saw a vision of the picture with the bubbles of light. I feel you'll continue to see more."

I was able to visualize and clearly describe these energetic objects and the photograph they appeared in, without actually seeing the picture in person. I did not know the name of them until two years later. They are called "orbs" and soon after that discovery, they began appearing in my photographs. They are confirmations that even though you cannot see something with the human eye, does not mean it is not truly there.

Southern Ohio provided the richest soil for the fermentation of spirituality. Some of these drivers called me a prophet. I replied, "Do I look like a prophet to you? I'm in the middle of nowhere, jumping on and off of a delivery truck for over ten hours a day."

When I returned to the more stagnant soil of Northeast Ohio, the title of prophet was replaced by terrorist. The conversation with many drivers went like this, as each person almost duplicated the dialogue…

"Your name is different. What country are you from?"

"Syria."

"Where's that?"

"Next to Iraq."

"What!? Are you a terrorist!?"

I would shake my head, shoot them a paralyzing look, and tell them, "A terrorist? What kind of question is that to ask, anyway? Use your common sense instead of listening to the media. Being Middle Eastern does not automatically make me a terrorist. I'm still your boss, so do your job and I'll do mine, no bombs included."

If I was asked one more time if I was a terrorist, I thought about using it as a scare tactic to get us back to headquarters in less time than the usual ten or eleven hours. Other drivers kept me out until 10:00 P.M. to gain a higher pay, making deliveries at night in some of Cleveland's worst neighborhoods. I was never scared, but certain special individuals along these routes would ask the driver what he was doing having me out here. There was one driver in particular who I was warned about, not only by other supervisors but by the drivers themselves. This driver was hard headed, stuck in his old ways, and disliked any management personnel. However, after his time study with me, which would determine how much he would get paid, he professed to all the other drivers, I would give a fair assessment. He could not explain to them why or how, he just knew it.

Other management witnessed for once he actually trusted and did not put up a fight. I was asked by them, "What did you do to him?!"

I was management level, and young enough to be their daughter. Whether the responses were positive or negative, there was always a common factor. I gained their reverence and had their respect.

What happened after this repetitive job assignment? Unbelievably an even more tedious project followed. I visited numerous, wide-spread company buildings to measure the operation capacity. I rotated through the different work shifts, my mind and body lost most function during the abnormal 3:00 A.M. schedule. At times, I could not keep my eyes open, driving as early as 1:30 in the morning to perform the beyond-early task. Though the premature rise was a major mind-numbing factor, the supervisors and managers were another source of distaste.

While I was ordered into positions that were not so fun, I always maintained my dignity and did the best I possibly could. I tried to cause change within this more than one-hundred-year-old culture. They, themselves, forgot the original perspective of their company's values and standards. They were reaping immediate rewards by conforming to the reality of current business practices, but at the expense of their integrity which was detrimental to their roots and the people within.

It had been two years. It seemed there was zero to show for that time period of my life. I saw nothing but judgment, a hierarchy of people in their lowest state, and an ego-driven system. Most of the time I sat there observing managements' behavior. There was a lack of listening, as everyone was in their own head and wanted to be right. The rest of the time was spent in a room of cubes with no windows. I wanted it to be a dream, but it was just as real as the unfruitful retail job. The mind was left stifled. The soul searched for a purpose in this experience. I had to find it to survive, that is who and how I am.

The conclusion was this corporation had strayed very far from its original ideals. In the beginning, I thought the reason for being here was about changing this lost company. The major lesson eventually learned was I could not change the culture alone. All I could do was plant the unyielding seeds of truth and nurture them during their fragile sprouting stage. In the end, the justice to a deserving workforce was not to be granted by me, but by all the people within this establishment. This change takes courage. Also known as bravery, courage is the state of mind, and the practice of the soul that enables one to confront fear, danger, uncertainty, pain, risk, or intimidation.

Courage is not about being fearless. It is about being afraid, and still walking forward and taking action. Courage, like self-discovery, is unique to each person. It may mean getting out of bed, climbing up the next peak, or having that difficult conversation. Once we have a clue to where courage is needed, we can summon and apply it to the specific situation. **When we lack courage, we settle for the reality handed to us by society, culture, family, and/or genetics.** We need to boldly follow through, otherwise, we are suspended in thinking, planning, and excessive worrying. This then creates our life as if living in a glass house, we can see out, but we are confined.

My physical appearance differentiated me at the new job, my interior makeup made me a lion in a sea of sharks. An intruder into their world, I arrived both to do a job and plant seeds of possibility for change. This was accomplished, it was time for me to leave this trespassed territory and practice courage.

My mind started to run. *I know it's time to leave. I can't explain it, but I just know... What am I going to do without a job? I have saved some money, which will help. I don't know about the MBA application for graduate school? It isn't finalized, and classes are starting in a couple weeks. Management is not going to be too happy, seeing they just promoted me to supervisor. Well, what can they really do? I think I'm becoming like them in order to survive. Another reason it's time to go. I don't belong here…never did."*

With the ultimate decision to quit, I stumbled upon some confirmations I was on the right path. One of these signposts was a series of encounters with an unfamiliar co-worker in a cafeteria lobby where I hardly ever ate. I walked past him many times, and always had this sense he was somehow different than the rest. The three encounters stayed with me to come alive in this recounting. It seemed as if something higher channeled through him.

I quietly sat in a plain cafeteria with two tables and a vending machine. However, my mind was not so quiet. I was contemplating the decision to leave the company, reasons for and against, why now, and the consequences that would result.

The formerly unfamiliar co-worker turned to me and in line with my thoughts, he asked, "Do you know who you are?"

I was surprised and with a gentle tone, responded, "Excuse me?"

"I asked you, 'Do you know who you are?'" using the same confident voice he had in his first question.

I internally answered, "*A failure would be correct to say.*"

I felt like a person who accomplished nothing but overcame so much.

I gave a sincere explanation of the reality, "I'm here, an employee of this company…just like you."

He asked, "Do you know who I am?"

My intuition responded, *"A minister of some sort…"*

I replied out loud, "I'm not sure. I don't know you. I have seen you around, but we've never spoken before."

"Hmmm…well besides being an employee of this company, I work with family counseling. I received my Masters in this field."

"Congratulations. That is an accomplishment."

"Thank you. I appreciate it…'Different' was part of the answer I was looking for from you."

"No, I'm not. I'm just trying to survive like everyone else in this place."

"No, you're not. Survival is the least of your worries. You want to make an impact. You want to change this self-destructive culture. And you have given everything you have and more to this institution to try to help them even as they beat you down. Is this not true?"

Softly, I replied, "yes, that's true…"

No one knew what I tried to do for this business, I barely knew. I did it so willingly, the attempts came naturally. I bypassed the mental beatings and saw the core and potential of the company.

He continued, "But you have come to a fork in the road, right? You've decided to leave?"

"How do you know all of this information about me which is impossible for you to have knowledge of?"

He responded, "How did you know I'm not just a family counselor but didn't say it out loud?"

"You're a minister…" I pronounced.

"Yes. Why didn't you speak up when I asked you?"

"…It wasn't the right time."

"Very good. Everything has a time and place." He continued, "Your eyes change colors. They just did now."

I replied, "Yes. You are one of the very few people to notice that…"

"So you're really leaving? 100% sure?"

"Yes, I'm putting in my two-week notice when I return to my original building. I am 100% sure internally. 100% realistically? No." I confirmed.

"I believe you should stay. You have what it takes to not only survive, but command change. You can go very far with this company."

With conviction, I responded, "No. It's time to go. I have done everything I could. I used to think quitting was giving up. But in truth, I learned you can come to a point where you realize you did your best and cannot do anymore. I fulfilled what I was meant to do here and the rest is up to the company and the people here. No more. No less. Staying here would either delay the inevitable or make me a captive. I have to get out now before more time passes. Otherwise, I will end up using time as an excuse not to leave as everyone else does."

"I understand. But I'm sorry this place is losing you."

"Well, I shook the foundations a little too much around here." I maintained, "I don't think they are going to miss me."

We both started laughing, knowing the large number of co-workers who disliked me.

When he saw I was beginning to have more confidence to quit, he began to tell the tale of his own story of leaving a previous company he worked for. I acknowledged, "As one door closes, another opens…"

"Yes. That's how God works." He elaborated, "It was not an easy decision for me to make because I had a family to support, but everything worked out. I'm here to tell you the choice is difficult, BUT what you feel inside of you is always right. I know you are afraid and keep playing out scenarios in your mind of what might happen. You have to follow that inner feeling even though I think you should stay here. I wish you the best and hope you will discover who you are to this world."

I thought we already covered who I was. Again, I asked myself how he knew about my thoughts. We engaged in such a profound interaction, yet we never bothered to exchange names. Self-assurance in the inner knowing was the true reason we crossed paths.

Many of us have a path we are expected by others and/or ourselves to pursue. I came

to understand through this experience, sometimes these expectations are false and are not truly what we want. Awareness of this, is found in the concept I call false dreams. False dreams involve expectations of ourselves, family, society, and/or culture. As early as childhood, we are programmed to think certain occupations will better fit our finances, intellect, and/or talents. The elements of glamour, money, and prestige allure us even more and contribute to building the structures of these false dreams. We disengage from our true passions and calling, to pursue this dream developed by a world we believe is supporting us.

Though family, society, and culture may have the best intentions for us, they do not know our truth. Only we know our own true nature and can discover purpose. Sometimes, we need no one but ourselves to perpetuate false dreams. We have views of our "ideal" selves and stubbornly stick to them, instead of being simply, who we truly are. Also, at times the mind's seduction of certainty, safety, and grandeur manipulates our inner desires. While we may fall victim to this misguided agenda, our inner knowing never disappears.

The time, money, and energy invested in our false pursuits can prevent us from hearing, and accepting what the soul has directed all along. You have the soul and the mind, and the middle man between these two is intuition. The intuition, sometimes referred to as our sixth sense or gut instinct, is an inner compass. It exists to provide guidance on our journey, and is **one of the main means your soul and angels communicate to your mind.** These higher sources are all forms of the divine. Intuition whispers the messages from the soul that lead us to true dreams.

Within each of our inner garden lives a rose, our truth. We need to not be distracted by the other bright and rich vegetation. Instead, search the grounds for the flower that possesses the essence of our personal truth, where the others lack even the scent. This rose symbolizes the beauty of who, or what, we are meant to be. Newfound, the process of cultivating such a delicate bloom requires the soul, out of this blossoms our truth.

While I adapted to the culture, conforming to the negativity was not an option. Introduced into a garden environment, a wild rose absorbs the pollen of any other rose in the zone. Nevertheless, a gardener can keep it true, through the right planting arrangement. I kept my internal garden aligned with what felt right, maintaining the essence of a pure wild rose, even in captivity.

A little over two years with the company, I began to awake each morning with a vague sense maybe it was time to leave. This was at the peak holiday season which meant twelve-hour days. These thoughts were not new, but there was something different about them. I was never truly satisfied at this company. In fact, I looked for other employment the entire time, to find every door closed. November and December months were filled with trying to figure out what would be a next step.

Three years prior to this time, I walked out from the last final exam of undergraduate school, vehemently promising myself I would never go back. Yet, here I was contemplating returning. The option was graduate school for business. There were several universities within driving distance to my parent's house that offered the master's in business program. However, the preferred school was financially out of range. I was dead set against attending the downtown Cleveland university due to two reasons. Firstly, the parking situation was horrendous. The second reason came from a past experience. I took a full load of college classes there as a high school senior and did not feel the school was adequate. I came to find out their Master of Business Administration (MBA) branch offered excellent instruction and was well-respected. This eased my mind, but a part of me remained skeptical.

A week before I made my decision to officially quit, a vision of a lion appeared in my mind's eye. It happened again on Monday, right before I was to hand in the signed letter of resignation. The strong and vivid imagery flashed so quickly I had little time to absorb it all:

> In the form of a spirit, I appeared next to a young woman dressed in a white robe, her hair pulled up in a thick bun with rings of gold thread wrapped around it. An instant later, I hovered in the air looking down on a landscaped green maze with this woman standing at the apex of the pathways. The view returned to the young lady and I became her instead of the observer. Now, I stared in wonder at the scene. I was completely surrounded by an expansive, bright green grassland. A few feet in front of me, stood a marble altar. A lion moved back and forth on this platform as two torches blazed at either end of his domain. The lion did not mean harm, but he commanded a sense of majesty. His essence challenged me to have strength.

This profound vision steered me to gather the courage needed to quit the job. The consciousness of the mind and soul commenced.

The Mind asserted, *"This is crazy. What am I doing? People are desperately looking for a job and here I am just voluntarily leaving mine. I make more than my parents, but I'm throwing it all away. Money is not the highest priority to me, but who in their right mind would give this up? My mom does not support me and my dad thinks I'm getting laid off. Fatima and everyone close to me thinks I shouldn't quit... I am on my own. After all these years of hard work, I'm letting go of a stable job that provided a respectable title, reputation, income, and benefits."*

The Soul called out, *"Courage...Courage...Courage. I can do this. I know everything will work out."*

In this same week of putting in my two-weeks notice, courses already began. I was still not officially accepted in the MBA graduate program, but decided to attend anyway.

Sitting in my cubicle, I looked down the aisle through the glass window of my manager's office.

The angels encouraged, *"It's time to go, Jasmine. Leave with courage. We come as support, but you have to gather your courage for the final decision of liberation from this situation. Go and we will be by your side."*

While the butterflies in my stomach were fluttering, I absorbed the angelic impressions. It was time to get this over with. At 1:30 P.M., I took a deep breath, stood up, pushed my chair in, and walked down to the door. I knocked, knowing there was no turning back now.

"Come in," I heard from inside.

I opened the door and was greeted with his smiling Irish-blue eyes.

"Hello, Sebastian. I need to speak to you. This won't take long."

"Sit down, Jasmine," he politely requested.

I objectively weighed the pros, cons, and options. I thought the decision through, and had internal resolve. However, entering the office was venturing into the unknown. I took a seat in the chair positioned across his desk.

Sebastian asked, "What's going on?"

"Um…Read this so I can calm my nerves," my voice quivered, "It explains why I'm here."

I slid the paper containing the typed notice across the surface of his desk. Sebastian scanned over the sheet. When his eyes looked up from the typed words, he met me with a smile.

He asked me one question. "Why?"

He received a blank stare from me. Then he elaborated, "I mean, I read what you wrote, but I need to be able to provide him with a clear answer when I am asked the same question. You say you want to pursue your Master's degree, but we can help pay for your schooling."

"The truth?" I replied.

"Yes, you can tell me anything. You know that."

More surprising than his smirk was how I now spoke with unwavering confidence. "Simply, it's time to go and everything inside is reassuring me of this."

Sebastian said, "I knew this was coming, but didn't think it would be so soon."

Within moments of finishing up the conversation about my resignation, a co-worker knocked hard on the office door. He announced an immediate meeting with all management in the conference room. I followed them around the corner, down the hall, and into the room, wondering what this emergency was about. The company decided to consolidate the state's two regions as a form of cost-cutting. Prior to my resignation meeting, I confided in a few people I was leaving. Word traveled fast. I stared around the room at the soon-to-be former co-workers, observing them watching me. The stunned faces seemed to acknowledge the timing of my announcement and this sudden major restructuring.

Later, a co-worker Alex, a self-proclaimed cynic, could not deny the coincidental timing of these occurrences. When we spoke, he told me, "Jasmine, I know you better than anyone here but when you told me you were quitting I thought you were crazy, completely out of your mind. I have to admit, I didn't think you would do it. Now…man…I don't even know what to say. I mean your two-week notice and the meeting were seconds apart from each other."

I responded, "I told you it was time for me to leave and I couldn't even stop it. Timing is everything. I hope you remember I only speak the truth, no matter how crazy it sounds or may seem."

"Yes. I see that now."

Three days later, I noticed an unpleasant change within myself. I went from complete self-assurance to intrusive second-guessing. My confidence was unexpectedly blown out of the water, finding myself floundering in a sea of indecision. Doubts renewed with an amplified effect. I could not get it under control. I was unable to sleep. Everything that made me strong somehow was nowhere to be found. I encountered times that were much more challenging than quitting a job. There was no understanding of what caused such a drastic shift. My whole system was in panic mode, yet this felt way beyond what might be termed as situational anxiety. This was different.

The negative change bled into the external environment, and Sebastian took notice. He called me into his office. "Jasmine, I have noticed you haven't been yourself. You have been late to work, unsettled, and distracted from doing your job. I don't know what's going on, but I can see you're not well at all."

"Yes…just going through some hard times. I don't understand it myself, but I'll make it through."

Sebastian added, "Well, I know I have made some rash decisions in life myself. So I'm here to give you the opportunity to stay. I wish someone else would have done the same for me."

As he spoke, I felt enveloped in thick black smoke, almost like I was drowning. My vision narrowed. All was black except a white dot at the very end. I focused on this one light. I could not remain at this company. Even with this dark mess, I knew I made the right decision.

I replied, "Thank you for the offer, Sebastian. I appreciate it, but I am still standing by my original decision to leave."

"I'm going to keep this open for you. You have three more days to think about it."

Three days later, my internal stability regained, I left reputation intact. Liberated from the recent dark turbulence, I confidently departed. Was I afraid? Yes. Was I losing a lot of money? Yes. Was the truth going to fail me as I took the risk of quitting in the middle of an economic crisis? Absolutely not. It was ultimately a leap of faith in something I could not see or touch. Even as I was given the option to retract my two-week notice, I still could not postpone leaving. I did not have a single regret. I wished the inner knowing to resign arrived earlier than it had.

January 13th, the last day at the company, happened to be the coldest day of that winter, under a rare-clear, blue sky and bright sunshine, lasting the entire day. Eventually, they officially accepted me into graduate school. Besides enrollment, I did not know what to anticipate about the future.

After a year or so went by, Sebastian contacted me. He read this particular chapter, which sparked something within him and planted the necessary seeds. Following my leave, he endured bitter treatment by the organization, pushing him to a major breaking point. Sebastian devoted over twenty years of his life to them, had a set retirement plan, and a family to provide for. He decided to quit. Sebastian informed me he is much more content, has more time to spend with his family, and even earns a higher income. If reality claims you are mistaken or just plain foolish, ignore it. Follow your instincts and persevere. You are in alignment with the higher plan, it will not let you down. You will find fulfillment.

Due to money, family, power, or loving someone, we often stay in our comfort zone even though it may be a miserable place. Nevertheless, remember this: **Opportunities are granted to us, but not necessarily at the most convenient times in our lives or when we are expecting it. They do not always come in a perfectly wrapped box where everything is in place. This does not detract from the new passageway. This is a test in our journey. It forces us to weigh our desires and decide to stay in the safety zone or to take a risk on what you sense, and feel is right. Trusting the inner knowing is never wishful thinking.**

Petals of Timely Connections

Many of us connect in similar ways within our experiences, though the details are different. These inscribed words are about your life odyssey. The waters in the previous chapters are on the surface level, being shallow in nature. At this point, moving forward, there is a sense of vulnerability as we approach the deep end. Take a breath, extend your arms, and push off as we dive further.

Everything and everyone you have experienced made you who you are. All of this is in-sync with your timeline. The power of what is behind it, is now illuminated. The phenomena of synchronicity enters center stage. **Synchronicity is a chain of related and unrelated people, events and/or occurrences that link together. It works by a series of what seem to be coincidences.** These casual happenings magnetically flow one into the right place, at the right time, and with the right people. There are many forms of synchronicity. Imagine a grandfather clock, a tall free-standing device. Within it are the heavy metal components that turn, wind, and click. These mechanisms run to move the hour and minute hands right on time. Although these pieces function differently, they operate together, synchronizing seamlessly.

Many inventions are the result of synchronicity. At one point, a person took notice of a need or desire, and then a solution presented itself. A Renaissance inventor's imagination was captivated by winged creatures in the sky. His observations of nature, specifically bats, inspired him to create a flying device. The bat's wings and physical structure were the answer to making flight possible. **We subconsciously send out signals for guidance and/or answers. The soul then creates a path of opportunities, and the mind zeros in, landing on the tracks.**

Even though we are not aware of synchronized navigation, in hindsight, many times, we can see how the divine plan played out. The coming timely connections would segue to the creation of this inscription. This required higher guidance to directly step in, so everything could flawlessly occur. The angels were once in the shadows. They now took on a fully engaged and involved role. This was necessary for two reasons: My mind had to take a back seat, so the guidelines I follow could adjust. Secondly, my soul would soon be invaded. It was a blessing to have the angels more present. Unfortunately, the very fact of why they were, was not pretty. They were the sand bags against the hurricane that hit. Even with this line of defense, the storm did its damage.

Step one, placing me at the February 14th wedding. It all started with a simple conversation and an inkling. Fatima told me about her friend's upcoming wedding, and the fiancée, Ziad, finally getting a job at a bank. I previously met him on the 4th of July when he shared with me his struggle to find employment. Generally, he was not talkative, or one to provide anything personal. It turned out Ziad was hired at the bank location I went to. I never saw him until a series of coincidences, a month before the wedding. The instant Fatima spoke of the wedding a knowing surfaced I would be there. At first, I completely shrugged it off. Yet, every time she brought up the subject, my intuition told me I would be present, while the mind stated this was not possible. Surely, all the invitations were sent out and I barely knew the bride. Not to mention my personal preference of not attending a wedding unless obligated to do so.

There is a divine voice always with us which speaks of potential, wisdom, and connectivity. This is also known as the inner voice, intuition. There is another voice that exists from our mind. This is the ego which has a perspective of limits, doubt, and fear. Part of life is learning how to discern the two. Once we do, we have a choice to make. Which one are you going to listen to? We will always hear the voice of the mind, however, we must at times reject it, and follow the guidance of the soul. As the day of the wedding came closer, the inner voice grew stronger. Nevertheless, I kept denying the intuitive inkling of attendance with the facts of reality.

After quitting the career job in January, two weeks later, I received the last paycheck in paper form in the mail. This meant I had to physically go to my bank. The location was five minutes away, the task was quick and easy. I walked into the bank, found no line and went straight to the teller. I finished the transaction, turned, and at a distance through the glass wall, I was surprised to see Ziad, the groom to be. He was sitting in his office with his face toward the computer screen. I was comfortable with Ziad from the first time I met him. I empathized with him. At the same moment I saw him, he looked up from the monitor and waved for me to come in. I nodded my head in acknowledgment, walked over and sat down in the chair closest to the door. We greeted each other, and I congratulated him on the new position.

When I informed Ziad about leaving my career job, he replied, "That's weird because a few weeks ago, I went to a 401K training on transferring funds after you leave your job. Maybe I could help you, how much do you have invested in 401K?"

"I don't know," I said. "I didn't start contributing to my 401K until a year and a half after I started."

Ziad responded, "Why don't you find the information and we can sit down and figure out what I can do for you? Just come in whenever you find it."

The significance of this encounter pertains to how it was placed in seamless conjunction with the coming events. I did not end up meeting with him about my 401K, until two months after his wedding.

Two weeks prior to the wedding, I got a call from an unrecognized number. I hesitated to answer, as this meant it was probably someone unknown. Usually I would let it go to voicemail, but a magnetic-like urge caused me to pick up the phone.

I answered and found it to be Ziad's fiancée, "Jasmine, it's Lina. You probably heard from Fatima about my Valentine's Day wedding?"

"Yes, I did. How are things going with that?"

She replied, "A lot of people haven't sent their RSVP back. On top of it, we've already paid for over one hundred forty guests and we may only have around one hundred people attending."

I said, "I understand. People don't realize you can't wait until the last minute to respond, or just show up with no advance notice."

"Listen. I know my wedding is in two weeks, but I want you to come. I just got so busy and overwhelmed, I forgot to invite you. I understand it's not right just calling you two weeks before, but I hope you can attend. You're like a sister to us."

"Sister?" I thought to myself, we barely knew each other.

I knew this invitation was not a genuine desire for my company, but someone to fill a seat. Nonetheless, I accepted because of a very present and almost heavy inner knowing that I needed to be there.

Lina exclaimed, "Okay, great! I want to send you an invitation, but I don't have any left."

I listened with one ear, while the other ear heard the voice of intuition. My gut reaction was she was not telling the truth. The inner knowing that came through trumped the mind.

I responded, "It's okay. I'll get the address and times from Fatima."

The mind kicked back into gear. Every day, I debated to go or not to go.

The Mind would remind me, *"She was insincere with the two-week invitation, and she lied. Twice."*

The Soul would encourage me to attend, *"I have never broken my word and if I didn't go, I would be doing just that."*

The inner dialogue between the mind and the soul was resolved three days before the wedding. For the first time ever, I forgot my bank card in the ATM machine. When I received the call from the bank about needing to pick it up, I was a little baffled. This was unusual and not like me at all. Plus, the noise the machine makes was a sure reminder not to forget your card. The time came to let go of the mind chatter and embrace the side of the soul.

When I walked in, Ziad stood at the counter instead of in his usual office spot. "Hey, Jasmine! How are you? I just noticed your name on this bank card."

"Yes. I can't believe I forgot it. I've never done that before."

"It happens. Lina told me she called to invite you to our wedding. I'm really sorry we didn't invite you sooner, but Lina took care of everything, so I had nothing to do with it. We really do want you to come. I would give you a card invitation, but they're all at home."

"It's okay. I understand how crazy it is to put a wedding together. I remember planning and decorating for my older sister's. I'll be there."

The lie I sensed from Lina was realistically confirmed. A dewdrop of genuineness came as a welcoming taste. Ziad's honesty clinched the win for the soul.

The big day arrived. After getting ready, I came down the carpeted stairs and headed to the family room where my mother was sitting.

My mother asked, "Are you going with Fatima?"

"No, probably not. She's acting weird about the whole thing. I'm already running late for the ceremony as it is."

As I buttoned up my coat, the room fell silent except for the inner voice. *"Follow truth and truth is what will accompany you. But challenge this fact and it will be lost to a world deprived of this treasure."*

Confused about what treasure my intuition spoke of and the truth of this world, my mother interrupted my train of thought with more questions. Hoping my senses were wrong about Fatima not wanting me to come with her and liking to give people the benefit of the doubt, I called. Instantly and sadly, I knew my intuition was right.

Fatima ignored my question about meeting and directed the conversation on random chitter-chatter. Then dramatically, she explained, "My brother and mother are driving me crazy. I'm waiting on them. They're going to make me late!"

Therefore, by myself and practically a passerby of the couple, I drove to the wedding hall. I pulled in the parking lot and waited in the car for Fatima to arrive. Thirty minutes passed, I was still waiting. At this point, I figured who cares if I did not know anyone and decided to walk in alone. Although it was mid-winter, the temperature outside permitted one to stay warm enough without a coat. I removed it while in the car, to uncover a royal blue knee-length dress, with off-the-shoulder sleeves lined in black jewels. I passed through the parking lot, and entered the hallway of the reception. I heard someone call my name. I turned to my right and found it was the groom, Ziad, surrounded by four other men. I became extremely shy when all of them stood silently and stared. My eyes dropped quickly, and I pretended not to hear Ziad's voice. Out of respect, I gathered enough courage to walk over to congratulate him. After I spoke, he asked if I found the 401K papers. I politely guided the answer to reminding him it was not the best time to talk about this. He agreed to which I smiled, nodded yes, and excused myself.

I walked down the lobby of the hall and over to the table that displayed the seating arrangements. With an eerie anxiousness, I found my place card. I went through the main doors, keeping my focus on the table destination. I ignored the many stares and head turns as I navigated through the tables. When I settled into a seat, I immediately noticed the artistry of the reception hall. Where the ceiling met the wall was a navy border with delicately carved ivory sculptures that beautifully, but simply, portrayed biblical stories. The dance floor was two tables from where I was seated. Each table was set for six, with a tall glass vase centerpiece filled with long stemmed deep red roses.

Twenty minutes later, Fatima's brother, Moe, and their mother arrived. Moe and I were in the same school grade but were never close. He replicated the life phases of Fatima; angry, Muslim religious advocate, tumultuous mother relationship. Leaving out, the low self-esteem Fatima embodied. He made a great friend, but a terrible enemy. At first, Moe sat right next to me. Then he moved when his mother pushed him to shift to the other side of the table.

With his deep, flat voice, Moe asked her, "Why?" and received that motherly look of, "Do what I tell you, or else."

I started laughing, knowing she did not want people to think we were together.

I questioned Moe, "I thought Fatima was waiting for you guys, where is she?"

He shrugged his shoulders.

With her own car, Fatima came in thirty minutes later, settled next to me, leaving one vacant chair between us.

I sat there quietly as people came to greet Moe and Fatima. One person, a cousin of the bride spoke to me. He annoyed me from the moment he opened his mouth. Not only was he loud and obnoxious but also, lacked the concept of any personal space. He angled and scooted his chair right up to mine. I gave Moe a look of, "Please, help me!" Moe grinned, pretending not to notice. Both he and his mother sat watching, amused by the bride's cousin endlessly talking and my obvious dislike for his presence. He asked me personal questions, I did not want to answer, then he went on about himself. At the end, he requested my number, something I tried hard to evade. As a private person, my code of conduct is to not give my number out. As a considerate person, I tried to prevent people from asking. I was trapped, cornered, and uncomfortable. I reluctantly gave it to him. I got rid of the cousin of the bride for the time being and that was all that mattered.

At weddings and most celebrations, dancing is a huge part of Middle Eastern culture. And so, the rest of the evening involved dancing with Fatima, Moe, and some of the bride's family. Throughout the event, the unwelcomed cousin would concentrate on me. His irksome behavior became nauseating over the hour. I would have left if it was not for the consideration of the bride and groom. At the same time, I was being held in place. There was something much more powerful in charge and at play.

Fatima was hardly visible at the party, and continued to sit with an empty seat between us. When the bride's cousin asked me to slow dance, I summoned the energy and told him no. I stayed clear of him the rest of the night. Relieved, I took a break from the dance floor, and stood next to Moe. We had our backs turned to the stage, which was a few feet away.

I said, "Moe, keep that cousin away from me. I can't believe you just sat there and let me go through that. I know it was enjoyable to watch, but you should have stopped it after the first ten minutes."

With a large grin on his face, Moe replied, "Okay, okay but it was hilarious. You should have seen your face. Don't worry, I'll help you out next time."

"You better!"

We returned to dancing and after a few songs, something drew my attention to turn, and look toward the direction of the band. I happened to make direct eye contact with the guitar player. His eyes radiated a strange familiarity, almost as if I knew him in a previous time. There was complete silence and the crowd faded. I had this same feeling once prior. It was when my parents were searching for a new house to purchase. After looking at several dozen, I walked into one house, and felt an immediate connection, a sense of being there before. This was the home they ended up buying, and became the living space for my siblings, their children, and a holiday gathering space. It was déjà vu for this house, and now this person. I thought it was odd he caught my attention, he seemed to come out of nowhere. In that moment, with so many people and things happening, it aligned for us to meet eyes. There was something unspoken there. After this shared instant, I returned to the dance floor.

The final part of the night arrived, the music stopped, and almost every guest left. Back at the assigned table, I collected my belongings and waited on Fatima to come back from socializing. I noticed a red rose of unique beauty in the centerpiece. I plucked the flower, placing it in my hair behind my ear. Fatima's mother noticed the rose hair piece and started pressuring for me to take the whole centerpiece.

I gently asserted, "I have no right to take it. They belong to the bride."

The bride's sister overheard the conversation and shouted, "Take whatever flowers you want. They're all going in the garbage at the end of the night."

I decided to make a bouquet for my mother. So, I went around to the tables looking at the red roses from each batch. The eye of the soul searched for a certain essence and the mind assessed the symmetry. The flowers filled the glass vase, water reaching the brim, almost overflowing. I arranged them, while Fatima sat across from me, and her mother two seats over from her. Fatima and her mother occupied themselves by chatting with the other lingering guests next to us. Behind Fatima, I noticed the guitar player walking in between the tables toward us.

The angels hinted, *"Take notice of the eyes. They are the light to the soul and truth of the first encounter with him."*

I returned to the roses, focused on creating just the right arrangement.

Making his presence known, the guitar player loudly said, "How have you been Fatima?? Long time no see!"

The sound of his voice pulled my awareness back up to his closer proximity. What I observed was quite a contrast to the brightly glowing person I first saw on stage. A different person was standing there, his appearance was dim and ugly. I could not figure out why.

The angels forewarned, "Have patience, the mind is quick to dismiss and form judgments, but you must follow higher guidance."

The guitar player touched Fatima's shoulder to greet her, and then kept walking until he stopped next to me.

I could tell Fatima did not remember who he was, although she replied, "Yes...How are you?"

"Good. Good." His attention swiftly turned to me. "And you are?"

In my head, I thought, *"None of your business."*

The angels countered, "Do not shrug him off."

I gave him my name and he gave me his, which somehow, I instantly forgot.

He asked, "How come I've never seen you before? Where do you go out?"

I replied, "I don't know, probably because I don't go out much."

He persisted, "How can I run into you then? Are you on social media?"

Step one of the unknown divine plan was to attend this wedding. Now step two arrived; Overriding my customary reservation to give out my number.

The angels impression came through again, "What of the truth you felt, the earlier inner knowing? Doesn't that take precedence over your actions in all times of your life? Do not make such judgments. Offer him your number."

I was extremely reluctant, but I bent and flowed with it. I answered him, "No, I don't do social media. You can have my number though."

To myself, I pronounced, *"What in the world has gotten into me."*

This was a precursor for something that ended up consuming daily life. It shredded an established code of conduct, rewrote my life recipes, and controlled every ingredient.

Fatima inserted herself in the conversation, "What nationality are you?"

He responded, "I'm Syrian. Actually half Syrian, half Lebanese but I usually don't say that."

I asked, "Are you Maronite (Catholic)?"

"No, I'm Druze. You probably don't know what that is."

"Actually, that sounds very familiar, but I don't know why. I can't remember where I've heard it before…"

He said, "Really? I'm surprised. There are only a few million of us in the world."

We heard a voice yelling in the background, and all turned to see the lead singer signal him to get back to work.

My inner voice jingled, *"The singer is jealous of the attention you and Fatima are giving to the guitar player. He feels, as the better-looking lead singer, he should be getting the attention."*

I smiled to myself, and thought it was amusing to watch men compete like children.

He explained, "Sorry, I have to go finish breaking down and loading the equipment. I'll get in touch with you soon."

He strolled back to the stage. If he did contact me, I would ignore the unknown number as it was my normal procedure.

Curious, I asked Fatima, "Where does he know you from?"

She replied, "I couldn't remember at first. Then I remembered he introduced himself when we were setting up for Grace's wedding."

When I reached home with the flower bouquet, I went upstairs and knocked on my mother's bedroom door. She welcomed me in.

Sitting next to her on the bed, I said, "I made this arrangement for you."

With a tired smile, she replied, "They are beautiful. Thank you, Jasmine. How was the wedding?"

"It was nice. I had a good time. We had two empty tables next to us. I felt bad for the bride. People don't understand the cost when they decide not to show up."

"I know. I'm glad you had a good time. I have to wake up at 6:00 A.M.. I need to go to sleep."

I shut the bedroom door and walked toward the bathroom to brush my teeth. I heard my cell phone ding with an incoming text message. It was from the guitar player, stating his name, Hisham, and that he would call me later in the week. As I read the message, I actually considered replying which confused me. I had prior clarity about not answering any of these men from the wedding. I shrugged it off and went on with my nightly ritual. Unknown to me, responding to the guitar player was step three in the plan.

I looked in the bathroom mirror and started to reflect about the events leading up to Grace's wedding. She finished undergraduate school in Columbus and was indecisive about going for her graduate degree. Her parents had a more prescribed life set out for her. During this break from school, she boarded a flight to Syria with her mother. We had a conversation right before she left. Outside her house, she embraced me and asked, "Please don't let me get engaged, I don't want to."

When Grace spoke those words, there was something behind them. Almost as if she sensed she was going to get engaged. With modern day arranged marriages, the man approaches the woman's family, if they agree, he has a sit down meet and greet with the daughter. If still interested, he asks for her hand in marriage. If the woman says yes, the engagement becomes similar to a dating period where it can be called off. I ended up hearing news of Grace's overseas engagement through our female cousins. For good reason, you will come to know them as the shallow cousins. I was not surprised by the bulletin, rather by how it was relayed. I was left in shock. Grace was not only a first cousin, but my confidant and best friend. My mind tried to wrap around why. After everything we experienced together, and the significance of this type of event, how could I hear about the nuptials from anyone but her.

I knew she was afraid of my disapproval of the engagement and I was probably the only one who could convince her not to go through with it. I thought Grace would always know I would honor and respect her choices, regardless of my mind's opinion or soul's feeling on it. We all choose to live our lives in the way we want or see fit. Who am I to question her ultimate choice or plant any seeds of doubt?

Grace returned from her visit, contacting me several weeks later. We arranged to meet at her parent's house. I entered and wrapped my arms around her with total love. During this time together, I did not ask Grace for any explanation about her engagement. She chose to provide the tale. We sat on the rug covered steps and I listened. She spoke of a dream where an angelic being appeared and proposed to give her answers about her life. The angel said, "You can ask two questions and I will give you the answers." For one of the questions, Grace asked if she should tell me about the engagement. The angelic being replied, "No." I did not believe one word of this account. I kept that to myself without giving it another thought, until I wrote this reflection. I recognized, Grace knew I felt dreams have power and angels exist. Sadly, she was using this knowledge to find a way out. No matter the emotional ties or history, I do not let anything cloud the truth.

Through all of this, I knew and maintained who she truly was and is. Grace is one of the most loving and kind people I have ever met in my life. She did not have bad intentions, but did have a tendency to go out of her way to exaggerate things, craving approval from others. During two years of attending college together, she became a true friend, a person who believed in me. Sometimes people see in us, what we fail to see in ourselves. I provided a sanctuary for her, where she could be free to be Grace. Not dominated by her family's control and pressure to conform to their expectations. Once she stepped outside this sphere she crumbled and never came back.

The day before Grace's wedding, a group of us spent the entire day decorating the hall. I was left in charge of coordinating the chaos of setting up an entire reception for two-hundred-and-fifty people from scratch. Hours were spent on the thousands of twinkling lights covered with tulle. We took these strands of light, and wrapped them around two gigantic concrete pillars. With more lights, we cascaded them from the middle of the room. There were thirty plus tables specifically arranged and draped with Mediterranean colored clothe, and candle

lit centerpieces nestled in glass stone beds. The middle school cafeteria was transformed and unrecognizable. Grace came by for fifteen minutes, asking if I minded her leaving so she could help with the tux fitting. How could I say no? I was not bothered by her leaving. What saddened me was the distance between us greatly expanded. The past seems to intertwine with the future, sometimes with thorns.

    Another doorway began to open, all because of the synchronized events that led me to attend the February 14th wedding. Except for Fatima and myself, no one would ever know what transpired during the four-year journey following the inner knowing. I wanted to put it in the past, keep it there, and move forward. With quitting the retail job, Fatima finding her love, and resigning from the career position, I thought whatever was driving me to act on these risks was over. Little did I know, there was great struggle ahead. The end was nowhere near and there was more to unfold.

Union with Halos and Horns

Internally, I managed to steer in calm seas and clear skies. Without warning, the dark clouds cascaded, suddenly my system had a hole in it. There is an emergency signal onboard ships that alerts the coast guard if the vessel is in dire need. The tidal wave came, my internal alarm was set off. Something was very wrong. Things went south so rapidly. For the first time, I could not swing into action. I grabbed onto whatever I could, trying to stay afloat, as everything was sinking.

During the first week of March, a gateway swung wide open to something I did not even believe in. I did not know what was happening. It felt like I was being suffocated on the inside. I had no hands to fight off the assailant. Insecurities flooded me, to the point where I could not sit down without feeling like I was going to erupt. At times, I felt like I wanted to peel off my skin, to somehow bring the suffering to the outside. There it would be visible to the physical eye.

The only solace I had, the ability to hear the angels and inner voice, was muffled. It felt like I was submerged under water, hearing only murmurs of voices. It is already hard enough to remain connected to them. One is born with natural talent, for example an Olympic athlete. Yet, they still have to discipline themselves, study, and practice. This is the same way intuition works. I was still practicing my skill but could no longer because of this foreign interference. I was truly alone now. Old doubts emerged, as I struggled to believe in myself. I thought insecurities were conquered, were put behind me. What was now being experienced showed the contrary. I internally struggled for clarity, some answers to this paralyzing black smoke.

I drew upon the character of being self-reliant. Days went by of trying to fight through and figure out how to clear all of this. The fumes just kept getting thicker. Still unable to understand, or cope with what was taking place, I reached out to the only person who could help and was trustworthy, Maya. I first went to see Maya for Reiki soon after resigning from my career job. She came into my life by serendipity. I shared with a former co-worker my interest in having a Reiki session. With the two-week notice finalized, that weekend, he gifted me a certificate to Maya's holistic center. Reiki translates to "universal light" and is an energetic healing method that focuses on the chakras, energy centers of the body. Think of Reiki as a satellite dish placed on a roof of a house. The chakras, the spinning wheels of energy, are fuses in this house, supporting our electrical flow. I never mentioned to the former co-worker, or anyone else, what I was going through. This random gesture of kindness saved my life.

Although I enjoyed the Reiki session, I was indifferent and did not anticipate booking another appointment. I figured I lived this long without Reiki, I would be fine without it. However, there were much higher plans in place and Reiki became imperative to my survival. During this difficult period, I experienced what felt like an intrusion on my mind, body, and soul for six days. An exam worth thirty-three percent of my grade was the breaking point. This test was to be administered in less than forty-eight hours. I could not focus or study for the life of me, there was an unknown obstacle preventing it. In all of this confusion, a higher message to seek Maya kept filtering through. I ignored it and continued to try to make sense of it.

The persistent practical thoughts never backed down. *"Focus harder. Try harder. Push through."*

Time ran out. I finally succumbed to the inner knowing and called Maya.

With her soft-spoken voice, Maya replied, "I'm sorry Jasmine, but I'm completely booked up tomorrow. What's going on with you?"

I answered, "I can't really explain it…I have a lot of anxiety and I can't seem to get it under control. I wish I could tell you I don't need to come in tomorrow, but I need relief from this…I just need a few hours to study for a major exam."

"I will try to fit you in sometime tomorrow. I'll call you back if any appointments become available."

I met with Maya the next day at her center. I walked in through the doorway feeling an immediate sense of comfort, an understanding that an answer was waiting. I checked in at the counter and settled in a chair next to the window. I stared out the glass panel, prepared for what was to come. I turned around without hearing a sound to find Maya approaching. When our eyes met, the familiarity of our souls was crystal clear. Without delay, the reality of the mind returned to remind me she was a person I had one Reiki session with.

We sat across from each other, with a small rectangle wooden table separating us. As Maya stared into my eyes, she asked, "So, tell me more about what you are feeling."

Hesitantly, I replied, "I'm not exactly sure…I can't seem to understand it myself, let alone explain it to someone else…" My eyes went down to the tabletop in despair. "I don't know…I just don't know…"

Maya encouraged, "Why don't you try to describe what it feels like?"

I took a deep breath and let the details flow. "I can't seem to grasp how it works. One moment I am fine, then something happens without my awareness and I find myself experiencing this pain. I tried comparing it to the shocking lower back pains I used to get from the years of lifting heavy trays as a server, but it's different. It 'feels' like a full body pain, but I know it's not truly physical pain…It's the oddest thing…"

Maya mostly listened to me during the appointment. The more I expressed what I was going through, the calmer I felt.

When I was finished, she said, "What I can tell you Jasmine is that this is all very real. I am not certain what it is yet, but I feel it will last for three weeks."

I returned home, studied with only a bit of anxiety, and the next day aced the exam. Unfortunately, the symptoms soon came back. The experience was a full-scale war, and the siege extended way beyond the three weeks Maya spoke of. It was like my entire being was undergoing an excruciating surgical procedure where I was wide awake, with no anesthesia to numb the pain. Week upon week went by, I stubbornly endured. I kept trying to rationalize these attacks. Once again, I resorted to calling Maya and I went through a similar conversation of detailing things.

In the coming months, Maya and I went through a process of discovery together.

One visit proved to be most significant. I entered the room, sat in the chair with the window to my back. I faced Maya with the antique table between us. Her deep-set blue eyes looked back at me, with a knowing.

Carefully, Maya began to explain, "You know dark energies exist. . . ."

Quickly, I responded, "Of course. There is dark and light in this world."

As I finished answering, I saw the unspoken words in her eyes, and the light in my whole being dimmed.

Almost unable to fully receive and absorb what I heard, I asked, "Do you really think… this could be what's been happening to me?"

She replied, "I do...Look at everything you have told me. If this was anxiety, you would have certainly felt this way before. From what I know of you, this seems uncharacteristic of your personality. You have been in situations when you were under a lot more pressure and stress, than you are realistically under now. Look at the circumstances you spoke about in Columbus, having to pay for your entire education and living expenses. Also, coping with school while having little support and relying completely on yourself. This would've been a prime period where this type of experience might have happened, and it didn't. Am I right about this?"

I sighed in sadness as everything inside of me confirmed her words. It felt as if a puzzle piece clicked into place. "Yes, you're right..."

Maya gave me a flashlight. I could see where I was going now. My eventual return to her, in hindsight, was fulfilling destiny. Maya became my confidant and healer, offering genuine guidance and providing temporary sanctuary. She had a stoic, yet therapeutic demeanor. I left the Reiki sessions with a renewed sense of peace. In this time, a prior disbelief was discovered to be true.

My fears were no longer shadows of my imagination, but full-fledged warriors of the dark. Disarming the black knights was not a possible tactic. I was their long-awaited fortress with no barriers for protection. I was left vulnerable to their onslaught, but this was serving a soul purpose. The entire experience was a no holds bar war for them, continuing for years to come. The battleground was my mind and soul, where I endured unrelenting assault.

My mother exacerbated the attacks with unceasing words of criticism and her screaming voice, deepening the severity. I was trapped, at the mercy of their whims. Every waking day, they unceasingly fed off my mother's hostilities. One of the strongest experiences occurred when she walked into the kitchen late one evening. She put the groceries down on the counter and began another rant. Her piercing voice kept rising as she continued putting the groceries away. She did not pay attention if anyone was listening, on and on my mother went. It was like being in a tub of water and a plugged-in electric appliance was thrown in. The shock waves within me increased, bringing my system to overload.

I weakly pleaded, "Mom, please stop."

My heart was electrified to the point of fainting for the first time in my life. I closed my eyes, and when I opened them again, my mother had not noticed a thing. I slowly got myself up from the family room couch and staggered over to the stairs. I crawled up to my bedroom with every last bit of energy. Unabated, she continued to yell. I laid on the bed and could still hear the intensity of my mother's voice ringing in my ears. The torture lifted, there was an immediate cooling of my inner core, and soon, peace.

I was riddled with internal suffering. The torment ebbed and flowed, responding to anything less than positive. This was fuel. At first like anyone, I was ill-equipped with no weapon or instructions to vanquish this invasive attacker. Just like a novice knight gathering their forces, the more battles I endured, the stronger I became. In retaliation, the other forces grew in cunning and strength, morphing into ever higher levels of interior distress. As I evolved, they evolved too.

Different forms of darkness do exist; spirits, beings, energies, and, what I came to discover, demons. People generally do not speak of demons and many do not believe they exist. I used to be one of those people. Let me be more clear, I knew light and dark existed, a yin and yang. However, demons were not in my frame of thinking or sensing. **How is it possible to believe and know in angels, but not believe in demons? This is because, how they were portrayed was false.** I thought of a demon as a formed figure with a hideous body. Movies, religion, and folklore depict demons as monsters from the underworld. However, they are faceless and bodiless. **The truth of the matter is, they are very much part of the hierarchy in our evolution. They are the internal motivation for fulfillment of our potential.**

I discovered two forms of demons exist: soul demons and mental demons. Soul demons are a species of darkness that have existed from the beginning of time. Naturally occurring, not created by the mind, soul demons are rare. They have access to your most intimate and deepest parts. They can reside internally and/or externally. **Archetypes of our mind, self-created mental demons are manifestations from things such as fears, insecurities, and unresolved anger. Although they are limited to the mind, they can create disorder and an imbalance through our perception.**

Soul demons do not possess a person, nor turn them into evil beings. A person does not become a marionette, a puppet being shaped by these dark energies. Rather, they are entrapped, mind, body, and soul. They feed off of negativity and infiltrate a person's being. Fears, insecurities, and doubts are amplified. This lifetime is extra challenging and heavy. **Many souls have chosen not just to grow, but to evolve. We evolve the most, through the darkest of places.** Some of the greatest advancements came through the darkest hour. Countless new techniques in surgery developed from remedying battle wounds during times of war. Many breakthroughs in treatment for viruses are the result of research done on the tragic HIV and AIDS epidemic. Numerous forms of renewable energy developed from the destruction of the environment.

Validating evidence of what was happening got brought to my doorstep. One came in the form of an encounter with a gentleman. I saw this middle-aged man many times as I walked in and out of a nearby school computer lab. There was something off about him, and much of it had to do with his lack of hygiene. Most people would easily take one look at this man and instantly dismiss him as crazy. After several run ins, one day, I ended up next to him. I sat down, making sure to have one computer station between us. Suddenly, he turned toward me, began revealing deep private insights about my life, he had no way of knowing. I tried to write him off as mentally ill as the secretary informed. This just did not sit right with me. I moved my face from the computer screen to look at him. I asked him how he knew of such things.

It became a thirty-minute conversation, and during this time, he transformed into a different person. He no longer had an unstable look in his eyes and his speech was calm without seeming erratic. I saw the true man behind it. He was centered, balanced, and sane.

He confessed to being in a mental institution. He had open brain surgery and underwent many years of severe shock therapy. The doctors found nothing off-balance or abnormal in his brain and all the treatments did not help.

For whatever reason, it surfaced in me to ask him if he ever tried to kill himself. He replied, "Only once."

It happened when his mother told him he was costing the family a fortune being in a rehabilitative institution. That spoke volumes. There was this clear sense, unspoken understanding we both experienced the same thing, but each made it out differently. There are no weapons to battle fog—soul demons. You must wait and move through until it lifts. It does and will eventually. If you lose sight of that, it will take you to a place of instability, as it did with this gentleman, sitting next to me in the computer lab.

He asked me how I survived them. There was a short silence, then he provided the answer himself, "You had faith. And you never let it go."

It is almost second nature to quickly stitch up our wounds, ignore them, and simply go through the motions of life. Sooner or later, this leaves us as a shell of ourselves. Demons are brought in, so we can no longer disregard what we need to face. They undo the stitches and force us to mend the damage.

I used to be in the eye of the storm, in the vortex where there was silence and peace. I was ripped out of this vacuum, pulled into the chaos of the tornado, and kept there.

Eclipse of the Sun and Moon

The moon possesses no light of its own. It shines as a result of sunlight reflected from its surface. During a total lunar eclipse, the moon can take on an array of tints, from citrus yellow to dazzling orange and from red to dark brown. In contrast, the sky of a total sun eclipse presents an eerie nightfall as the sun's rays are covered by a black globe of the moon. What is about to be shared began as a glistening moon eclipse. Later, the dark globe of the sun eclipse covered the surroundings. Ultimately, it was about the sun relishing in her contribution as a guardian of the light, while the moon was glowing ultra-violet rays in the pitch dark.

The wheel of life churned. I quit a career job to return to school. My mind resisted enrolling in the Masters of Business program, but my soul knew it was right. Initially, I did not see the purpose of cycling back into the education system. It was hidden, as so many occurrences are in life. Nevertheless, I trusted in the soul guidance, the inner knowing. It does not lead us down a false trail. **The key is to follow what feels right, stay connected to your soul, and you will receive confirmation.**

In the last week at the career job, I was still not sure the right decision was made to leave and enroll in graduate school. I headed there, driving a different route then I did most of the last two and a half years. On a main road, something pulled me to look to the left. I turned to see a brick building with a glass encased stairwell in the middle of it. It seemed familiar, but never noticed it before. A vision flashed of a dream I had two years prior. I was standing inside this exact building, on those stairs, looking out through the glass. In the same dream, I recalled seeing construction vehicles digging up the soil. The foretelling dream calmed my mind and was reassurance the right choice was made. I later discovered this structure was built the same year I had the dream. This would be where the majority of the MBA classes ended up taking place.

During this time period, homelife involved being around two adults who were very different from each other. They were together but separate, locked in ceaseless combat. Both were detached from the soul and driven by the mind. **When your soul is not connected to your mind, it becomes like an open window to a house, permitting anyone or anything to enter.** Bad things happen.

What entered through these two individuals' unlatched windows, were shadows. Genetic DNA is a human sequence of physical attributes, while spiritual DNA is energetic strands of connective matter. As genetic DNA is recognized and analyzed, spiritual DNA is very much as integral to our makeup. Spiritual DNA threads through generations, and continues through family members just like the gene pool. There are recessive and dominant genes in the physical body, and there are recessive and dominant energies in our spiritual being. With the presence of certain spiritual DNA in the bloodline and a disconnection between the mind and soul, my parents were more prone to dark dominant genes.

Fumes from the havoc leaked through the air, making our home a flammable habitat. It came from all fronts. My mother and father alternated striking the matches through their words and eruptive behavior. It burned deeper parts of me, leaving my body charred. There was no escape from the dark smoke externally, or internally. Both of these environments were the source of fuel for the soul demons. On the interior level, they had extremely low quantities of material to access. Growing up in a large family, and being compared to my sisters, I knew I needed to develop differently for my well-being. I did not have character challenges such as jealousy or envy. I walked humbly through life, never forgetting my roots, and treated every individual as I wanted to be treated. I was not a conflicted person, maintaining serenity within and responding with a calm demeanor to the outside world.

Since the soul demons had very little to go on, they scavenged for any and every vulnerability. It was a three-pronged event consisting of the mind's battle with insecurities, the body's extreme physical discomfort, and worst of all, the evaporation of the only assistance I had. They took any ordinary interaction and amplified every negative emotion that resulted, minimizing the positive. They whipped up anger and irritation to exaggerate situations. If given wrong directions, the typical me would be slightly frustrated, but consider being lost an adventure. However, with the soul demons present, they would take advantage, hone in on the frustration, and magnify it to aggravated road rage.

They took a real event, and twisted it into a negative virtual reality. This causes the mind to be overtaken by fear and doubt. My natural giving nature turned into a sense of being taken advantage of. This was not like me. I give freely, even when terribly lacking in the financial department. When soul demons entered the picture, they converted an ordinary concern about money, into an emergency matter that required immediate evaluation.

They pulled out insecurities, mutating them to torturous levels. I watched my grandmother, on my mother's side, go from being a physically strong person built like an ox, to a grown woman in diapers. She was a cold and mean grandmother yet, this did not change how I looked at her. I had compassion seeing her in this aged state, stripped of power. With this empathy, there was also an insecurity about growing old. The soul demons drew this out and exploited it to an agonizing degree. There were moments in time where it was as if I was dragged from my physically young body and placed into a tattered and haggard old woman's body.

The suffering took the air out of the room. The breath out of my body. All of these things created a total imbalance, an elimination of peace. I tried to return to the equilibrium I strongly knew since childhood. Yet, it was no longer in reach. **As a child, we experience more of an awareness, than a knowing. We are born with the mind and soul merged together. This does not mean the mind is fully mature, and completely in the wisdom of the soul. It is that we have a direct and more clear connection to divinity.**

Early on, I learned a way to keep the balance within and follow the internal guidance. At the age of nine, I opened a pot full of freshly barbecued meat. I reached in, took out a chicken wing, and paused. My mind said, "Wait a minute." It looked like actual human skin with goosebumps. From then on, I stopped consuming meat unless there was absolutely nothing else to eat. The next awareness arrived a couple years later, when I bit into a free fast food burger. I looked at it, ready to take the next bite, when I saw a piece of fat hanging. It churned my stomach. My meat eating days were completely over. I was teased by the family for being the "picky eater," but stood my ground. These instincts were so powerful, they were not a choice. **Growing up, the divine cord gets covered with layers piled on by the external world. The mind and soul unmerge, creating a distance between them. The child awareness changes shape and translates into a knowing.**

The inner knowing moved from being behind me, to the forefront. It appeared in real time, playing alongside reality. This commenced the four-year journey with Fatima, and it came time to quit the career job. In December, the inner knowledge became tangible jewels for this childhood friend, and in mid-January, the two-week notice finalized. I thought life would return to normal. However, the testaments of the inner knowing were not finished yet. They merely paused, and began setting up a new venture.

In three days' time since the February 14th wedding, I declined a call from an unknown number. As the voicemail notification popped up, I had a strange sense I should have taken the call. I listened to it and found it was the guitar player from the wedding, Hisham. A back and forth inner dialogue ignited whether to return the call. This debate was confusing because I did not have a second thought about him after we met. Beyond my awareness, there was a higher scheme unraveling.

While driving home from class, I experienced an odd and strong tugging sensation to call Hisham back. As I resisted, it intensified. It was like sitting at an overcrowded sporting event. Each time you attempted to leave the seat, the crowd would jump up to cheer. You would be unable to get out of the chair, let alone the row. You could only remain in the seat and continue to watch the game. My mind tried to make sense of it, bringing me back to previous times where I experienced something close. What I have come to call "the soul force," began to participate in its full capacity at this time in life. **The soul force replicates the energy of a positive magnet and negative magnet, together. It assists in aligning your soul chart to this three-dimensional reality, maintaining the direction of your right and destined path.** Many of you have encountered this alluring field of energy and like me, have not recognized it for what it was. Instead of peeking through a window, the soul force entered by means of the doorway and joined with the angels and intuition.

I continued to reject the idea of calling. I did not have a care besides getting through the graduate courses and figuring out what I was going to do next. In that same time of resistance, there was a peculiar pressure in my chest growing heavier. I did not understand why or where it came from. By ten o'clock at night, I gave into the overpowering magnetic persuasion. When I pressed the call key, the pressure immediately lifted.

Hisham picked up the call and it was oddly comfortable speaking to him. The conversation somehow led to me telling a bizarre story that involved a manipulative cousin. This menacing relative held certain abilities I could barely fathom. One was knowing I spoke about him when he was not physically there. I never trusted him, but there was a need for an open mind. I listened to his story, as if I was a lie detector. There were no indicators of fabrication. While the cousin served in the military in a special forces unit, he was incarcerated for an indiscretion around the age of twenty. One night alone in his cell, he bargained with a higher source. As he spoke, he knew something was listening. Never before were his words so sincere, as he surrendered to the stark reality. He was facing over a decade of time behind bars. In exchange for his freedom, he promised to become a better person. Less than a few months later, he walked out a free man. His wish was granted. He accessed knowledge and unlocked it for me, years before I discovered it was real.

As weird as this experience was, it provided beginning proof for my mind, there was more to us than our five senses. During the phone conversation, I shared this spiritual happening with Hisham, something I kept to myself and protected. It was a component being set in motion, for a plot that would create more chapters and testaments in this book. Hisham denied my cousin had these abilities and argued he was just very observant and excellent at reading body language. I expressed my disagreement, then remained silent as he continued to rationalize the story. The conversation later on revealed Hisham wore many masks.

The following day Hisham sent a message, asking if I was free that upcoming weekend. I wondered why he reached out again, after such dismissiveness over the phone. I replied yes to his question and he offered to pick me up. I accepted, yet puzzled as to why I was okay with having a complete stranger come to my parent's house. I treasured privacy to an exceptionally high degree and rarely let anyone visit.

Regarding my worries, a whisper chimed in, *"Trust yourself. He will do no harm to you."*

Around 7:30 p.m. Hisham called, saying, "I'm outside."

I replied, "I think you're at the wrong house. I don't see you."

When he started laughing about waiting at the wrong house, I began to feel more at ease. As a guide post, I turned on the lights that hung on a miniature maple tree outside on the front yard. Hisham pulled into the driveway.

As I walked toward his car, the Mind asked, *"What have you gotten yourself into? Now you can't even escape because he is waiting right in front of you!"*

The Soul responded, *"Follow your intuition. Do not give into fear. Instead, enjoy the time offered to you. Laugh. Be merry. Remember, truth is waiting for you to embrace."*

You stand on a path, to the left and to the right are voids. Truth stands ahead but so does its treacherous companion, reality. Where do you venture? It is possible to retreat and go backwards, but why turn back a clock which is perfectly synchronized?

I took a deep breath and warily climbed into his SUV. He drove to our pre-planned destinations, while the conversation flowed. It was two souls, once well acquainted, were meeting again. The ease I felt in his presence allowed me to speak freely.

Without any sense of restraint, I expressed my opinion about the band's performance at my cousin's wedding. "You guys did a terrible job at that wedding. I danced only twice during the whole three hours and I love to dance. I was embarrassed for you all."

Without appearing to take offense, he responded, "I think it must have been the speakers or something. The stage was so small and we had a hard time setting up…Wow. We must have been pretty bad if you didn't dance."

Though very honest and blunt, I am usually very conscious of my words. I did not think twice. My train of thoughts about my frankness were disrupted when Hisham announced his need to stop at a office supply store. When we parked in the lot, I decided to stay in the car while he went inside. My eyes followed him as he walked toward the store entrance. I thought about how his physical appearance seemed to change before we arrived. There were moments when his demeanor appeared camouflaged and other times he seemed clearly familiar.

After a coffee stop to drop off the posters, we went to an Italian restaurant. I asked, "So, if you have been with the band for over two years, you must have played at my cousin's wedding in November?"

"Probably."

"Strange…I never saw you there…When everyone got impatient about the band taking so long to come out on stage, I did something about it and went back there. I yelled at the lead singer to get out there and play. Do you remember that wedding? There were more than three-hundred Syrians present."

Hisham replied, "No, not really…I play at so many weddings they all seem the same to me."

I received a hint from the angels, "The electricity fiasco."

I exclaimed, "Wait, I remember! It was a wedding where half of the string lights were out and then the electricity went out. You guys started packing up the equipment to leave! I went up to the lead singer demanding he stop packing up. When I got an arrogant attitude in return, I softened up and pleaded with him to give me some time to get the electricity back on. Which it did. Yet, I still do not recall seeing you there."

I noticed a change in Hisham's eyes. I had a sense he remembered and saw me beg Shadi, the lead singer, to stop removing the equipment. Hisham went from denying he played at this wedding, to admitting he did, but still reinforcing he did not see me. Let me recall for you, some details at what ended up being this light malfunction wedding. Fatima was not familiar with many of my family members, so she stayed close by my side the entire time. This wedding setup is where Hisham went up to her for the first time, and introduced himself. He somehow recalled Fatima and her name years later at the recent February 14th wedding. It seemed his memory was pretty sharp. I did not have realistic proof for this instance he was lying, but the storyline to come will hold evidence.

We parked in an empty lot and walked across the street toward the strip of bars and lounges. I followed him down a set of steps that led to an underground wine bar. The place was dimly lit with an oversized bar that took up almost the entire room, surrounded by cocktail tables. He escorted me through the narrow pathway to sit down at one of the tables. My eyes wandered, observing the people.

When a piece of art caught my eye, I asked, "Do you see the girl with the tattoo on the back of her neck, sitting on the bar stool?"

"Yes."

"It's a beautiful rose," I stated.

"I don't find tattoos attractive on women. Do you have any tattoos?" he inquired.

I answered, "No, but I thought about getting a small cross on my lower back. I would never do it though. It's not my style. You know, I once saw a guy with full-size angel wings tattooed on his shoulder blades. Extreme, but I have to admit it looked incredible. Do you have a tattoo?"

"No. Excuse me, I need to use the restroom."

He pushed out his chair and I watched him walk to the other end of the lounge. I doubted his answer, sensing he actually had a tattoo. I did not have real validation to this instinct he was lying about not seeing me at Grace's wedding. The intuitive notion about the tattoo was a different matter. Later, he bent over, revealing a tribal design on his lower back. This was the very beginning of a presentation, displaying a good soul, does not mean a good mind. Why did he lie about such a thing? I do not know.

When my eyes caught sight of the tattoo, I asked him the question, "Why did you say you didn't have a tattoo?"

He uncomfortably answered, "I don't know…I guess I lied…You know how girls get when they find out you have a tattoo. They want to see it and make you show them."

I just shrugged. In actuality, I figured a woman would never need to ask since most men show them off. I kept the response to myself and nodded my head. I knew it took some courage from him to admit to the falsehood.

Last stop was a hookah lounge. Hisham opened the door for me, and we entered a foyer, containing a glass case of Middle Eastern desserts. Off to the right sat a male bouncer. We went through the door way past him and walked into a heavy crowd of people. The lighting was very dim, with strobe lights circling the room. I looked ahead to see two women on the dance floor sloppily belly dancing. Trailing behind Hisham, we passed the line of tables and crossed through the dance floor to a booth.

Before we sat down, he introduced me to his cousin, Samir, who was sitting in the booth. He was a petite-framed man with thick black hair and a nasally voice. I smiled and attempted to hear him over the loud music, at the same time had an impression he did not like me. When we settled in, Samir immediately started talking in Hisham's ear. I turned away from them, sat silent, and calmly watched the commotion in the lounge. I questioned being in an atmosphere with people that were so disagreeable to my taste. This is a location I would not come to willingly to. This is a person I would not even speak to in the first place. These were not people I would choose to be around. I was lowering myself.

Interrupting my thoughts, Hisham leaned over to say, "Now I see what you were talking about. You told me you get extremely quiet when you're not one-on-one with a person. I can see how people misjudge you for being stuck-up…You really are shy, huh."

"Yes… I know. I'm a private person and when I'm in a new group, I observe and listen. Unless someone asks me a question, this is the way I am."

"I'll be right back. I'm going to say hello to some people across the room."

As soon as Hisham left, his male acquaintance slid over on the bench, stopping right next to me. Ignoring my guarded look, he asked, "What was your name again? I didn't hear it with the music so loud."

I desperately wanted to get out of there. I got myself into this situation and I was going to find a way out. Without a car, I figured I could call one of my cousins to pick me up. I thought it was a great idea, but there was something higher in the works, practically prohibiting me from pressing the send key to connect the call. I was left confused as to how this was possible.

The male acquaintance disrupted my confusion and getaway plan, asking if I wanted to dance. I was cornered again, blaming myself for being in this predicament. He persisted. About half an hour passed, the friend asked once more if I would dance with him. I felt bad for rejecting his requests, so I decided to hit the dance floor. Though awkward, the movement of my hips did not reveal a hint of it. Two young women he knew joined us, which made it more tolerable to stay on the dance floor. The song ended, I thanked the heavens, and we sat back in the booth. Within a few minutes, Hisham returned with a possessive look on his face. The comrade sensed it was time to scoot to his original position.

I pondered how I could make this night end. My planning was interrupted once more when Hisham proceeded to reach under the table and intertwine his fingers with mine. It was shocking and after a few more confused moments, I pulled my hand away. It felt wrong, his intentions were wrong. I convinced him to end the night early. During the car ride, I was eager to get home. As he turned off his head lights and pulled in the driveway, I dreaded what I knew was coming next.

When Hisham attempted to kiss me, I dodged the move and burst out, "Nice try."

He was visibly surprised for a second then brushed it off by chuckling. I surprised myself when I said it out loud. **I did not understand why at the time, but knew the only reason this outing happened was because of something higher than both of us.** That aside, there

were realistic variables to consider: He left me with strangers at the hookah lounge for over thirty minutes, tried to kiss me even though I pulled my hand away from his and continued to evade any physical touch. You might think after all this, I would definitely never hang out with such a person again. This was not the case, there were many purposes to be fulfilled.

Almost a week passed, I went about my business, attending classes, and studying. Intrigued by the spiritual aspect of the Druze culture, I decided to research the background. I clicked on a guided link and reached the section on the Syrian Druze leaders and the fight for the independence of Syria from France.

Then an intuitive message came through. *"Hisham is closely blood-related to the Syrian Druze leaders and his family is tied to the heritage of the Syrian Druze."*

Doubts about my intuition surfaced. I never reject the truth, but I do let it run its course. The next day after these inklings, I received a late evening call. Hisham notified me his work was cancelled and asked if I had any plans for the night. School assignments were caught up on and I was free. Still uncomfortable with the idea, I agreed for him to pick me up again. He arrived and headed to a district of lounges.

As he drove, I opened the discussion to the topic of the Druze religion. "Because I like to know a little bit about everything, I went on the Internet and researched the Druze. I found a really interesting article."

Hisham responded, "Most of those articles are false and depict Druze in a negative way."

"I think this one might have provided some true insight about your background."

He inserted, "Did you read the part about how we have a law stating we can't marry outside our religion or convert to another one?"

I did not understand where that came from, responding, "No, I didn't finish reading the whole article. I must not have gotten to that part..."

Hisham asked, "Did you read about how the Druze fought for Syrian independence?"

"Yes. I read a phrase I can't forget for some reason...it went along the lines of 'no Syrian group played a more heroic role in the fight for independence from colonialism than the Druze.' It left an imprint... somehow I knew it was true."

"Wow, I didn't know that," he continued, "Well, my grandfather fought in that war and he was one of the leaders. One of my uncles was a spy for Syria and the other one held a high military position."

The inner voice was utterly right. Not only was he Druze, but he came from a lineage of Syrian Druze leaders.

After our twenty-minute drive, we made it to a part of Cleveland I had never seen. The array of lounges were uniquely designed with a historic village essence. We entered one of the nestled pubs to view a life size tree, framed by a glossy wooden bar. A brick fireplace sat off to the side. We sat in close proximity to the fireplace with no one else around. That night, we conversed as if we knew each other for a lifetime. It got quiet for a few moments, I slightly turned my head to ask Hisham a question. I found him abruptly leaning in and landing on my lips. I was blindsided, and after a brief instant leaned away. There was not a single ounce of awkwardness, until this second attempt at a kiss. This spoiled the innocent and care free time. I pretended it did not happen. We exchanged further dialogue until the clock struck 2:15 A.M. It was time to leave.

Once we reached his car, he asked, where I wanted to head next. It was a Thursday night in a city with limited social scenes, plus I did not go out much. Hisham affirmed everything was closed and threw out the statement to go to his house. With a look of apprehension, my heart dropped to my stomach. I knew, without a doubt, what was on Hisham's mind. Yet, found myself saying that was fine.

The angels arrived and evoked, "Follow truth. No fears. You are in safe hands. Relax. He is to be trusted."

There was higher power reassurance, on top of that, a strong magnetic push to go. I was still hesitant to accept Hisham's invitation to enter his house. I temporarily suspended the mind's analyzation, to make way for what was right on a soul level. I followed Hisham to the doorway of his home. He held the door open for me and, with somewhat eased nerves, I stepped inside. While he gestured for me to sit on the ivory sofa, he introduced me to his cousin, Jalal, who sat on the nearby black futon. Jalal looked up at me, said hello, and returned to the television screen. He was tall in stature, with a lean physique, and wore sleek framed glasses that settled on a broad nose.

Hisham said, "Jalal, she's Syrian. Do you want anything to drink, Jasmine?"

I replied, "No, thank you."

I came to find out Jalal respectively loved and admired Syrian women. When Jalal heard those words, he turned his attention back to me and began asking questions such as, was I "born in Syria?" and when I "came to America?" After that, the conversation alternated between us watching a movie and engaging in random discussions. Hisham kept giving Jalal looks, insinuating he wanted him to go upstairs.

My intuition glowed as I began reading Jalal's thoughts. "Maybe I should go upstairs… no…I'm enjoying the company and she doesn't seem the type to sleep with him…At least not right away. She seems different than all the other girls he brings home… plus she's Syrian."

Jalal seemed a person of great and solid character. He stayed for another thirty minutes. Having reached the pinnacle of ignoring Hisham's persistent hints, Jalal said good night and we watched him walk up the wooden stairs. The room fell silent and Hisham leaned in. I convinced myself to go with it. It was okay for the moment, did not feel right or wrong. Within a few passing moments, it changed.

I pulled away and without hesitation pronounced, "You know I'm a virgin, right?"

When I spoke those words, it referred to our common traditions. In Middle Eastern culture, it is a well-known custom a woman stays a virgin until she marries.

His eyes widened as he absorbed the words and responded, "What?"

His body reacted unconsciously as he slid himself away.

Unfazed, I verbalized his stunned reaction, "You didn't think I was…?"

"No, I thought with you growing up here almost all your life and going away to college for four years, you wouldn't be."

"Interesting, I understand. But I choose to stay true to my upbringing and, above all, to myself."

He did not get what he wanted, I thought that was the moment to go.

The angels provided a whole different message. *Stay relaxed, do not rush to judgment.*

Without an apparent reason, I looked over at him, and found myself saying, "I'm sorry…"

He moved his eyes from the ground to meet mine. The apology provided just enough light to his true core. "You should never be sorry for such a thing. It doesn't matter, anyway."

Hisham changed the subject, we started to watch television, and conversed like newly acquainted friends. A two-note hum came to my lips, out of nowhere, and caught his attention.

Hisham asked, "What are you humming?"

"I don't know…I wasn't even aware I was humming."

"Well, it's very pretty."

The night gave way into morning. Suddenly, I realized how much time passed. As both of us were surprised, he jumped up and stated the need to take me home. He was concerned about my parents seeing me arrive so late. He turned off the headlights and pulled into the driveway.

Naturally, I said, "Next time, we should have Jalal watch a new movie with us."

Immediately after that statement, doubt returned. I questioned myself as to why I brought up the idea. Most likely, I was never going to see or hear from him again.

Hisham replied, "Yes, definitely. I will let him know. I will call you tomorrow."

I figured he said that to be polite. I kissed him on the cheek and said, "Okay. I'll talk to you then. Goodnight."

The next day, Hisham did call. We met up five various nights within two weeks, chit-chatting, watching movies with Jalal, and eating ice cream until 4:30 in the morning. The times were full of contentment, the words spoken never led to deep conversations. There was an understanding to what we were experiencing. A light switch was flipped. Hisham's opaque character took a temporary step back. A type of transparency illuminated his authentic self. Before the February 14th meeting, we discovered we crossed paths many times. He played at two weddings I was present at, went to the same wake less than a year before, and attended the same techno show in Columbus years prior. It truly was like two old friends who were meeting again after a long separation.

Three weeks later, I went to an Arabic concert with my brother-in-law, Nasim, and my older sister, Genevieve. Hisham also went to the concert with a group of his friends. We never came into contact, even when we looked for one another during the intermission. When the concert was over, I walked down the long staircase to the sight of free dessert samples. Genevieve ordered me to keep moving. Already past the display, I ran back through the crowd and snapped up a piece. Returning toward the direction of the exit, I found Hisham right outside the glass doors.

After I introduced him to Genevieve and Nasim, I explained, "Okay. I have to leave with them."

Hisham asked, "Why don't you just come with me and I'll take you home?"

My eyes filled with hesitation. I was assured, "He is trustworthy."

In faith, I replied, "Okay. Nasim, I'm going to just go with Hisham."

Worry and protectiveness appeared on my brother-in-law's face, while my sister kept nagging him to leave.

"Don't worry," I reassured Nasim. "I'll be fine. Get home safely."

Joey, the drummer of the band and a close friend of Hisham, drove us to an international night at a west-side lounge. As a group, we went inside for twenty minutes, they ordered drinks, and walked back outside to the lounge's patio. I spent most of the time chatting with Joey who remarked about how my eyes told a story of their own.

After an hour, I sat on a wooden bench next to Hisham, I heard the inner voice yell, *"Look immediately to your right."*

When I moved in the advised direction, I saw one of my first cousins, Majid. What were the odds of seeing him when I had not went out for over five months. I was thankful I saw Majid before he saw me.

I turned my face back to Hisham. "One of my cousins is here. I have to go say hi before he gets the wrong idea."

Alarmed by my swift response, he answered, "Okay…"

Sometimes I wondered about things that happened since meeting Hisham. One after another, the timing was impeccable. I approached the outside line of people waiting to have their identification checked. Majid greeted me with a peck on the cheek and I did the same.

Majid asked, "Who are you here with?"

I replied, "With some friends."

"Where?"

I pointed, "They are right over there, around the bench."

Majid shouted, "They're all foreigners. You know foreigners want only one thing!"

"Majid, I'm a foreigner." Though I had a quick come back, fear materialized.

He countered, "You're different!"

Knowing there was verity to what Majid said, I looked back at Hisham and internally felt, "He does not have those intentions with you. Trust."

Majid exclaimed, "Wait. They're all guys!"

"No, they're not all guys." I gestured at the female with the short black hair.

"Come with me and I'll introduce you to them."

Majid put on a macho act, aggressively shaking the hands of Hisham's friends, announcing he was "Jasmine's cousin." He followed it up with an interrogation of where my car was, who was taking me home, and who was going to drive.

Without taking offense to this behavior, Joey stepped up to the plate. "I'm the one driving."

Majid's phone rang, interrupting his next words. He said, "Jasmine, wait here! I'll be right back. I need to pick this girl up who can't find her way here. Do not leave! I'm going to walk you to the car."

While this was taking place, Hisham's temper was flaring. "I can't believe him!"

Joey cooled him off immediately. "Come on, Hisham! If you saw your cousin out with a bunch of guys, what would you do? Honestly, I would have done worse than what he did."

We waited and waited. I called Majid repeatedly as Hisham's friend, Fadel, needed to get up early for work.

Hisham moved to my side, whispering, "Jasmine, energy, energy. I can feel everything you're feeling."

I looked at him and reflected. I thought he did not believe in those types of things. Was

he not the person who kept providing realistic explanations for every mystical occurrence?

I called Majid once more. Patiently, I asked, "Majid, where are you? I'm still waiting."

With no reservation, he replied, "Go ahead. Drive home safely. Bye."

There is a difference between a person's attitude and their true character. Ironically, Majid put on this display, to protect the public appearance of my virtue, only to drop everything for a random woman. I was following my soul's knowing to continue to interact with Hisham. Almost a week following the Arabic concert, I awoke to an uneasy knowing. I was blindfolded, being guided by something divine that I trusted. My mind recognized I was being led to darker areas. I was determined to stop what was happening, before it progressed any further.

As of late, it seemed anytime I deviated from the necessary steps, I experienced an uncomfortable physical signal. On a Saturday afternoon, in the middle of a Pilates workout, I received a text message from Hisham. I picked the phone up and pushed ignore. Before setting it back down, my heart started to pound. It was physical, but even deeper, as if my chest was being squeezed. It reminded me of when I resisted calling Hisham back after his first initial contact, but more intensified. I placed my hand against my chest, attempting to somehow calm the discomfort. After a few minutes, the aching eased to where I could breathe better. I went back to what I was doing. The longer I ignored responding to the text message, the stronger the throbbing became. I occupied myself with anything I could find.

A cousin was having a birthday party at the unpleasant hookah lounge and I did not want to go. This cousin and her sister are referred to as the shallow cousins. I can see the true core in everyone. It does not mean I like them. They based their whole life solely on superficial things such as makeup, clothes, and their bodies. In addition, they are well-known for gossiping about everyone and intentionally manipulating stories, stirring the pot. I had the misfortune of experiencing this first hand and refused to interact by word or deed. There is no need to lower oneself to the level of another. It does no good.

My mind repelled against the force of the soul to attend. Even with both the aching discomfort in my chest and the powerful force field, I refused to comply with the push to go to the birthday party. In recent weeks, Nasim, my brother-in-law, opened his own immigration law practice. I sent messages to everyone I knew in the Cleveland area with an ethnic background. I let them know if they needed an immigration lawyer, I personally knew one. A former co-worker responded, saying he would keep that in mind and asked if I had any dinner plans.

Light and dark have different energy frequencies. Instead of looking at the spectrum of colors, I felt the vibrations of each color. I knew the difference in every wavelength. Positive, neutral, negative, and anything in between. At once, the timeless analogy of a demon on one shoulder and an angel on the other, came alive in real life.

The angels intervened, "We do not recommend you go out with him. You will pay heavily later on, when it comes back to haunt you in an unforeseen way."

I ignored it and with no other plans, arranged a meetup at a local restaurant with this former co-worker. At this point, the pounding in my heart started to increase again. I did not heed the warning of the angels and disregarded the inner knowing. It provided the dark entities with an opportunity to speak:

> **Breaking it now is the best for all. Come on, Jasmine! Break the connection. Look at the reality of the situation. You have only known him for three weeks. He is just a guy you met at a wedding, nothing more. What is the purpose of continuing this? Look at how much you will lose and the very little you will gain. Why delay the inevitable behavior he will act out? You have hidden behind the truth for so long but soon you will pay dearly for your loyalty. We will be waiting for you again and again. You will falter, and we will catch you, imposing our command which you deny. Fail not to forget our wrath, for each time we return, we will come back stronger and cut deeper. We laugh at your allegiance to truth for it will bring you much more pain than we are even capable of!**

There seemed to be a significance to the connection with Hisham, so much so it provoked the presence of both the encouraging angels and the hindering demons together. I was left out of the loop until the very end. All of the soul demons' prophecies came true beyond my imagination.

The former co-worker and I arrived at the restaurant, sat at a back table, and began chatting. In brief, the conversation simply involved me asking questions and him responding.

The real dialogue took place in my head. *"God, why do I have to try so hard to keep this conversation going? I feel absolutely no connection toward him except boredom. There was a connection and comfort when it came to Hisham...what makes Hisham different?"*

The angels provided a key. "It is the unique, powerful connection you share with each other."

The answer resonated and rejuvenated my mind. I ended the dinner early, finally giving into the energetic pressure, to appear at the shallow cousin's party later that night. I convinced one of my older cousins, Mansour, to attend the party with me. Mansour was a person I trusted and enjoyed his company without having to keep my guard up. After he climbed in my car, we drove to the hookah lounge.

Mansour yelped, "Slow down. There is always a cop waiting in that parking lot."

I replied, "I know. Don't worry."

He said, "The light is about to turn red. Hurry up, but don't speed."

"Mansour trust me. I'm a good, safe driver."

"Be careful turning this corner."

"Okay. What is going on with you? You don't have to tell me if you don't want to, but I've never seen you so paranoid about driving before."

"I got pulled over for drinking and driving. My driver's license is suspended except for work driving privileges," he said.

With a laugh, I pronounced, "Now we have the story, STOP thinking about cops, we have seen three in less than ten minutes. You're attracting them to us."

Did he listen? No. Five minutes later, we saw a police car parked on the side of the highway. Through our thoughts, positive or negative, we can and do, attract things into our lives. Have you ever noticed times when you started to think about something, and it begins to show up around you? For example, you find a car you like, are attracted to. Therefore, an automatic connection to the vehicle is made that vibrates out. Before you hardly noticed that model on the road. Now it seems like wherever you go, you see that car. **This is a response matching your vibrations to what you are thinking and how you feel. It does not decipher between fear and courage, or know the difference between good fortune and misfortune. So, if your mind is focused on something constantly, whether you are aware of it or not, this is what you end up attracting more of. Channel your thoughts to something that makes you feel lighter. The vibes you put out, are the vibes you receive.**

Mansour and I walked in the hookah lounge and spotted the long row of tables. All the cousins were seated, on the verge of boredom. I ignored the negative attitude of the two shallow cousins and spent some time with the others. Different people, same place, still equaled the same undertone of grime. Again, the want to leave and why I was there returned. The strangest thing was Mansour disliked this place and the company more than me. He also could not verbalize the words to go, even with his friends waiting for us at another place. When they repeatedly texted and called Mansour, I kept offering the option to depart.

Later, I asked Mansour why he did not want to leave. He replied, "I don't know. I guess I had a feeling we needed to stay for some reason."

There was a "meant to be" occurrence this night, involving Hisham. He and his group of friends were at their usual weekend booth, located right next to the stage. When I noticed Hisham leave the table, I took the opportunity to greet his friends and cousins. I walked across the dance floor and sat next to Joey. I thanked him for preventing the situation from escalating last weekend with Majid's protective behavior. The embarrassment from Majid, leaving me hanging for a love interest, was another story. As I tried to end the conversation with Joey and leave the booth, Hisham entered the other side. With the table separating us, he stood greeting new arrivals, ignoring I was present.

Joey yelled for his attention. "Hisham, look who it is!"

He turned toward me, giving an unpleasant look of 'what are you doing?'

Deciding to intervene, Joey shouted, "Hisham. It's Jasmine!"

Hisham realized that his disapproval was apparent. "Oh my God, I thought you were someone else. I saw blonde hair and thought it was our friend, Kate."

It was a fact we have no resemblance, whatsoever, to each other.

He came and sat next to me, asking, "Are you having a good time?"

I gently responded, "No. Actually, I forced myself to come here for my cousin's birthday. It's a cat fight over at my table."

"Where are you sitting? I didn't see you anywhere."

"The table directly diagonal to this one, the entire table is full of my relatives."

Unconsciously, I expressed an internal feeling, "I want to leave."

"No, you shouldn't do that. Just give it a little more time."

I tilted my head down, and recalled the earlier heart throbbing.

Intuned, Hisham asked, "What's wrong?"

I returned my eyes to his face and found myself saying, "My soul is tired…"

I thought, *"Where did that come from?…why did I tell him something I haven't even revealed to myself?"*

He responded, "Why? You have everything a guy could want. You're intelligent, pretty, educated, and on top of those things, you're Syrian."

If he only knew the extent of this journey, and how bizarre it became.

While I listened to his words, I noticed a different look in his eyes. "You've been drinking?"

With a sense of guilt, he replied, "Yes. What are a bunch of guys supposed to do on a Saturday night? We started drinking before we got here. How can you tell?"

"Your eyes show everything."

As the music faded into the background, I knew he was about to speak the words that came from his fear. "You know, Jasmine, I'm not ready for a relationship. I like the way things are in my life. I'm thirty-two and don't have any commitments or things tying me down."

I did not understand where this was coming from. There was nothing spoken or unspoken about any sort of relationship.

Then he said, "Remember when you told me about your cousin and his powers?"

I nodded yes.

He continued, "I tried to make you believe there was some realistic reason for how he did those things. That he was good at reading people through body language and eye contact. I actually knew those types of things were real. I've had experiences in my life with energies and things reality can't explain."

I asked, "Why did you do that?"

"Because I couldn't let you inside that part of me. You would be in too deep. I had to protect myself, so I tried to convince you it wasn't true."

I acknowledged with, "I understand."

My mind did not function from a place where I would cover up who I was, but I understood this was how his mind worked.

The inner knowing came through, it was right to tell, "I went to dinner earlier tonight with a guy I used to work with. I sat there forcing myself to keep the conversation going and I was bored out of my mind. I wanted to decipher what made you different. I compared him and the experience to you…I needed to know how and why the connection to you is not like anything I encountered before."

I still did not know the full answer, but I let go of the resistance. His facial expression completely changed when I shared this casual meetup. I began to experience the throbbing in my chest again. I tried to take some deep breaths and soothe this sharp physical reaction. One of my male cousins walked over and spoke in my ear. He warned of my uncle's irritation and said they were about to leave. I knew this needed to be finished. I acknowledged what he said and told him I would join them in a few minutes. I turned back to face Hisham.

He immediately said, "Jasmine, I don't know why I'm telling you all this…probably because I'm tipsy so I'm more honest. I know I'm going to end up hurting you. I know myself. At the same time, I feel like I need to protect you. I want to push you away, but I want you in my life."

The sensation in my chest intensified, leaving me puzzled to what it was and why it was happening. Hard as I tried, there was no stopping the pain.

The angels requested, "Focus on him."

I knew what Hisham was about to attempt, and an instinct kicked to gear. I jumped into the waters to pull him out of his fears. "Hisham, don't push me away. Listen to me. We can be friends. Don't just cut me off. There is no need for that. I make a good and loyal friend."

He replied, "Yes. I could tell that about you from the way you spoke about your cousin and the advice you gave him."

Literally at the exact moment, the same cousin that came over previously interrupted again. He said, "Jasmine, we really have to go. Your uncle is about to lose it. He is waiting over there."

Returning to Hisham, I said, "I'm sorry, but I have to go. They're waiting for me."

I walked out of the lounge with Mansour on my right side. The pains and confusion continued.

Mansour asked, "Are you okay? What's going on? What happened in there?"

Trusting Mansour, I gave him a quick rundown of the conversation that just transpired, describing the uncomfortable feeling that took physical form. The puzzle pieces of this experience were beginning to come together. **Disguised as physical throbbing, it was a signal that occurred each time I tried to go against the inner knowing, or things were deviating in the wrong direction.** The aches did not stop. They merely continued to return and inflict confusion. Eight months later, I came to call these the "discomfort of knowing," a binding which ran as deep as the soul, reaching the physical body. The experience was extreme in this case, but you might have encountered something that resembles it. You are about to get in your car or enter a building, and your body begins to signal you. You feel anxious in your stomach or heaviness in your chest. These are realistic cues for you, guideposts that detour or set you in the right direction. Understand when you do have these physical sensations, many times there is a higher meaning.

Like the moon in a lunar eclipse, darkness fell and toxic rays permeated. The battle of light and dark played out in its purest and most paralyzing form. I discovered myself exposed to things I did not believe in, or thought existed. At the same time, I found myself dueling with the external reality and the internal knowing. This was all part of a grand plan to bring more chapters alive. The four-year journey with Fatima ended and a month later, the inner knowing returned, knocking at the door. There was more evidence that needed to be unearthed about the truth of this world. Fatima was replaced with the character of Hisham, a person entrapped by the mind.

Unleashing of Medusa's Rumors

Although intrigued by the mythological creature, Medusa, I did not know she transformed from maiden to monster until I researched it. As one of three daughters, Medusa was the only mortal child of the sea titans, Porcys and Ceto. In her original form, Medusa was a maiden of rare beauty with long silky hair which was her most valuable asset. She bragged of her beauty being greater than Athena, the virgin goddess of wisdom. The sea god, Poseidon, desperately desired Medusa and so he ravished her while she was praying in the temple of the goddess Athena. Appalled and outraged by this sacrilegious act, Athena transformed Medusa's beautiful tresses into serpents. The now hideous monster gained the destructive power of being able to turn anyone to stone who looked directly into her eyes. A hero, named Perseus, approached Medusa as she slept. With the help of Athena's silver shield, Perseus killed Medusa by looking at her reflection in the armor and beheading her.

We go through life and it sometimes offers challenging events. Looking straight at these happenings can turn us into "stone-like" figures, overwhelming us so much that we disconnect and no longer feel. **Mirrors are presented, through people and incidents, to show reflections of our insecurities and wounds.** This is to keep us from being overloaded and hardening completely.

The past damage of abandonment, which happened at an early age, was heightened during the first two years of college. In order to keep me close by, my mother forced me to accept an academic scholarship package from a college less than two hours from home. I fought against this with everything I had, sensing continuation of comfortless high school years were on the horizon. The only thing that stopped this resistance happened while driving to the required campus visit. I sat trying to convince my mother to understand where I was coming from. As we entered the city of the college and approached the campus, there was an intense magnetic pull within me. It internally came over me to stop struggling and accept what was meant to play out. At that precise moment, I became still, and swallowed this difficult pill.

A couple years later, I came to call this college "the black hole of Ohio." Many students who attended, specifically from the east coast area, would nod their head in agreement. On the flip side, I observed some students enjoyed all it offered, from academics to social life. Nonetheless, my two years at the college fell short of what others experienced. For the first three months, my landscape was filled with a lush patchwork of relationships. I became friends with three separate circles: my roommate, a group of girls that lived down the hall, and others from another dorm. The gals down the hall did not care for my roommate and froze her out. I took the initiative to introduce them all to each other and they got along beautifully. My roommate suggested we share clothes and it seemed to be a fun idea, so I agreed. The first gust of the windstorm came through. Eventually, the roommate and the ladies formed their own clique, omitting the person who brought them together. Later, after mustering up the courage to ask my roommate, I found out what was going on. She tried to avoid answering but the sneaking and excluding had gone on too long. I stood still waiting for a response. She finally confessed, at some point, she changed her mind and was uncomfortable sharing her clothes.

I said, "You did exactly..."

She finished my sentence, "What they did to me."

The second gust came when I befriended a classmate in the first semester of a biology class. For several months, I would return to my dorm room to find messages from him. He introduced me to his roommate who played on the football team and we all spent time with each other. Then, it suddenly stopped. When I crossed paths with him or his roommate there was total avoidance. Enough was enough. After six months, an encounter allowed for some closure. I decided to speak up, asking him in a very general way, what happened. He rambled, while I remained silent. He spoke of a conversation he had with his roommate, about his growing concern for my well-being.

Making it out like he was looking out for my best interest, he said, "You got too attached to us, you were becoming dependent on us for things."

You see, the facts about me were very much the contrary. I came out of high school a bit introverted, with no friends except Fatima. My shyness kept me to myself, although it was effortless to make friends. I relied on myself and never needed a shoulder to lean on. There was no justification for what he was saying, I was baffled. This classmate left the next year due to low grades. He returned for a visit and ended up professing how I was a "perfect ten" in his eyes.

I was blindsided from both of these situations, especially because they entered during a time of vulnerability. College is a new opportunity to step in with openness and an optimism it will be different than high school. You crave real connection, since your child-like essence, which roots us into all that exists, is somewhat dissolved. You take the risk to find this realness by trusting in others. Then you come crashing down from the reality of these interpersonal relationships. This whipping experience sent me reeling backward and left me wondering if it was worth it to ever trust people again.

The one blossoming orchid was Sarah, a beautiful soul. She became a person who provided a little light to this darkened landscape. Unfortunately, she soon drifted away after a raw conversation about her losing her values and most of all, herself. She did not really like what I had to say at the time. After four years of no contact, she returned.

Sarah explained, "I met this guy who made me realize what you said to me was for my own good. I see now that you just wanted me to know my worth."

Although the distancing saddened me, without judgement I embraced her, with understanding I stayed neutral and did not hold onto any questions about the situation.

Those experiences became a catalyst for a belief, since I was the common denominator in all these situations, I must have been the cause of the broken relationships. As a result, I lost much of my sense of humor and carefree demeanor. If it was not for my cousin Grace, the deep impact would have remained. Subsequently. I grew to recognize these early college situations, were "built-in" hurdles on my map of life. It was about testing and finding who I truly was, despite the events telling a different story. **All these examinations of loss served as a lesson that many people will move through your life as temporary connections.** I successfully came to understand this principle, yet, I questioned if there was something I could have done differently in each scenario. Maybe even prevented the loss of these friendships. I carried this in the deeper recesses of my mind and it continued to haunt me.

If we look directly at the pain, disappointment, or damage, we tend to shut down or disconnect. People walk into your life to be reflections of these wounds without you being completely immersed in the thick of it all. Hisham was one of these characters. The bandage covering the hurt of being deserted was ripped off. Since I met Hisham I saw him transform into a different person, opening up, and letting me in his world. He was simply himself, not watching or filtering what he said. He mentioned connecting to some people of Syrian ethnicity on social media. Pulling up the site, he asked if I was related to any of them. I remarked, one of them was my first cousin, Grace. He commented how attractive she was, and then added he could not believe he expressed that to me. He invited me to come down to his studio and listen to songs being created. Hisham never shared his music with anyone until the finished product, revealing this as a big deal. His friends would be shocked to hear he actually did this. He showed me photos of his childhood and family, telling me stories of his mischievous behavior.

So swiftly reality came knocking at the door. I left all control of the communication with Hisham. I called and sent text messages only on necessary matters. When I found good news and wanted to share it, I restrained from reaching out. The past wounds of the college relationships were opening. I tried to hold them closed with one hand, attempting to conceal the gashes. I did not want them to negatively impact relations with new people.

I encountered Hisham a few weeks later after the cousin's birthday party at the hookah lounge, when he asked me to meet him there. The early afternoon sunlight was trying to pierce through the faintly lit lounge. Hisham, his cousin Johnny, the girlfriend, Samir, and I sat in the booth.

Hisham asked, "What are you planning to do tomorrow?"

I replied, "I'm not sure? Nothing I know of."

Then he hurriedly said, "What do you think about going to Michigan with me?"

I thought he was playing around. I answered, "I don't know. Call me early tomorrow and we'll go from there."

That following day, my mother reminded me of a family baby shower we were expected to attend. I went without reservation. At the shower, I enjoyed the atmosphere and the delicious sweets. As it started to wind down, I felt an ache in my chest, and had no idea why. There were different degrees of pressure, a squeezing. In my stomach, it was a queasiness, or an extremely full feeling. **These uncomfortable cues are the language of the body, the connecting doorway to your soul, and its landline for communicating.** Has anyone brought up a topic in conversation and it causes a physical reaction where you feel something is not right or off? The body knows things that the mind is not aware of.

When we returned home, I wondered why Hisham did not contact me. I started to connect the dots, there was some sort of connection between these physical symptoms and Hisham. Late in the night, I received a text from him, asking me to meet at the usual hookah lounge.

My dislike for this particular lounge did not change, I set those feelings aside as the angels informed, "You must go. It is urgent for many reasons you will see. Do not mind the environment. Focus on seeking the truth."

To offset the distaste for the lounge's atmosphere, I arrived around midnight, leaving less than two hours before closing. I walked in alone, while this growing feeling of anxiety became my sidekick. I found everyone at their regular booth, noticing two neighboring tables full of familiar-looking Syrian men. I saw some around town, others were distant relatives, or came from the same small village as my father. They watched every step I took. I ignored their stares and sat down. Hisham introduced the woman next to him as a friend of the group. I greeted her with a smile, and she returned a sincere, "Nice to meet you."

After a little conversation with the her, Hisham started talking. He remarked, "She can speak fluent Spanish, and for some reason she thinks Fadel understands it. So she sat there speaking Spanish to him for 15 minutes, and he just nodded his head, pretending to agree with what she was saying. To this day, she is still convinced Fadel can understand Spanish."

I laughed visualizing Fadel, the keyboard player in the band, nodding his head and her proceeding on, clueless to the fact he did not understand a word she said. I looked over at Hisham to find him looking out into the distance of the room, lost in thought. He returned to my eyes a different person.

Hisham said, "You know, Jasmine… I'm way ahead of you."

My intuition spoke of what he implied with those words. In hopes I was wrong, I asked, "What exactly do you mean by that?"

He replied, "This whole thing taking place between us…I know what's going to happen. You're not aware. You don't know and see things like I do."

I responded with assertion, "Hisham, do not underestimate me. Don't think I'm not aware of anything because I am aware of everything."

He continued, "I'm not underestimating you. I just know more than you do of what's taking place."

Though puzzled about exactly what he was talking about, I did not read into it. There was an instinct he was projecting his own matters upon me. A male acquaintance came over to ask Hisham to temporarily accompany him.

"I'll be right back," he said.

I acknowledged by nodding my head.

It was like an open tear which did not bleed, but stung. I sat there not knowing what to do. The metaphysical and physical were two separate dimensions, now they were completely fused together. The four-year journey with Fatima was always kept private and apart from our outside reality. I was able to keep her afloat, while I dealt with finding a career, facing family pressures, and coming into my potential. My spiritual world and reality were interlocked, and I could not unmerge them. His words, the physical aches, and the inner knowing, whirled within me.

I sat in the booth, focused on the crowd ahead and the loud Arabic music playing. Throughout the conversation with Hisham, I continued to sense the stares from behind me. After he left, the chance arrived to directly return the looks and deliver the unspoken words of "Stop looking, mind your own business."

Hisham came back, sat next to me on the end, and did not reopen the subject or speak a single word.

Eventually, his Spanish-speaking friend leaned over and whispered into his ear. He turned to me and said, "Jasmine, she wants me to dance with her."

Without hesitation, I sincerely replied, "Go ahead, go dance with her."

When they began to dance, I slid over to the edge of the booth which touched the parameter of the dance floor. I needed to get out of this place. The throbbing in my chest was too much. I fought the urge to escape.

Hisham came over and took hold of my hand, "Come on Jasmine, dance with us."

"Hisham, I really don't want to dance. I'm not feeling well."

He persisted, and not having much energy left, I gave in.

As this was happening, the entire group of Syrian men turned their attention once more, closely watching us dance. We formed a triangle dancing and after thirty seconds, the song to my relief ended. When we returned to the booth, Hisham decided to leave and disappeared into the crowd.

The place was closing in thirty minutes, he was nowhere in sight. The little girl inside of me came alive, searching for sanctuary. I was transformed back into that six-year-old self again. I began to relive experiences as a watcher of my past.

Sitting on the cold concrete steps of the playground, alone, the little girl

stared out. She was physically different from most of the people in the village. The adults would praise the girl for her blonde hair and light blue-grey eyes. Amid the dark-brown hair and brown-eyed children, she stood out like a giraffe in a herd of zebras. The children took notice of her uncommon features; the girls excluded her from their jump rope, while the boys left her out of the hide-and-seek games.

 In reality, it was my appearance that set me apart from others. **In truth**, it was my internal makeup. As a child beyond her years, I was acutely aware and observant, thinking in a way which separated me. Three boys started to laugh and point in this little girl's direction. She tried to look the other way, as a malicious grin plastered each boy's face. She froze when they drew closer to the steps. All she could do was internally scream for help. Leisurely, one walked by with the other two boys behind him. He picked up speed, whipping his hand out, smacking her over the head, while the other two pulled her hair. Meanwhile, the other students looked on and did nothing. The boys skipped away as if they did nothing wrong. She looked around wondering why no one helped her. Was she so different? She wrapped her arms around herself and salty tears ran down her rosy cheeks.

 The principal caught sight of me and walked over to question what took place. Frightened to speak the full facts, I softly named only the first boy who caused the most pain. As fate would have it, this boy's aunt was one of my teachers. Although the boy received a minor reprimanding from the principal, the boy's aunt decided to retaliate. Entering the classroom and settling into my seat, the hollow icy desk sent shivers through my small body. When I dropped a pencil on the floor, I heard the teacher's voice demand me to approach the front of the class. I obeyed her orders. She asked me to take out my hands and open my palms. Again, I followed, unaware of why this was taking place. The leathery stick flew up in the air and repeatedly landed on my palms, to the point of both hands bleeding.

 My mind took refuge in nature; a place which I knew would not harm me. I spent much time alone. I often ventured by myself far from the village homes to pick wild roses and daffodils, ignoring the frightening stories of animals in those areas. While the fragrance soothed my mind and soul, the rose itself, to this day, symbolizes my freedom. The petals represent the delicacy of life and the architectural form of the flower emulates the beauty of life's organized chaos. Nature was a haven to this little girl.

Now all grown up and in a crowded hookah lounge, I was nowhere near nature. It was a shock factor; how could my two worlds be one? I stopped wondering where Hisham was and followed Fadel. From the war-torn country of Iraq, standing five-foot-nine with thick black hair, sprinkled with grey on the sides, Fadel was a multi-talented musician. Even though he was uncomfortable, and hardly ever spoke around me, we shared a mutual respect for each other. He had a love for music and the divine gave him a voice which mirrored that love. The smile on his face never failed to reflect this image. We waited in the exit area for everyone to regroup. I wanted to say goodbye to Hisham and deal with this pain later, when I was on my own.

Hisham came from behind me. He wrapped his arm around my neck and moved me closer to his side.

Elated, he spoke, "It's nice to be with the prettiest girl in the place."

My body tensed up, like a cat not wanting to be picked up. I was sure my face gave away my uneasiness.

With a slight snicker, I asked, "Do you feel good about yourself now?"

Thinking about it for a moment, he replied, "Actually, I do."

As I tried to push him away from me, he began, "Jasmine, are you coming over to my house?"

With the throbbing pain in my chest still present, I said, "I don't think that's a good idea. I don't feel too good. I should go straight home."

"No, you're coming over! You have your car, right? Let's go."

I did not need to agree or disagree with him any longer. I had my own car which meant I was not powerless to drive straight home. My free-will was intact, well that was what I thought. Destiny had something else in store. I walked to my car, parked in the far back lot behind the lounge. The pressure that started in my heart, moved down into my stomach, increasing in intensity. I would stop and try to collect some strength. The pauses gave me just enough of a break, to regain my energy before the discomfort of knowing resurfaced. The magnetic soul force and the angels revisited me during this walk. The angels reassured me, while the soul force pressed for me to drive to Hisham's house. I could not refute their urging or power, so I headed to his home.

I moved dizzily through the doorway and toward the kitchen. I tried to focus my energy, not wanting to lose my balance and fall.

Hisham offered, "Here, taste this sweet," while he cut a piece with a fork and moved it toward my mouth.

"I can't, Hisham. I'm not well at all. My stomach is in knots."

"Come on, Jasmine. It's your favorite."

The last bit of my energy expired, my body lost its balance. He swooped to my side, held me up before I could catch myself, and walked me over to the couch.

I said, "I can't believe I'm letting you see me like this."

"No, I'm actually glad to see this part of you. It's nice to know you're not superhuman."

The reference of superhuman took me by complete surprise.

He was not the vulnerable one anymore, I found him saying, "What I said to you earlier was harsh. I didn't mean it to come out that way. Come on, Jasmine, let me help you with your pain."

I relaxed the recent fortifications, letting go of the stubbornness.

He asked, "Where does it hurt?"

"Right here," I pointed.

He placed his hand on my stomach. "Okay, release it, Jasmine, and I'll absorb it."

I hesitated, thinking, *"No way. Whatever this is could harm him."*

"Don't worry. I can handle it. Let it out."

Within a few moments the throbbing lifted. It seemed his touch removed the pain. How did he know what this was? What to do for it? I guess there was more depth to him and his abilities than I knew.

The next day, I met with fellow students to work on a group marketing project. Still recuperating from the discomfort of knowing and strange onset of high anxiety, my phone rang. The identification screen showed Othman, my cousin. Thick eyebrows, pale skin, a boastful stride, there were no features that showed we were related. I had a feeling the call was linked to last night.

I answered, and heard, "Hi, Jasmine. How are you?"

"Fine. I'm working on a school project with my group. What's going on?"

Suspiciously, Othman asked me, "What did you do last night?"

"Nothing special. Why do you ask?"

Ignoring my inquiry, he continued, "Where were you?"

"I was at a hookah lounge. I met a friend there. You know Hisham, he was brought in our conversation when I came to visit you at your new house."

Disregarding my response, he went on, "You tell me your side of what happened. Then I will tell you what I heard."

"Othman, there are no sides to the story. Nothing happened so there is nothing to discuss."

"We need to talk in person. Call me as soon as you finish with your group."

I did not know what he was talking about or why he was speaking to me as if I was under cross-examination. One group member's slow ways and lack of typing skills, combined with his manic mood swings and threatening words, increased the tension. Almost daily, I was dealing with the soul demons. From the flaming high anxiety to drowning in insecurities, their torture weakened my strength, and made the situation seem intolerable. My mind could not regain focus.

During my first year-and-a-half in Columbus, Othman and I attended the same school. I cooked for him on countless occasions. He also slept over on the couch many nights. He knew I always carried myself with complete respect, and I rarely ever drank. Othman even commented once he would want a wife just like me. Now, here he was, questioning my character.

I immediately called Othman when finished with the group meeting. "Okay. So what is going on, Othman?"

He replied, "I can't tell you over the phone."

"Fine, when and where do you want to meet me?"

"I can't tell you until I finish watching the soccer game."

"Othman, are you serious? You act like this whole thing is an emergency and then you tell me I have to wait for you to watch a soccer game?"

He ignored my frustration and answered, "I'll call you later."

Around seven o'clock, Hisham called me to come over and join him for dinner with Jalal. On my way to his house, I debated whether to tell him about the call from Othman.

When I arrived at his house, the inner voice persisted in vocalizing, *"Tell him about the phone call from Othman. Build his trust for you. He cares. Do not hesitate to express yourself. Speak of the incident before he thinks you are hiding things from him. The road of courage has begun."*

My mind decided he did not need to know. I constantly steered clear of unnecessary commotion. My family's loud spectacles were enough theatrics to last many lifetimes. I lost one of my favorite cousins at the time from a dramatic episode. During a typical family gathering, Jonathan's father and my mother clashed over an issue involving Jonathan's mother. I witnessed harsh words being exchanged, then my uncle slapping my mother across the face. Jonathan's family stopped showing up to the holiday celebrations and then they vanished. Jonathan continued to come to Thanksgiving and Christmas, by himself, but by the time Easter came around, he disappeared as well.

As Hisham and I sat on the couch, I gave into the persistent higher nudging. Hesitantly, I opened the topic for conversation, "Hisham, do you remember when I spoke of my cousin, Othman?"

"Yes."

"Well, he called me earlier today and asked me what I did last night. He said something along the lines of 'you tell me your story and I'll tell you what I heard.'"

Hisham questioned, "What is he talking about??"

I replied, "I have no clue. I think those Syrian guys, who sat right behind us last night, have something to do with it. Othman is supposed to call me back soon."

"Do you know any of those guys?"

"Not really. I think they're all related to each other, and some of them come from my village, but I don't know anything about them, even their names."

My phone started ringing, it was Othman. Hisham walked over to the kitchen to prepare dinner.

Othman said, "Hey, Jasmine, I'm just going to do this over the phone. I was sitting at a coffee shop with a group of guys when they started talking about last night and dropping your name. To make sure they were talking about the same Jasmine, I asked them to tell me what you looked like. Then I knew it was you."

I asked, "How do they even know my name?"

I moved to the open kitchen area and sat on the bar stool.

Othman continued, "That doesn't matter. They didn't know I'm your first cousin and I didn't let them know. I wanted to find out everything. They said you were hanging all over a Muslim guy you have been dating for six months. They also said you danced with him the entire night."

As I sat on the bar stool, I watched Hisham in the kitchen get tenser with each passing moment. He appeared to energetically read the situation, although he could not hear the other side of the phone conversation.

I explained, "Othman, first of all, I told you about my friend and you know who he is. Second of all, how could I be seeing him for six months when I told you I met him on February 14th, which was only two months ago? You know me. Do you really think I would hang all over a guy? Come on, Othman. I have a hard time even hugging or allowing people to touch me. I danced with Hisham and a girl for thirty seconds and we were far apart from each other. Last time I checked, Arabic dancing doesn't involve the type of movements you are describing. So how does that make any sense??"

It did not. Othman became aggravated with the common sense of the explanation. He remarked, "They said you go over to his house all the time and people have seen you there."

"I do go over to his house, but not all the time. He has become a good friend of mine. No one is here except his cousin and he wouldn't say anything. So, I don't understand how they could claim such a thing."

Agitated, Othman asked, "How well do you know this guy, Jasmine?"

I looked up at Hisham's face to find the answer. There was a recognition with my soul he was trustworthy, loyal, and someone I came to know deeply in a relatively short amount of time. I followed that feeling.

I replied, "I know him well enough."

"Trust me, I know these guys. They look out for their Syrian girls. Jasmine, people think by seeing you with this guy and figuring you've been dating him for six months that you're engaged. I don't care. Do whatever you want because I know you don't do anything bad. I pretty much lived with you for two years and know you better than anyone. Just don't be seen in public with him where Arabs are and don't let people see you at his house."

I said, "I understand, Othman."

"You know you're like a sister to me and I'm just looking out for you. I have to go. I'll talk to you later."

I hung up the phone and sat in disbelief at myself. I instinctively suspected it was Shadi, the lead singer of the band, who started this rumor. I recalled the instance where Hisham and I were in conversation, when Shadi suddenly dropped by. He seemed a bit taken back by my presence, I gave him no attention besides a hello and a smile. When Hisham went to get drinks from the kitchen, Shadi began to tell me his life woes, and showed me pictures of his newborn son. There was this feeling present the sharing was not about entrusting me with private information, rather a scheme for sympathy and attention. I decided to leave and gave them time alone.

"He really kept going, huh?" Hisham commented.

As I responded with a yes, I looked away, not wanting him to read what I was feeling. I just chose to believe in a person I have known for two months over my own blood, whom I was close to for six years.

I was afraid, but the angels reminded, "It is the truth that you continuously strive to live by."

As I moved to the couch, Hisham followed behind, sandwiches in hand. "So tell me what he said."

Giving him Othman's replies word for word, I left the Muslim issue out and the advice about not going out in public. "So, they knew I came over your house…"

I did not provide insight on the collaborator. I let him figure out that piece on his own. I was just a person he met at a wedding while the band is a part of him. Why would he even believe me? He barely knew who I was. I do not impose or expect another to have the same feelings as I do, whether it comes from the soul or not.

Fired up from what he heard, Hisham stated, "I can put a stop to this really quick!"

Surprised, I asked, "What? How are you going to do that?"

He began to stand up. "I'm going to call Shadi right now because he must be the one who twisted things about you coming over here."

I grabbed his arm and shook my head, "No, please don't do that. It's unnecessary and will resolve nothing."

"Oh, it will make him shut his mouth and fix up what he said," Hisham exclaimed.

I snatched the phone from his hand. "Hisham, please calm down and sit back down."

A confounded look came over his face. He realized my sincerity and cooled off.

Retaining his composure, he said, "I guess we can't go out to that hookah lounge anymore, or anywhere else they go."

"That would be a good idea. Othman recommended the same thing before he hung up."

That day, higher guidance stepped in, encouraging me to share a past experience. I confided in Hisham about being molested at a young age by a cousin.

Unfortunately, his reaction was, "You're over it, right?"

I then witnessed his eyes shifting in panic of what my disclosure might have appeared to mean.

I reassured him, "Don't think because I told you this, you need to comfort me, or I'm becoming emotionally reliant on you."

Through writing this book, I discovered just how deep the impact was from being molested as child. **Our sexuality is one of our direct links to divinity, hence, an embodiment of sacredness.** As children, there is a purity to us, the divine channel is at its strongest. **Being molested as a child not only causes wounds to our divine cord, but a scar forms.** Currently, I do not know of anything else which gives rise to such damage. **Scars do fade. They are warrior marks.**

Without me opening up about the childhood molestation, this imperative subject would not have found its way in this book. Hisham's reaction was pretty poor, but somehow it allowed more of his true self to the surface. Now, his behavior was changing. While in a class, I received two phone calls and a voicemail from him. When I listened to the message, there was worry in his voice. I was surprised. The higher guidance was right on many levels.

Walking to my car, I returned his calls. Hisham answered, "Hello Jasmine! Is everything okay?"

"Yes. Sorry. My phone was silenced. I just came out of class and noticed the missed calls."

"Not a problem. I'm in the middle of practice right now with Fadel and Joey. Give me a second to get out of the room and find somewhere quiet." Hisham explained, "I'm over at Fadel's house and I'm walking up the stairs to the family room...Okay, here we are. I spoke to Shadi earlier and told him he needs to keep his mouth shut about you. He swore that he didn't mean to say anything. He said his sister-in-law asked him a question about what was going on between us. Shadi just told her he didn't know but that you come over to my house."

I asked, "And you believed him?"

"Yes. I really believe he was telling me the truth."

I coolly responded, "Okay."

Hisham continued, "I told him he can't do things like that. This girl's reputation is on the line. She also has a huge family to deal with who all live in the area. Shadi promised he wouldn't speak a word and he would try to fix what he did."

"Good."

He said, "I guess you're like a superstar now. It must feel good to get all this attention."

Candidly, I replied, "No. I actually don't care for those kinds of things. I enjoy my private, loner life where no such attention exists."

My intuition blared in the background during the conversation, *"Shadi was not revealing the whole truth and jealousy was partially to blame for what he did."*

There is a major misconception surrounding "psychic" notions. **Even people who possess strong intuition or enhanced awareness can fall prey to deceit.** When a person is spiritually gifted, they cannot always sense, read, or foretell everything or even the majority of things, for that matter. Everyone has limits to their abilities. For example, when a person claims they can read your mind, they cannot simply stare at you and "hear" your every thought. Tuning into other people can be like tuning into an old-fashioned radio station. You scroll through radio frequencies to find a steady signal. As you turn the knob, you pick up mostly static, but some voices or songs filter through. You finally come across a channel where you can hear clearly. This is how the method of scanning and tuning into a person works.

Months later, the falsely-created rumors got carried halfway across the world to "Medusa's caretakers." In addition to the group of Syrian men, which I will call the goon squad, my family members started their own version of the rumors. Of course, the two shallow cousins were behind circulating this rumor to the family. Like bees drawn to a succulent flower, it was too irresistible.

I wish I could say the friendship with Hisham grew, but that is not exactly what happened. Alas, my interactions became a playground for the soul demons. I continuously questioned where this following of inner guidance was going? They saw this as an opportunity to capitalize upon, flooding me with increased fear and doubt. The soul demons took reign with these lapses of the mind. They convinced me it was time to permanently shut down the soul connection.

We come to prevent this matter from transpiring and see a means to an end to these disappointing notions. You think the truth will set you free from a will lost to your truth, but we are here to tell you otherwise. Do not resist our case. It holds a reality undeniable even to your humble servant soul. You say he will see and return to his truth, but we tell you he runs from every truth at his door, refusing to place the key in the lock. Why do you think you are so different? You know he offers nothing but future pain, yet here you are pathetically following an invisible and undesired path. We ask you, "Why?" You that is stable and on a righteous path. We offer you only truth and that, you cannot deny.

The soul demons were relentless in their intent to keep me from achieving the ultimate truth. During the entire drive to Hisham's house, they instigated the idea of severing the tie. The logic in their manipulating words reached me due to my many moments of weakness, where I lacked confidence in the inner knowing. Their torment was not limited to words. At times, their attack was like a bullet was ricocheting within my being. It traveled through my organs, piercing every nerve. Other times, the experience resembled a hot liquid, oozing and consuming my being with a scorching sensation. This fight between darkness and light was almost intolerable. They nearly persuaded me to end the friendship with Hisham, thus preventing these testaments from occurring.

I sat next to Hisham on the ivory-colored couch, ready. I opened my mouth to deliver the scripted words, however no sound came out. I tried again and again but could not voice what I came prepared to say.

The angels intervened. Each attempt to verbalize was followed by their voices:

Do not do this! You have been fooled! This is not the truth and definitely so not your will. Do not fall prey to the demons' manipulation. They penetrated you deeply today, but we have come to rescue the truth within you. My love, he who is not tested cannot withstand the wrath of the demons, but do not fail in your truth. We come as companions in the fellowship of the light. Do not be deterred by their deep invasion. Fall on your truth and it will always catch you even when you so desperately fear your own demise. Do not say something you will regret later. We advise you to follow our message for we are present on your behalf.

To secure my allegiance, they sent a profound angelic vision. The image displayed the messenger of the divine, head bowed, as golden long locks flowed around his face. The wings were flexed to the front, enclosing his entire tall body. The edges of the wings met at his hands which were in prayer position. The feathers alternated two shades of glowing black and white. They reflected the keys of a piano being played by invisible fingers.

To a small extent, Hisham was a relief from the soul demons. The moment I stepped into his home was the moment they withdrew. After weeks of enduring their onslaught, I had the courage to confide in him, about what I called "them." Hisham listened with his face turned away from mine. In a couple of sentences, I struggled to explain what I was going through.

He met my eyes, saying, "You are safe here. Nothing can hurt you when you are with me."

By the outside world, the friendship was twisted into an ugly nest of lies. Unleashed and out of control, these rumors had a life of their own, and I symbolically refer to them as Medusa. Sadly, it was not only the external environment that distorted the genuineness, but Hisham himself. He forgot his words to protect and became the assailant. You see, Hisham had a problem. He knew the truth but instead, let his mind lead. Just as he became more open, he disappeared. Fear took the reigns. Fear can be defined as an unpleasant emotional response, caused by a perceived dangerous setting involving a person, place, or thing. It can be a positive protection mechanism, preventing one from a hazardous situation. **Nevertheless, fear along with doubt, mostly block us from actualizing our potential and sabotage fulfilling our purpose.**

You are standing in the middle of a colosseum arena. It is completely clear and empty. You know what you are doing is right, you trust in your instinct, and you have complete clarity. There are concrete gates found along the perimeter of this arena. Behind these doorways are banks of water. Through the mind, fear enters, and the gates open, flooding our system with insecurity, doubt, and/or confusion. Those fear banks will always be there, but they can be kept at bay. Pause, regroup with the mind, and restart with a new soul approach.

Dream: The Key and the Jewel

    The moment you encounter someone and connect eyes, there is a vibrational resonance between you and that person. When there is not a familiarity present, there is not a soul connection. This does not mean they are not significant. They are just not soul-wise, energetically connected to you. However, when you do share this soul energy, the imprint of the person is remembered, and a link occurs. Sometimes it is a temporary meeting, but it never truly leaves you. You hope you will see them again. Other times, it is a long experience where you are bewildered why you feel the way you do. In this longer-term case, the best thing you can do is let the scenarios and people run their course. The supreme purpose will reveal itself, in time. This is what I tried to do, while I inscribed these undergoing events.

    More foretelling dreams unraveled. They built my trust and validated this new direction of the journey was the right course. A prophetic dream returned one late evening. I was in my bedroom, sitting on the floor, leaning against the base of the bed. I had the phone pressed against my ear as I was talking to the college friend, Sarah. I listened intently to Sarah's stories when I noticed the chest across the room. It sat there for over a year, and suddenly it took on a different light. The chest box was mounted on a dark brown rectangle base. The feet of the box were gold lion-like claws, supporting the main structure. The shape of the container was similar to a pirate treasure chest. The exterior surface of the body held an antique design of pink stemmed roses and old manuscript writing. There was a bronze lock latch on one side and a handle on the top.

    Somehow looking at it set me back to a memory of a dream. I could trace it to around the age of thirteen. The recollection was so strong I interrupted Sarah to listen. I explained to her what I just experienced and how I saw a snapshot of a waterfall, a jewel, and a key. I could not figure out why the remembrance was springing forth, but as the conversation continued, the entire dream revealed itself. I began recounting it, talking faster and faster.

    I appeared standing in a light-tinted grass landscape. The horizon presented a setting sun that radiated like the satin-red, glowing-orange, and rosy-yellow colors of a ripened peach. Its light touched upon the vegetation, highlighting the blossoming fruits of plums, cherries, and pears. Wildflowers laid scattered on the sides of a nearby dirt path. Covered with thick, green plant life, large hills sprang up. When my eyes moved upward, I found olive trees planted in hundreds of rows, as far as I could see. The air was heavy with the scent of wild roses. I turned in all directions to figure out where I was.

The land felt familiar, but I could not identify the location. My eyes settled ahead and focused. A few feet ahead stood a short wall made of large white stones. The top layer of the stones met grassland. At the end of the semi-circle shaped green area, I was met with a dark-red clay cave structure.

A disembodied voice began to unravel the details of the place, "This is a very sacred shrine, which has been used for thousands of years and still exists to this day. Many people walk by it but never catch sight of it. A special energy barrier exists for protection and allows only certain chosen individuals to see it."

As my heart rate increased I felt the lure of the site in my bloodstream. Excitement turned to determination to enter the vicinity of the shrine. I began to walk toward it, when I suddenly heard a masculine voice yell from behind. "Wait!! Don't go any further!"

I turned around to see a young man dressed in a brown robe, running and jumping through the hilly landscape. As I observed this scene, my mind did not know him, but my soul identified him as an old friend. I shrugged off his insistent voice and turned back to the original destination.

Within a few steps, I found the old friend right in front of me, blocking the passageway. Irritated, I moved my head slightly upward to meet his face. I encountered features I never saw before and yet, looked so familiar. He stood with tawny-colored skin and dark cinnamon brown hair. My mind calculated he was around six years older than I.

I thought, *"Who is he?...Where did he come from?"*

The divine voice commented, "He is a long-awaited friend and a truth you will encounter in the future."

He repeated, "You cannot go any farther!"

Defiantly I replied, "Oh yes I can. Just watch me."

"Who is he to tell me what to do?! I don't have to listen to him just because he's older."

The divine voice answered, "He holds you as a lady of his dreams, but also as a person he must defend even from himself,"

When I tried to step forward, his hands rested on my shoulders and held me in place.

In a caring tone he spoke, "Let me explain why you cannot go in there. Yes, you are one of the special few who can see this holy structure, but you're truly not ready to enter at this time. Your mind and soul have not aligned enough to handle the power of this sacred shrine."

"Who is he to protect me? I don't need protection, let alone being told what to do."

The omniscient messenger replied, "He is a truth but a figure you will be challenged by. Take his hand."

I began to listen to this old friend's words and stopped my progress to the shrine. He nodded his head in acknowledgment of my decision. He stretched his left arm out, and opened his palm toward the fertile green earth. "We both belong to this land but originate from different areas. I have traveled from a place far away from here, where the people have a different makeup."

Suddenly, the sound of approaching voices arose, drawing closer.

Startled, he said, "I have to go before they see me here."

Concerned by his words, I replied, "Why do you have to go? You are safe here. These are my people and they will accept you because you are with me and a friend."

"No. They will not. I am different, and they do not welcome what I am."

The divine voice confirmed, "He is correct."

"I understand," I answered, "But how are you going to make it back home if you live so far away?"

"I didn't travel here by walking. I came here in a special way."

"In what way was that?"

"I transported myself here by using my energy and I'm going to transport myself back."

"Why do you have to leave so soon? Can't you stay here with me for a little longer? We can hide somewhere safe from everyone."

"I cannot. There are many children in my family and I have other responsibilities there. My father owns and has special rights to the land."

A distinctive knowing came over me, "my people" were not truly "my" people. They were going to turn against me as fast as the wind changes course in a storm.

I thought to myself, *"I want to leave with him. I don't want to stay here."*

The omniscient source agreed. "You will be safe with him."

I pleaded, "Please let me go with you?"

"I'm not sure if I can transport both of us. I never tried it before... It is worth a try."

He stretched out his right arm toward me. "Take my hand, hold on tightly, and do not let go."

With no fear or doubt, I clasped his hand.

In the second part of the dream, I was removed and watched it as if I was a director of a film. The scene entered a view of dark-grey jagged mountains clustered together. At the base of these rock structures, extended out a relatively smooth slab of stone. This sat above a large basin of water. The view moved to the right, showing a booming waterfall. As the field of vision shifted downward, a separate smaller waterfall, closer to the basin was visible.

The focus returned to the cliff slab, where I recognized myself as older, in my twenties, with longer hair. Then the movie screen perspective disappeared and I returned to looking through my own eyes. I stood in front of a different man than the one who stopped me from entering the shrine. I was unable to see his face, but saw the rest of his figure. I found this to be the same man who appeared in the last two prophetic dreams. He was presented in the exact same manner, facial features blurred, outlined features of dark hair, olive skin, tall stature crystal clear. He reminded me of someone close to my soul, but still far away from my mind.

An inner sense arose I was not going to see him for a long time. I asked, "How long is it going to be before I meet you?"

He bowed his head in sadness. "I don't want to give you the answer because it will hurt you."

I requested, "Please just tell me. I can handle it."

With difficulty, he struggled to answer, "We will meet again, many years in the future."

I replied, "You are going to wait all that time? You are not going to forget me?"

He assured me, "Yes, and I will be waiting for you. How can I forget those eyes of yours?"

I extended my arms to rest on his shoulders, squeezing him tightly. I hung on for dear life.

As the dream returned to screen view, I watched the embrace, their pulsating energy echo throughout the surroundings. The scene faded the pair into the background, and moved the snapshot on to the large waterfall. A treasure chest came forth from within the waterfall. It drew closer to a more zoomed in view. Hovering in mid-air, over the water basin below, the chest unlocked. Two objects emerged from the box, and emitted a white-gold light. The screen focused in on the objects as they floated above the open chest. Suspended in the air, was a golden key, and a massive red jewel. They returned to the treasure chest, it locked itself, and merged back into the waterfall.

This dream foreshadowed more than I thought when initially recounted to Sarah. Hisham physically matched the person in the first portion of this dream. When he spoke of coming from the same land but different areas, in actuality, we both came from the same country but distant regions. During the dream, I did not know what he meant when he said "different makeup." Present day, this was solved with the knowledge of our varying religious backgrounds. When I referred to the distant voices approaching us as "my people," I recognized the first setting of the dream was placed in the village of my birth. Traveling to Syria in the next coming months brought further insight. When I arrived, I found the Syrian village held a negative perspective on the Druze religion. The validation needed completion and a phone call from Hisham provided that opportunity. The consciousness of the Mind and Soul ensued.

The Mind began, *"Don't tell him! He will think you are a dreamer. He won't understand the dream or your questions. You speak of angels, gifts, and a knowing which he sometimes chooses to deny and sees it as your own special way of thinking. I am not going to allow you to add to his twisted proof. Do you understand how his mind works? Unlike you, he doesn't follow the voice of the soul, he lives in a reality that owns him. You are a temporary passageway to what he perceives as truth for him. I beg you not to follow through. You will only gain dissatisfaction from your release of the dream's prophecy."*

The Soul conveyed, "Speak your truth. Complete the purpose of the dream. Though he collects facts about you, which his mind twists, his judgment, his reality, is irrelevant to the journey to truth."

I asked Hisham, "If I describe a place for you, can you tell me if you've seen something like this in Golan Heights?"

He replied, "Yes, sure."

I gave him details of the stone cave structure and the two waterfalls.

He responded, "First, where is this coming from?"

The Mind urged, *"It's not too late! Don't tell him about the dream. You can sway the conversation in another direction! The possibility to avoid sounding foolish is now here for the last time."*

The Soul encouraged, "Swallow your fear and courageously address the dream's prophecy."

I said, "A couple of days ago I remembered a dream I had when I was thirteen-years-old and you were in it."

I elaborated about the man who blocked me from the shrine. I could not believe I shared that portion of the dream with him.

Hisham remarked, "Oh, really? How do you know it was me in the dream?"

"Because it looked exactly like you."

He paused for a few seconds, then continued, "Okay...You know what? It sounds familiar, but hold on. Jalal is next to me and he knows the area better than me."

He repeated the description for Jalal, and returned with, "Yes, he said there is a place which matches your description."

This was more proof of how prophetic dreams depicted a place never witnessed with the physical eye, but existed half way across the world. Not only this area, but my village territory was also pictured. In addition, I came upon the existence of the cave like shrine with the white stone wall during the trip to Syria. Prophetic dreams validate there are things beyond the physical dimension of what we can taste, touch, smell, hear, and see. **The more our minds are in a space of curiosity and not so set in the five senses, the more these soul elements organically present themselves.** This dream continued to reveal its meaning.

The Chaos of Isis

Two variations exist on the myth of Isis, an Egyptian Moon Goddess. The first depicts Isis and Horus, her son and the sun god, as both liberators of the people. The second portrays the sun god as Ra, who was the most powerful of all the gods. Isis took over his reign by creating a venomous snake which bit Ra, causing him immense suffering. Isis carried an antidote but would only give it to Ra if he spoke his true name. This secret true name was the source of his power. Left helpless to cure the poison, and at the point of death, Ra whispered it to Isis. While Ra recovered, Isis gained the great powers he held and used them for the benefit of mankind.

We have a tendency to not reveal our true identity. Living in your true self requires being vulnerable. **The mind fears judgment and what it perceives as a loss of power.** It brings to life what I came to understand as the lower self of a person, and with that there is also the higher self. **The higher self is part of the soul, the original version of who you are as created in divinity. It is propelled by true authentic connection, purpose, and service to something higher. The lower self is part of the mind, encasing our human qualities, good or bad. It is influenced by control, comfort, and fear.**

When two souls connect, and we experience another's higher self, it flows naturally. There is a warmth and unspoken trust. There is a sweet curiosity. That person is uniquely them self, it is thrilling, joyful, and liberating. **Most of us perceive this experience of the higher-self as a romantic connection as that is what our mind can configure. It is beyond that, and more often than not, it has nothing to do with romantic or sexual.** The lower self on the other hand is disjointed and cold. Belonging to the mind, many times contrasting to the soul. **When one of the two within this kind of connection drop from higher soul self to lower mind self, there is a huge difference and the other person feels it, whether they are fully conscious of it or not.**

This is what happened with Hisham. It was disheartening and a shock. As we sat in front of the computer screen, Hisham pulled up and showed me an internet article he found about the Druze religion. He discussed the thousand-year old marriage law, and whether people follow it in modern times.

Hisham pointed, "Here is the law that doesn't allow marriage outside our religion… the other day I spoke to my mom and asked her about this…" He hesitated for a few seconds. "I have mentioned and talked about you a couple of times. She told me it's fine to be friends with non-Druze, you can date non-Druze, but in NO WAY can you marry a person who is not Druze."

I sat quietly, surprised he revealed this part of himself. I knew he held it close to his soul.

Hisham said, "Too bad people can't even convert. My mom said there are reasons…. and I understand."

He divulged more as the night unfolded. The topic soon turned to immigration.

I explained, "In order to stay here, one of my cousins married a lady older than his mother. It's not easy, I would never want to be placed in that position of marrying someone for a green card."

Almost automatically, Hisham replied, "I got married to a stripper."

Caught off guard, I replied, "What? You're kidding, right?"

Uncomfortably, he answered, "No. It's not like you don't understand how it is, or that it's really that weird of a thing to hear."

"Yes, but a stripper?"

"She was my friend's girlfriend. After we got the marriage license, I never saw her again until the immigration interview. We divorced less than two years later."

I knew it took courage and trust for him to tell me, so I lightened the moment by remarking, "Samir told me about his immigration problems. I tried to make him feel better and gave him advice to not give up."

Shocked by my words, he said, "What?! Samir told you about his immigration issues? When did this happen and where was I??"

My attempt to help diffuse the conversation did not have the intended effect. "Yes… He confided in me, you're the first person I spoke a word to about it. It was the time you went into the guitar shop to buy a piece of equipment, while Samir and I stayed in the car. You were in there for a while. Is something wrong with that?"

"No…it's just Samir doesn't trust anyone, and he especially doesn't like talking about his immigration situation."

"I guess Samir trusted me and felt comfortable enough to tell me."

"Yes, I can see how you come off like that to people."

Hisham relaxed enough to tell me more about his immigration-based marriage. His willingness to trust me with this knowledge allowed our mutual understanding to grow, or perhaps survive a bit longer. The timing of him sharing this information coincided with an event which triggered Hisham's lower self. Prior to me entering his life, he stayed untouched, everything was safe and emotionally risk-free. He let his mind create a facade, where the emptiness could never be filled. His soul was buried in the process, and this is why these voids existed in the first place. The soul connection shared brought him back into his more authentic self, his higher self. The soon to be ill-fated occurrence plummeted Hisham back to his lower human qualities.

A few days after Hisham opened up, I awoke with a sense of uneasiness, a hint of looming chaos. For some reason it seemed easy for me to tune-in to his circumstances. I sent a text message to Hisham inquiring if everything was okay. He replied he was leaving the house to give Jalal some privacy. He was not telling me something. There seemed to be more that was unsaid.

The next day provided some answers to these inklings. I was at home getting ready when I received a call from Hisham. I was immediately aware something was wrong.

Hisham announced, "I'm going to be leaving the country soon and won't be able to come back. I want to see you before I leave."

With sudden concern, I said, "What? What happened?"

He said, "I came back to my house around seven last night and found a notice from the immigration department. My neighbor told me an agent came to his house and asked his wife about me. He also told me, a couple weeks ago, he saw a person taking pictures of my car. So once they find me, I'm gone. When I saw your text message last night asking if everything was okay, I thought, 'How the heck did she know?' "

My mind went into confusion. The angels tuned in, "Collect yourself. Do not let the circumstances lead you away from the truth. You know he is overwhelmed at the moment. Fall onto us for guidance as to your next move. Do not let him detour you from what we speak. He is stubborn to our words, but you are not."

I decided to ask Hisham, "Okay. I thought you were legal with a U.S. work visa?"

"I have a valid work visa which makes me legal. The problem is I had an injury on the job and haven't returned to work for over four months. Even with the worker's compensation claim being processed, the permit might be invalid now."

I started to think what I could do and if I knew anyone who could assist. To be of any help, I needed to stay composed.

I said to Hisham, "Listen to me. My brother-in-law can help. I will call him right now, find out more information and figure out what to do next."

"No, no, I don't want to get more people involved with this and I'm not going to let you do that. There is no reason for it. There is nothing he can do."

He was resistant, but my determination was stronger. I asserted, "Hisham, you have to trust me. I know my brother-in-law can help. Please, just let me call. I'll tell him some of the general information, and give him your number so you can speak to him."

"No, I don't think that's a good idea. I've spoken to three lawyers and no one can get me out of this, Jasmine."

The angels declared, "Keep fighting! Don't give up! Return to your inner knowing. Follow this truth. Forget about what he speaks. You know his core. Proof or no proof, persist."

"Hisham, what do you have to lose from this? Absolutely nothing. So just let me make the call and we will go from there."

Contemplating my words, he finally relented, "…Okay…fine."

I called my brother-in-law, Nasim, and gave him a brief rundown of the situation. After fifteen minutes, I received a return phone call from Hisham.

"I spoke to your brother-in-law and he needs the numbers on the different immigration forms, but they are all in my house and I can't go there."

I offered, "I will go to your house and you can walk me through where everything is."

"Jasmine, I can't risk you doing this. You have already done enough."

"No. I want to do this. You don't need to ask, I'm offering. I'm a U.S. citizen. There is nothing they can do. I'm just a person at a friend's house," I insisted.

He got quiet for a few seconds. He responded, "Okay…but I locked the door and the key is with me."

"Where are you? I can meet you, pick it up, and head straight to the house."

"I don't know about this, Jasmine."

"Just let me do this for you!"

As I drove to meet Hisham, the angels spoke, "Come with no fears, but do not be afraid to show your emotions. He needs to see your truth, your care, and your conviction at this time."

The car offered me temporary shelter in the whirlwind of events. I turned right onto the street adjacent to the coffeehouse where he was waiting. When I parked, Hisham signaled for me to stay in the car. I watched him walk over with the key. He appeared disheveled and his eyes looked worn down. This had to work.

I said, "I will give you a call when I get to your house."

I pulled out of the parking space and hit a red light. With this delay, I opened my palm, examining the key. The dream of the key and the large red gem flashed vividly in my mind. I relived the opening of the chest and the release of these two items. The key I held in my hand reflected the golden key that came out of the box. The rest of the drive involved contemplating ways and people who could help Hisham. There had to be a way.

The angels encouraged, "*Your inner knowing has never been proven false and it never will be.*"

I parked my car on the side street, called Hisham, and told him I arrived.

He instructed, "Go upstairs and stand in front of the large black dresser. The second drawer to your right has a pile of papers. Those are all the documents."

"Found them. I'll call you back soon. Let me speak to Nasim."

I hung up and called my brother-in-law. Nasim directed, "You will find the numbers in the top right-hand corner or within the beginning of the boxed area."

I read off the necessary information. While doing this, I had thoughts about the key in the dream and the key Hisham handed me. What was happening in present day was symbolized over a decade ago. Suddenly, I remembered the sweet woman Nasim introduced me to at a fundraiser a week prior. She spoke of specializing in immigration affairs, but I could not remember her name. When I met her, she and I instantly took a liking to each other.

A friendly soul, she searched for her card, sincerely telling me and oddly stressing, "If you ever need anything, do not hesitate to call. Wait, I don't seem to have my card on me… That's strange. It doesn't matter. Nasim has my contact information."

Remembering this potential resource, I instantly called Nasim back. "Nasim! I just remembered the nice lady that you introduced me to at the fundraiser!"

"Oh yes, I forgot about Mariam. She might be able to help by calling her immigration contacts."

I contacted Hisham, telling him the news. The angels reminded me, "*Keep him afloat. He is drowning in his fears.*"

I reassured him, "Hisham, I have a strong feeling this whole thing is going to work out. I just know it. It doesn't matter how the situation seems right now. I'll be there in ten minutes."

I parked my car in the same spot as before and saw him approach.

His first words were, "Your brother-in-law said Mariam is waiting for me and to head over right now. You want to come?"

I thought, *"Thank you for asking me…"* and answered, "Of course."

"Leave your car here and we will ride with Samir."

I gave them a rundown of how I met Mariam less than a week ago. With a glimmer of faith in his eyes, Hisham remarked, "Talk about timing, huh?… You meeting her just last weekend and this taking place now."

In the driver seat, Samir asked if I knew where her office was. I could not pinpoint the exact location but recalled the surrounding area. I guided Samir with a picture of it in my mind. "There's the sign! Turn right into that parking lot."

Samir parked the car, we got out, and he decided to lead the way down the ramp, saying, "I've been here once. I think the office door is down here."

I shook my head as I watched Hisham follow him. I spoke, "No, I think it's this one, Samir."

"You have never been here before. How do you know?"

I answered, "I don't. I just have a feeling."

He turned his head and re-examined the building. "Oh yes, you're right. I don't know why I thought it was in the other direction."

The three of us walked in and were directed to Mariam's desk. She met us with a large smile and welcoming voice.

Hugging me, she exclaimed, "How have you been? It's so good to see you again! I just got off the phone with Nasim. Now tell me about this case and exactly what took place."

I responded, "Hisham, it's yours to tell."

He gave her a summary of the events leading up to now.

Mariam stated, "Okay. I understand. Let me make some phone calls and see what else we can do...I need the I-9 form."

Nervously, Hisham began to rustle through the large pile of papers.

I memorized the order of the documents when Nasim asked for them, and calmly said, "I know where it is."

After giving her the I-9, I handed her every form Nasim requested to make sure all areas and questions were covered. She proceeded to make the required phone calls.

Hisham turned to me and quietly pronounced, "My neighbor is checking up on me every ten minutes, you broke into my house, Samir left work, and now we're here at this office. All of this for me."

I replied, "Of course, you're my friend, that's what friends do."

Our attention returned to Mariam's voice, "Okay, I left a voicemail for the person who can provide the real status of the case and he'll contact me within five days. Sometimes he gets back to me in less than two. It all depends on his workload."

We left in higher spirits and drove to Samir's apartment. This time with Hisham driving. When he was about to make a left turn into the parking lot of Samir's complex, we saw a van parked on the side of the building.

With a frantic voice, Samir shrieked, "Oh my God! There's a black van next to my building! They're after me now! Keep driving!"

He immediately called his wife. "Kelly, I'm going to tell you something. I want you to listen very carefully and do exactly what I tell you. Slowly go to the window and look down right below you. Do you see the black van parked next to the building? …Okay. Now look to see if there is any writing on it."

"Yes, it has a cable company's name on the side," she responded.

These guys had lost it. I laughed so hard at the both of them, I could not breathe. As a result of my laughter, I listened to them tell and lecture me about what it was like to be a fugitive immigrant. I still could not stop laughing to explain how entertaining they were to watch in this paranoid state.

The next few days of waiting for the status of his case from Mariam were grueling for Hisham. He was faced with three alternatives: Go back to his house and wait for the agent to show up again, relocate to another state, or stay in the Cleveland area in hopes the new immigration reform bill would be signed into law. Hisham was truly grateful for my kindness and support during the immigration chaos. Yet, I found his lower self resurface with vengeance. **When driven by ego, a person wants a tighter grip of control over their circumstances and their feelings. The unknown and being in the soul space is too big of a risk.** They succumb to the conscious and subconscious mind.

We shut down and escape our true feelings. We try to make up for the lack, through pleasures of the body and musings of the mind. It is in our nature to experience a spectrum of feelings. We must bear the good, the bad, and the ugly. Hisham reverted back to living the life of a pirate, taking anything needed to survive or satisfy his ego's needs.

By this time period, the impact of the soul demons mutated from an electric shock effect to scorching lava effect. You are locked in a burning tower. The red alarms are going off, you scramble for a way to get out. You try every stairwell, every exit, but you are trapped on the inside. The fire is blazing, taking over the space as the sirens pierce your ears. I tried to separate from and block the burning darkness, but was unable to do so. I was powerless. I recognized I literally had no control over my own being. This new awareness fueled the soul demons' attacks. I was left raw and exposed as they burrowed deeper into my psyche. On the other side, the discomfort of knowing intensified in proportion to the dark energy. These uncomfortable pains balanced the scales. As strong as the soul demons were, there needed to be something to counterweight their heaviness.

A layer was peeled back, revealing an ugly truth. I came to understand when the soul connection occurred between Hisham and me, it fully unlocked another opening for the onslaught of the soul demons. This weakness was exploited. When the demon thrashings subdued, it allowed Hisham to see the contrast before and after soul demons. There were changes to my physical features, so much so Hisham noticed in the middle of his immigration crisis and the

reign of his lower self. It convinced him there was something to this, the very real existence of these dark entities.

He tilted his face, and commented, "Wow! You look so much younger…more like your real self…. Seriously, you look almost ten years younger."

Drawing back his head, he looked into my eyes for something. Hisham acknowledged, "I can really see a difference in your face. They really messed with you, huh?..."

Until he saw physical evidence, Hisham's mind dismissed what I previously explained to him. "Yes Hisham, I was telling you the truth."

During this conversation, I did not identify them by name, I pronounced the dark entities as "they." He then casually revealed how they bothered him during his sleep, at a younger age. He explained how he suffered from insomnia for two years.

While I faced the soul demons head on, I never knew what to expect. Yet, that is part of how I survived them. I had no expectations. **There is power in being present, and remaining in the now.** Staying in the present moment is easiest when doing something enjoyable. When things are difficult or extremely uncomfortable, it is challenging to remain present. Despite this, it is important to do so. Allowing our feelings to flow through during the moments that do not feel good, ironically get us closer to freedom.

The dark experience reinforced that way of existence, as it was already a way of living for me. **What does being in the present moment really mean? I discovered the essential answer is about being plugged into the soul.** You are standing still, and you can see an aerial view of what is around you, a complete three-hundred-and-sixty degrees. In this entirely encompassing perspective, you feel the vastness of the intricacies of life. You taste the full flavor of food, you receive enjoyment from the smallest things, your thought process is lighter and clear. **There is an appreciation for every step, dark or light. Because each step has led you to where you are now, and will take you where you are destined to go.**

Ascendency of the Queen

It was like being in the middle of heavy, pouring rain. The droplets blur your vision. What used to be clear become a haze of dancing shadows. The terrain is blanketed in slick mud. You attempt to get up and move forward only to slip down on your knees. Your hands strike the ground catching the rest of your body from collapsing. I turned my face toward the sky, only to have the rain beads merge into my tears. I once sat on a throne where nothing touched me. From this seat, I was protected from such chaos, and I could somewhat see where I was going. In this newly dethroned place, I looked around, surveying how I got here, and if I would ever rise out of it. If I would ever see the breathtaking view again and feel the warmth of the sun.

I was slowly, but surely, broken down. Every insecurity and doubt was a living, breathing, daytime nightmare. My body became the capsule and my soul, the channel to an internal hell. In the form of mental demons, the mind is capable of creating the same constructs of suffering. Soul demons are similar to a spider's web. There is structure and order in their arrangement, and the fibers excreted from the spider create silk fabric. On the other hand, mental demons are like a bird's nest. There is disorganization and disorder, and the various materials gathered from the outer surroundings produce a mangled mess. It is generally understood, mental demons cannot be absorbed or transferred from one person to another. The same goes for soul demons. Soul demons do not appear out of thin air, they are specifically assigned to a person before coming into this world. I know the depths of soul demons, and if I had any enemies, I would not wish this upon the worst of them.

Everyone has a money cord. This rope is a connection to anything financial. Both soul and mental demons pull on this cord, but for vastly different motivations. Mental demons utilize the money cord as a source of disruption. The mind wants instant gratification, to fill the voids and escape. It places a value on money to gain this. This is a potential scenario, you buy an expensive piece of clothing you want on impulse. The mind creates an illusion you will feel better having it. Then this purchase places a strain on necessary expenses. It is a temporary distraction, causing more grievance than anything truly satisfying. Soul demons pluck the same money cord but is based off survival elements. For instance, you worked and saved to pay for a home. The time comes to settle and there is still not enough. The soul demons introduce perpetual worry over the lack of funds.

Mental demons are a result of trauma done to yourself, or by the outside world. This causes a fracture and destabilizes the mind. They are purely from the ego, and unlike soul demons, take over without any rational material. I gained this further knowledge and awareness about mental demons through someone actively dealing with them. Thanks to them, I was able to incorporate it in this book and shed light on the subject.

This is not a romantic story, nor a novel. **This is a testament.** I do not add spice, or remove ingredients from the events, just facts served on truth's time. I tried to hide my gems; the private and raw experiences which were locked away. Despite much resistance and many attempts to stop this, extraordinary forces got involved and here I am baring them. **Higher guidance continued to intertwine and untangle the workings of the mind,** through Hisham. They placed me right smack dab in the middle of his path. I could not be on the sidelines. The effect would not have been the same. I had to walk beside him, experience it first hand, and not just observe it.

I will share with you a few instances of a person whose loyalty did not lie with the soul, but rather, in the mind, trapped by the pitfalls of the ego. Even though his reaction was guarded when I disclosed about being molested, the divine intervened and encouraged me to share once again. I threw caution to the wind and opened up. This experience involved a visit to a first cousin's new house. It took me over a month to find the time to congratulate him and deliver a house warming gift. I was on the phone with him trying to find the house as it sat back behind another house. I pulled in the long driveway, parked, and went up the steps with a gift bag in hand. He opened the door and immediately I knew he was in a weird state of mind. I instinctively sat on the other couch while we watched a movie. He started on about the lead actress's body and looks, and how he wanted somebody like her. Then he brought up past girl-friends. I sat and listened quietly. Somehow it led to him boasting about how he gave the best massages.

I laughed and casually replied, "That's nice. Good for you."

He then offered to give me a back rub, which I declined. He heavily persisted, and I thought to myself, *"What's the big deal? It's a simple back rub."*

He was close family, practically a brother. I did not think I would end up with my bra unstrapped. This cousin never reached out again, I heard he left the country, and I did not see him until two years later in Syria.

I took a seat next to Hisham, and reluctantly spoke of what happened with the cousin, in as little detail as possible. He responded by blaming me, claiming I was the one who led him on and therefore, at fault. Most people would be insulted and walk away. Typically, I would have as well. Although I still did not know why, there was a purpose to sharing. I continued to follow my inner knowing, letting the character of Hisham play out. It was like being left in the dark, stumbling around looking for a light.

It was four months since our first meeting, Hisham began to create a web of skewed and tainted perception. I was caught in it against my will. My birthday was approaching, it provided a temporary window into Hisham's core, and a slight reprieve from the soul demons. Three days before my birthday, late in the evening, I received a rare call from him. He informed me he was going out of town to renew his passport and wanted to celebrate my birthday that same day. By this point, I had not heard from him in a great while and was not sure how he remembered my birthday. It got brought up in conversation only once.

I arrived at Khalil's doorstep where he greeted me with a smile and a hug. He escorted me to the family room and relayed Hisham just stepped into the shower. When Hisham put his house up for sale and moved out, he became Khalil's roommate. Also Druze, Khalil was a long-time friend of Hisham's and I found him to be a humble and kind person. Fadel, Joey, and the newest acquainted friend named Mahir, arrived. I sat on the furthest corner of the couch and watched the different religions mingle together. It was refreshing to see such an assimilation between Christian, Druze, and Muslim.

Fadel interrupted the chatter to tell me, "I think Hisham is calling for you."

The room fell silent enough for me to hear my name from the upstairs level. "Jasmine, can you come up here for a second?"

I walked up the carpeted steps and knocked on the white painted door located right at the top of the staircase. Hisham welcomed me in. "Why do you still knock even when I always tell you it's okay for you to come in without knocking?"

My eyes shifted downwards and back to him, "Because that's the way I am…"

I took notice of the clutter in his room. Clothes were piled up against the wall, shoes were scattered across the room, musical instruments were mixed with his other belongings, a few collecting dust. It seemed to reflect his disordered state of mind.

He grabbed a white gift bag off the floor next to the bed. "Here, I got this for you."

"Hisham, thank you, but I can't accept this…"

"Why? Come on, Jasmine. Don't do this. Please just take the gift."

It was uncomfortable to accept gifts from others. The past showed me, there are usually strings attached and a sort of debt owed. Out of consideration, I said, "Okay, I'll leave it here and take it when we get back."

He conceded, gathering up his wallet and keys. We headed back downstairs where all the guests were waiting. I never did take the gift and have no idea what it was.

I gazed around at the genuine affection of everyone. After I lost Grace to her overseas engagement, and Sarah moving to another state, I had no close friends or any sort of companionship left in town.

At the same moment, Hisham remarked, "It's nice to have people who celebrate your birthday not because they have to, but because they want to, huh?"

"Yes…" I softly answered.

I watched everyone down their last shots of alcohol and out the door we went. I walked down the driveway and over to Hisham's car. I caught sight of a recently bloomed white rose bush in the front yard next to the vehicle. Before I opened the passenger side door, I paused to pluck one of the delicate flowers. Placing it behind my right ear, I returned to the car.

Khalil took notice of the white ornament in my hair and asked, "Did Hisham get that for you?"

Without thinking, I replied, "Hisham? No. He's not sentimental like that."

The inner voice picked up, *"Hisham heard you say that and it hurt him."*

My mind went on high alert, and I searched the area for him, finding him nowhere in sight. My intuition appeared to be false, but you will discover as I did, appearances are deceiving.

We arrived at the hookah lounge and found the place unoccupied except for a few employees. We sat in the usual booth. Hisham sat to my left and his friend, Mahir, to my right. Mahir was the shyest and most soft spoken of them all. At this birthday celebration, he came out of his shell when he heard news of my upcoming trip to Syria. He pulled out a photograph and showed it to me. The picture was of a young, very fair-skinned woman with straight, blonde hair. Although it was over nine years old, he kept it in his wallet for remembrance. Now, an opportunity presented itself with my scheduled Syria visit. Mahir asked me to track down this lost love who he had not seen for over six years. I figured he felt I was trustworthy and nonjudgmental from his quiet observation of me.

I asked, "You mind if I take a closer look?"

"No," Mahir gladly answered.

I took the photograph from him and brought it closer to my view. When I sensed Hisham's wheels spinning, I showed him the small portrait.

Brushing off the whole matter, Hisham expressed to me, "He doesn't really expect you to find her."

As I gave back the picture to Mahir, I knew better than to disagree with Hisham. I was aware of his lower state of mind, how he misconstrued who I was. My instincts told Mahir really wanted me to find his lost love. Reality suggested I was not the one who grew up with or knew anything about him. The rest of the night continued with enjoyment of everyone's company.

Unfortunately, after this celebration things changed even more. Throughout almost the entire time of knowing Hisham, he second-guessed my qualities. Now, it intensified. We have different pairings with people from family to strangers. My pairing with Hisham was not chosen, it was divinely orchestrated. I **choose** to follow my soul which placed me in his orbit. In order to prove his false assumptions a "trial" began. The wheels of Hisham's mind could not stop turning.

A couple weeks later, I was at Khalil's house, Hisham and Samir were there as well. Khalil wanted to watch a video of their friend's overseas wedding. I did not like watching weddings since attending and working at so many as a server. This never took away from the fact it was a sacred union of two people. Khalil placed the recording in the player. The scene showed the bride on horseback and the couple throwing hay at each other.

I immediately took notice of the bride's very revealing dress, and after making sure I was seeing it correctly, I remarked, "You can see right through the top of her dress…"

Khalil watched it before, and casually commented, "Yes, you can. I never noticed that."

With a suspicious look, Hisham turned to me. "You're sneaky, aren't you?…Yes, you're really sneaky."

Jolted, I looked around to find a reason for the ridiculous charge. There was nothing that hinted of wrong doing, Samir and Khalil did not react and were completely fine.

Not understanding where it came from, I responded, "Hisham, I have been accused of being many things in my life. But never once, not even by my cousins who dislike me, have I ever been called sneaky."

He returned to the television screen with no reply. His mind was made up before I even spoke my words. He placed me under a microscope, examining everything I said and did. His mind was on alert, anticipating the next move in its twisted and manipulated illusion.

The next few days included more of his fabricated thoughts. In Middle Eastern culture, men typically pay for everything with any female companion, including cousins and friends. One instance started when Hisham went to the gym right next to my parent's house, which was much further away from the many surrounding where he lived. When he called to meet, he pretended he forgot his wallet, and asked if I would cover the tab. This was an immigrant on the run and the same person who was offended each and every time I tried to pay for myself or refused to order anything. He was testing to see if all those times were just an act. When he failed at this, he then insinuated I did not respect my cultural role as a woman, and suddenly found his wallet. He performed character tests, searching for evidence of falseness.

Months before, I casually mentioned having dinner with a former co-worker, the same one who gifted the Reiki certificate with Maya. I spent hours helping this friend select designs for his condo, and as a show of gratitude he took me out. Hisham randomly brought up this event. In his backwards reality, going out to dinner equated to a desire for men's attention. He cultivated prior irrelevant actions of mine to confirm I was not who I seemed to be.

When the mind has such a hold on one such as in the case of Hisham, every person and encounters warps to fit the misguided reality. This treatment was wrong, it was unacceptable. Throughout these interrogations, I did not justify or defend myself. I am fully aware of life's many facets and the masks people wear. I never tolerated behavior or treatment like this from others. I was compelled by divine breath, which encouraged standing solid and not walking away.

The proof he saw for over five months of spending time in each other's company, could not override his entrenched beliefs about women in general and now me. Hisham no longer saw me in the same light. His own clouded goggles distorted the view of the person he knew. His soul that came forth, was submerging back in the dark again.

Hisham relented somewhat after subsequent days of examining. I wish I could say this character test period was a mistreatment as it appeared in reality. That would be false. In truth, the soul demons played on every one of his acts. You are immersed in a large vessel containing boiling water and the lid is put on. The heat creates fourth degree burns, the layers of skin break down, exposing the muscles, creating the gradual meltdown of the rest of the body. There was no way to get out of the dark cauldron or escape the soul demon's boiling water.

The truth never evades me, but at times, it does confuse me more than I would like. From beginning to end, this meeting was a clear and sacred alignment of our souls. However, his mind polluted the waters. Discovering much later part of the purpose was to help him reconnect with the core of who he truly is.

>The angels declared, We come to you with the truth. Forgive his deeds for he is unaware of the consequences. Bring him to the light for he resides in darkness. He is oblivious to what he is doing. He is suspicious because of events in his own past. You are not blind or stupid but a servant to the truth, which will set you free.

When the number of these tests began adding up, I sensed there was a specific incident which caused Hisham's behavior. I followed my gut instinct, doing my own detective work with my senses to discover when and where this started. The clues repeatedly led me to the time of meeting Johnny, a cousin of Hisham. On the exterior, Johnny was sweet, but my sixth sense picked up the opposite knowing. The perception and my intuition did not match. I was open and extra-friendly that night to Johnny and his girlfriend. I even started the conversation between us and went out of my way to make her feel comfortable. It was apparent though, she was uneasy about something.

It was ironic Hisham kept contacting me, even though he acted like I was unimportant by this time. A few days after he 'forgot his wallet,' Hisham sent a message and invited me to a party that was at the usual hookah lounge. The higher forces were very much present, calling on my required attendance. I called three cousins, trying to persuade them to go with me to this Hawaiian-themed gathering. Each one had legitimate reasons why they could not attend, so I gave up and decided to go by myself, somehow knowing there really was no choice in the matter but to go.

I wanted my old self back. I wanted to return to "the queen" who was present in Fatima's story and who courageously resigned from her career job. I was far away from that place now. Where was the person who would not put up with this treatment for even a minute? The strong woman who commanded respect from every single person when she walked in a room? The human being who knew what she deserved?

This brought me back to the age of twenty-one where serving people was the source of income for survival. One event stood out, catering at a gala filled with a wealthy crowd. They each had an overload of needs and special requests. This type of environment did not intimidate me. I breezed through the tightly packed tables to the kitchen area. Grabbing glass cups, I turned to see a fellow server heaving and crying. She explained how she was being commanded in every direction by the guests and scolded at the same time. After comforting her, I took initiative, told her I would tend to her assigned tables in addition to mine, and for her to do what was needed in this back area. Upon approaching her tables to introduce myself, I witnessed what was overwhelming. Nonetheless, I made my presence known and offered my assistance. As I replenished the water for one person, my head swiftly turned to see a seated man, raise his arm, pierce his fingers together, ready to snap them. He locked eyes with mine and slowly lowered his hand. He replaced the entitled gesture with a polite wave, asking for my help. The rest of the night was smooth sailing, as the co-worker was baffled and impressed.

My sails naturally drift with the winds of higher guidance. Whenever there was an interference from the mind, I redirected to the true flow of the soul. After everything Hisham did, I refused to allow the course to head in this direction. I reasoned it was not too late to make up for all of the lost time spent following the inner knowing. I was like a fish caught on a hook, fighting to escape. I devised a plan to finally put an end to all of this, set myself free, removing the ties which bound me. The ultimate truth of this testament had something else to unravel.

I stepped foot into the hookah lounge with a smile and thoughts of ascending back to the throne. Hisham was busy behind the bar. I wanted to do this immediately, but patience was vital in awaiting the time to arise. I headed to the end of the room and down the aisle where his friends and cousins were seated. I stopped at the first booth past the bar to find Khalil sitting alone. I was surprised to see him, but comforted by his presence.

Khalil pronounced, "Jasmine? I didn't recognize you with your hair straight. Who are you with?"

"I came by myself. No one wanted to come with me."

"Come and sit down. You want anything to drink?"

"No, thank you. I want to stand."

Out of the blue, Khalil bluntly asked, "Jasmine, why didn't you take the gift Hisham gave you for your birthday? I saw it sitting next to the couch and asked him what your present was still doing here. He told me you wouldn't take it. You know he took me with him and spent time picking everything out. You should just accept it."

I did not want anything from Hisham. He had done enough. How can I accept something from a person who treated me more like a foe than a friend? Once again, the divine rope tugged at my soul. Khalil was right. I should accept it, not for me, but for the sake of Hisham.

The angels expressed, Remember who he truly is, Jasmine. Despite his actions, he cares deeply for you, as you can see from Khalil's experience. Don't forget his core. Don't let his behavior change what you know inside of you that is the truth. Don't give up on him for he is lost in the darkness. Continue to be *his light, an unwavering testament. The 'reality' is a mild, yet harsh, reminder of the impossibilities, but look onto the truth for it shall be the triumphing reality.*

The fish reel started to be cranked in. Uncomfortable with the message from the angels, I changed the subject. "So how was the trip with your wife?"

Blushing, Khalil replied, "I didn't go on it with my wife. You must think I'm a bad guy or something?"

"No, not at all. I know you said you were separated and in the process of getting a divorce. Just because you're not divorced on paper doesn't mean you're not truly divorced."

He needed to reassure himself and me, so Khalil clarified, "I dated her for six years before marrying her. After we got married, I learned how different we were and what we valued. I couldn't live with a person who cared so much about money and shopping."

"I understand. You don't have to explain yourself to me. I'm assuming your parents didn't know you married a Christian?"

He answered, "I didn't tell my parents but my sisters knew. They met her when they came to visit."

"What would your parents have done if they found out?" I asked, being he was Druze.

"What could they really do? I'm their son. They probably would be upset in the beginning, but eventually get over it. You know, a major Druze leader married a Christian."

I inquired, "But I thought your community would disown the person and the children?"

"When you have power, it becomes a different story. Many of the older Druze families in Lebanon converted to Christianity to gain political power. All the powerful positions were held by Christians. So, this was their way of getting in."

I asked, "They might have converted, but they didn't practice Christianity, and they maintained their Druze religion, right? I read that Druze have done that in the past with the European missionaries to preserve their religion."

He replied, "They began to practice Christianity and considered themselves Christian. It doesn't matter that it was against our religion. They did it."

I understood very well how power and money work. I was surprised by this new information, it completely contradicted the way Hisham presented it.

Samir interrupted the conversation between Khalil and myself, greeting me with a hug and kiss on the cheek. "Hey! How are you, Jasmine?!" he exclaimed, embracing me with happiness.

I returned his enthusiasm, "Good. How are you, Samir?!"

Samir inquired, "Jasmine, I want to ask you a question. Fadel and I were just talking outside. It's so weird how you came into Hisham's life right when all this immigration stuff happened. Where did you come from?"

Smiling, I answered, "I don't know. Good timing, huh?"

"Yes. It's like it was all meant to be. You know the first time I saw you, I thought you were stuck-up. I didn't like you. I even leaned over to Hisham and told him, 'Are you kidding me, Hisham? What are you thinking?' He told me he was surprised I felt that way about you."

This present-day conversation with Samir, revealed why Hisham was taken aback by Samir confiding in me about his own immigration situation.

His statement did not faze me. I was actually amused, and replied, "Really, why did you think those things about me?"

Samir realized maybe he was too blunt. "I mean you were nice-looking, but I didn't like anything else about you. When I sat in the car and listened to you as Hisham told you about the immigration thing, I saw how much you really cared about him and what kind of a person you are. I figured out I was wrong about you and that's when I started to like you. I got into two big fights with my girlfriend because of you."

I laughed, "What did I do?"

Samir elaborated on the jealousy this woman had for me. Apparently, she disliked the attention he gave me. Another reason was because I did not greet her one night at the lounge. Samir told her on both occasions, no matter what she thought about me, she had to respect me because I was friends with Hisham.

I remarked, "I don't tolerate people like that. Sorry it caused you to fight though."

Approving of my answer, he confidently said, "Don't worry about it. I have another question for you."

"Go ahead and ask." I replied.

"What do you want in the future?"

Beat down from the soul demons and being bound to my divine promise, I responded, "Samir, I can't give you an answer to that. I take everything day-by-day as it comes. I have learned to go with the flow of life."

Not long ago, Samir was a person upset with Hisham's change from partying and being available, to more reclusive once I came into his life. In the beginning of us becoming friends, one night Hisham decided to have everyone over his house instead of going out to the hookah lounge. Samir resented me because he thought I had something to do with Hisham staying at home. When Hisham went down to his studio in the basement, I was left upstairs with Samir and Jalal. Samir felt he had an opportunity to express his repressed feelings.

I sat on the couch next to Jalal, Samir was on the other side of him. I kept to myself. Out

of left field, Samir remarked a term in Arabic that roughly translates to being cursed at birth by a mother's private area. The context of it inferred that I was a whore. I watched Jalal take his nails and grip Samir's leg, warning him to shut his mouth and never speak to a woman in that manner. I never said a word to Hisham about Samir's disrespectful reference. I was exposed not only to Hisham's contaminated reality, but also the others who contributed to it.

This growth in Samir from extreme dislike to a more open minded and trusting person, showed I was actually having an impact. The soul-driven rod pulled harder, reeling me completely back in. While writing this account, I recognized something was taking place. I experienced the soul's essence and lived in a higher vibrational state. Hisham's soul wanted to catch up. It got me involved to make this happen. I was a helping hand and a chained soul.

There is a quality that makes each one of us innately royal. It is in our makeup and just like one of physical royal blood, it cannot be removed. What diminishes this soul royalty is our mind and the external environment. You feel something is right, and you take the necessary actions. The results are not too pretty. At this point, the mind steps in punishing. It perceives your measures as compromising yourself, or not a good deed. You must trust yourself. **You played a role, it does not mean that is who you truly are. When you are following closely to your soul, you are doing exactly what you are meant to do, regardless of how your mind or others see it.** We just have to peel back the layers, adapt, and stay connected to our soul.

A queen is a queen no matter if clothed in silks or rags, her current status, or if she no longer sits on a bejeweled thrown. I was stunned and bewildered by the grey-shadowed surroundings. Nevertheless, I was quick to accept current reality, evaluate it, and act accordingly. I could not crush the burning quest within, or make it go away. It just was, whether my mind liked it or not. I would eventually return to the rightful seat as we all will, no matter how long it takes.

Descent into Valley of Shadows

After almost twenty years, I had the opportunity to go back to Syria, and fulfill a long-time wish to return to my origins. I wanted to reconnect to that little girl; to see the green landscape, taste the fresh apricots, plums and pomegranates, and touch the stones and rocks that covered the vast lands. My mother joined the journey to Syria for one main reason, I wanted to give her a break from the small grocery store that consumed her life. I never imagined it would lead me to meet a mother I would no longer recognize.

Three days before the scheduled flight, more stitches of my wounds came undone. In the last six months, it was as if my skin was peeled off, leaving every organ and nerve vulnerable. The trunks of the past came to the surface and opened up. As the mind engraves the images of distressful events, the soul and body store the feelings of them. The issue arises when we bury these feelings and impacts too deep inside. They become trunks of gems, submerged under the ocean floor. Initially, I was distracted by personal and outside survival, letting the trunks accumulate. Recent occurrences, sometimes related to these chests and sometimes not, forced me to look within. There was still a choice, a willingness to deal with the effects. I could have easily been reactive or ignored it, yet decided to face it, bringing the heavy trunks back to the surface of my mind and cleanse the debris off the gems.

I began to become conscious of the cause and effects of my past. I unlocked the trapped memories in order to feel the gems inside and liberate the experiences. It takes courage. The release is difficult when the feelings rush out and the contents are exposed. Nonetheless, this is vital. **If you keep your feelings submerged, you become a version of yourself that is an imitation, a cheap knockoff. The effects go further, pouring into the degree of fulfillment we feel.** For example, you land a job, which is an accomplishment in any form, but you do not feel true satisfaction from attaining it, or it is very fleeting. The reason for this is underneath the surface. There is a disconnection within which places us in a state of survival mode. We are so focused on getting through, that everything else falls by the wayside. Once our mind connects the dots of our programming, the dust settles, and the picture is not as bad as we perceived. The soul fills in the wounds.

When you are in a situation that pricks and pokes at your hurts, sensitive areas, the ego has an urge to take over. It wants to protect. We detach, avoid, become uncommunicative, compulsive, and/or withdrawn. We do this more than we realize, we do not want to feel the pain. The minute we start feeling on a deeper level, whether it is at work, in a relationship, or in any situation really, we shut down or react. It becomes a cycle, an ingrained pattern. All we can do is be aware of ourselves when this almost automatic behavior happens. Observe it. Start here. Just begin to notice it. Do not analyze; that is going back into your head. We are in the mind enough. Observe without judgment.

While I had enough courage to look at myself, Hisham did not. He held onto the illusion of his old lifestyle. The women, the cars, the constant partying, socialite status in his city. Even though he knew there was so much more on the other side.

A few days before my departure for Syria, Hisham invited me over for a barbecue at his house. In the backyard, I saw Samir's former girlfriend also arrive. The tension between her and Samir was so thick, you could almost slice through it. It became so uncomfortable, I escaped into the house.

After a few minutes, Hisham came to find me. "Jasmine what's wrong? Why are you in here when we're all outside?"

"I just didn't want to eat the food outside. You know how I don't like meat."

With a slight aggravation, he said, "So you're going to eat this leftover pizza instead of what we grilled?"

"Ummm…yes…" I replied.

"Why would you do such a thing?!"

The fear of confrontation stung me to my bones. I muttered, "Can we please, please not talk about this anymore. It's not a big deal."

"Why do you always act like this when there is a disagreement?"

Softly, I spoke, "That woman does not like me, and your cousin is acting differently because of her. I think I should go."

"Jasmine, you're a queen. Don't let her make you feel like this. Who cares what she's doing. Just come with me and relax."

I was not sure where the queen remark came from, his behavior the last few months spoke the opposite. We walked back outside and returned to the bonfire. As nightfall mercifully settled in, a surprise was in store. I sat in a chair between Hisham and his friend, Mahir, who I took comfort in.

Seeming as if Mahir was contemplating something, he asked, "When are you leaving for Syria?"

I answered, "The day after tomorrow, actually."

"Can I ask you for a favor?"

I responded, "Sure, if I can do something for you, I will."

He said, "Remember when I showed you the photo of Layla? I do want you to try to find her, so I can get in touch with her again."

This proved the inner knowing from my birthday correct, when Mahir first requested to find her. Out of the corner of my eye, I noticed Hisham's look of astonishment and realization of Mahir's original intent. I gave Hisham a quick acknowledging glance and my eyes spoke, "you see, he was serious."

Mahir explained how he left the Golan Heights area thirteen years ago to attend school in the city of Damascus, where he met her. After dating for two and a half years, he moved to Canada and tried to bring her there. He tried for almost three years, but eventually told her to move on with her life and they lost touch. I felt only true love would bring a person like Mahir to ask a practical stranger to help him find what he lost.

Mahir provided more details, "She is half Christian and half Alawiyyah (Muslim). Her mother is Christian and her father is Alawiyyah."

I inquired, "Where is she from?"

"She's originally from the city of Sophita but moved to Damascus where she lives now."

As Mahir answered, I recalled I was going to Sophita and remarked, "Interesting. My village is only thirty minutes away from Sophita, and I have to take a friend's niece a gift there. What is her name again?"

"Let me get a piece of paper," he said while running into the house.

There was silence, not a word was spoken. Mahir returned with pen and paper in hand.

"Can you write everything in Arabic and English?" I asked. Continuing, "Okay. Sophita is the key to this, that's where she's from."

Mahir exclaimed, "No. No. She lives in Damascus now."

Hisham squeezed himself into the conversation, "Yes, but Sophita is the best place to start and Jasmine already has plans to go there."

I was surprised by Hisham's input. The next day, I went to Sabah's house to pick up the gift for her niece. I sat next to her on the pale-yellow sofa, drinking coffee.

The angels entered, *"You can trust her. Tell her the story. Show her the piece of paper with the name of Layla."*

I resisted, as this was Mahir's private issue and not mine to tell someone else. The angels were persistent in the message.

I verbalized, "Sabah, I want to show you something and ask you about it, but you have to promise me you will keep it private."

"Sweetheart, you know you can trust me. That's one of the things that makes me different from many of the people you know."

I pulled the paper out and filled her in on the details of the story. "So, I'm going to start in Sophita when I drop your gift off to your niece."

Sabah exclaimed, "Jasmine, my niece is a lawyer there. She can access records discreetly!"

"Can we trust her?"

"Yes. Don't worry. She is my favorite niece and will not say a word to anyone. She will probably need her mother's maiden name. I'll call her tomorrow and let her know you need her to find someone"

"Thank you so much, Sabah. I have to finish packing and my family is at my house right now waiting for me."

She walked me out to the car.

On my way home, I called Hisham and told him the news. "Hisham, talk about timing and what's meant to be. Of all the people I'm going to see in Sophita, it's someone who can access public records. Does Mahir know Layla's mother's maiden name? Sabah told me I would need it."

With some reservation, "Wow, that's crazy, huh? I guess it really was perfect timing and meant to be. I'll ask him, he's right here."

Of course, Mahir knew the name. These beautiful coincidences were few and far between during the Syria visit. With my mother accompanying, there was a change in her that coincided along the surfacing of the soul demons. Although one-sided, our relationship was relatively good. She called me "her angel" and trusted me with her thoughts like a best friend. In preparing to leave for Syria, the switch was completely flipped. I came to call it the "black veil of ego," which led to a series of clashes.

The ego can be defined as the self-conscious function of the mind, a sense of self. It processes our surroundings, and creates our perceptions of reality. For example, the ego perception my mother channels is an inflated feeling of pride, concocting reasons and justifications for her ways. This type can be acknowledged as "false ego." It is mainly formulated by outside influences. The false ego creates an illusion of one's desires, by superficial attachments. You want this specific car model, and think it has everything you like, and you see it as "perfect." You purchase it and after a short time, it is not giving you the gratification you were after. Why is that? It goes back to false ego, which makes something appear to be other than it is. It is an optical illusion and not the original preference. We think we want or dislike certain things, but it is just artificial. As this false ego exists, "true ego" also exists. This is a participant in knowing yourself, what you truly like and dislike. You find a car that calls out to you, and after purchasing it, you feel the satisfaction for the full length of the car's life with you. You are in direct alignment with your soul, your true self.

The night before leaving, my mother and I packed and weighed the luggage. Everything was organized and ready. Yet, this became an opportunity for my mother's newest strike.

She looked over at me, staring at my facial features. "You know your lips are too big. They are like Black people's lips."

I was caught off guard, replying, "I like my lips. You're the same one who thinks my shallow cousins are pretty just because they're tall. So, what you think is beautiful, really isn't…"

She stayed quiet.

My mother's family was the same way. My grandmother spoke disgusting words no child, or even adult, should hear. After she had her third stroke, my grandmother was left almost speechless. She had a total of nine children, seven of which lived within fifteen minutes of my mother. Growing up, each of her brothers and sisters felt the need to criticize their nieces and nephews.

My uncles would constantly comment on the girls' weight fluctuations with statements like, "Look how fat you've gotten. How much weight have you gained since the last time I saw you? Why don't you put her on a diet or something."

Their view of "fat" was simply a girl undergoing a physical change due to her hormones. Their perceptions were their ego's doing, to fit the girls into their likeness. Their harsh words did not stop at the physical level, they compared and criticized the words we spoke, our grades in school, and what schools we should attend.

Even Fatima, with an extremely dysfunctional family of her own, would say, "Man, Jasmine, your family is so judgmental. They make me self-conscious and uncomfortable. I feel like they're watching everything I'm doing."

Until I left for college, we saw my mother's family two to three times a week, alternating visits between her brothers and sisters. They were very abrasive, but I always understood they were my mother's only companionship. They thought they were just being honest. I never saw anything wrong with the hard truth, we need a tough push sometimes. However, it is not honesty being spoken. It was harshness. This false ego my mother and her siblings lived in was hard wired. They knew no other way, and never learned to be any better.

The day of the flight to Syria foreshadowed the trip to come. On our way to the airport, we stopped at a store to buy a memory card for the camera.

My mother started her frantic show. "Come on! We are going to be late! We need to get there two and a half hours before our flight!"

I calmly responded, "Mom, please, can you stop. We have plenty of time. Don't start your crazy worrying and rushing, stop listening to other people who make you worry more."

I looked over at the passenger side where she sat, internally wondering why this distress was necessary. Nothing could ever stop my mother from worrying about every single hing in her life. Worry is the state of engaging in chains of mental thoughts and imagery. **I see two forms of worry: destructive and constructive.** With destructive worry, an imbalanced uneasiness of the mind lives. It afflicts one with agitation, anxiety, and creates a negative disturbance within the mind. Constructive worry is more of a concern, where attention is given, and proactive steps are taken. **Accordingly, you can suffer and agonize yourself from destructive worry, or be in a state of constructive worry, where you take action whenever possible, releasing control when necessary.**

My mother contained her destructive worrying while we waited in the Cleveland airport. This wait was not a long enough time period for her to start a new round. The layover in Chicago provided the chance.

She ranted, "What happens if our luggage doesn't make it to Damascus when we land? Your aunt said that's what happened to her. She said it also happened to her daughter and the luggage was not found for a week. Do you know we live four hours away from Damascus? That means we have to pay another hundred dollars to return and pick them up."

Patiently, I pronounced, "Mom, can you stop talking about negative things? You are going to attract them to us and they will end up actually happening. Enough."

Again, nothing stops my mother. Each layover and flight brought on new worry.

This was the start of the descent into the valley of shadows. Things would begin to unravel in the coming forty day stay in Syria. The truth is, the majority of the occurrences that took place there, were a direct result of following the inner knowing. Alas, do not take these real-life stories as the complete verity of Syria. I was meant to go through these awaited trials to serve as another piece of evidence to this testimony. Syria is a beautiful country with many ancient secrets.

There is a seven-hour difference between Cleveland and Syria. We did not make it to the house in the village until 3:30 A.M., Syria time.

I awoke the first morning to my mother yelling, "We have guests over!! Wake up! They want to see you!"

This trip was supposed to bring some sort of peace, but my God, I could not get a moment of silence. These were not three ordinary village guests, they were old female neighbors. As a child, I viewed them as dark witches. When I settled on the sofa and looked around, I remembered a memory and recognized as a six-year-old I was on to something.

Each one had a remark as my mother blindly smiled, seemingly grateful to have them as company, "You're too skinny." "Your skin got darker. Stop going in the sun." "Your hair is not light anymore."

My child-held sense of their ill-intentioned makeup was proven right. During the stay in the village, I heard many unfavorable true stories about these women from my relatives. How they wished harm on others and deliberately damaged people's lives. One female cousin, who wanted to become a nun since she was a child, volunteered a sad tale:

"He was about to ask for my hand in marriage. Then one day he changed his mind. We called his parents to find out what happened. They said he was stopped by the neighbors, who were waiting for him at the end of my driveway one day. They told him foul things about me. These women convinced him I was no good and should find someone else. After him, nobody came to meet me. I found out they had done it to all the men who came asking for me before this last one. Now I'm over thirty-years-old…"

The chance to reconnect with the ancient land of youth arrived. The soil held **historical energy** that was not in the slightest bit made of light. The soul's divine channel was all I had in this country, as my intuition seemed to completely leave me during this time.

The Forty Days and Forty Nights

The days fluctuated in level of difficulty. Yet, every day proved to be an injunction to stand in front of a country and its people wrapped in a cocoon muted of light. The experiences were a series of trials, coupled with the unrelenting struggle against my mother's lack of knowing and absence of common sense. What kept me sane? **The only two things I had power over, my thoughts and prayer.**

One of the greatest powers to invoke change in anything is to shift our perception. This in turn generates a chemical transformation, an alchemy from within. Prayer is the main element and catalyst for this chemistry. **Prayer is a calling out, connecting to a greater source by means of songs, sanctioned words, or meditative communication.**

In order to douse a fire, you need to pour water over it. Instead of cursing a situation, person, or holding onto anger, pray. Send compassion and forgiveness, this is positive reinforcement. Even if your mind is in resistance, connecting to compassion, connects us to divine power. Therefore, the most powerful source of energy comes through, moving us past the pain. It will transmute the anger, hurt, pain, worry, fear and beyond. It does not change the behavior of a person or the situation itself, but with repetition, it transcends it. From this place, you are no longer fueling or fanning the flames.

I petitioned numerous prayers during the forty days. Even without sound, through our intentions and thoughts, we can send out messages to the cause or need. No religious practice or connection is necessary. The more it is repeated or sent out, the more powerful the prayer becomes. Like throwing pebbles in a pond, the prayers ripple to the furthest edges of the universe.

I called out for help to have the ability to speak Arabic fluently, as I once did as a child. I was now back in my native land, unable to ask questions, reply in complete sentences, or converse with others. I was frustrated beyond expression. Aside from our eldest sister, none of the siblings knew how to speak fluent Arabic, but we did understand it. In a conversation with my mother, she revealed why we lost the ability to speak it. It was due to her extreme dislike for my father. He represented everything she despised about Middle-Eastern men, which became predominantly expressed when they were living in the United States. My mother allowed the loss of the Arabic language, while my father was too busy watching television to take notice.

The process went past the reality of learning a language. The strangeness of the whole thing boggled my mind. Some days, the Arabic came naturally. Other days, I was unable to remember a single word. This bizarre occurrence sent me back to my sixteen-year old self. I excelled in school without studying, even tutored others while still learning the subject. Math, science, history, and grammar came effortlessly. During my sophomore year in high school, this natural ability changed. I discovered my mind seeming to be working against me. The subjects and the course work did not change, but my cognitive processing did. Although I maintained excellent grades, the ability to absorb the material became trying. Instead of soaking in the information, it slipped away. I was letting myself down. The fleeting recollection of the Arabic language brought me right back to those same feelings of disappointment. I was now determined more than ever to recover my lost native tongue.

The internal friction was very much present, and continued on a deeper level. I brought with me what I came to call "Mary Magdalene's sadness." My eyes would speak of a tragic sorrow. Prior to leaving for Syria, I discovered one of my reincarnations was in fact Mary Magdalene. I never wished to be her or any historical/famous figure. No matter how enlightened or prestigious a person, I refrained from putting anyone on a pedestal. I honor them for the imprint they left, but keep the humble roots. We all come from the same source. The heavy sadness increased in Syria, being closer to her native soil. What wants to be written from that time, is a reclaiming of her true legacy. Mary Magdalene was not a prostitute. The reality is in that era, or any present-day culture, a prostitute would not be present or allowed to be beside a mother while their child was on their deathbed.

Reincarnation, or past lives are a universal truth. Do we really think, we can learn everything in a single lifetime? The mindful awareness is spreading due to the effects from the many lifetimes trickling through into present time. Reincarnation is when the soul, upon the death of the body and mind, comes back in a new lifetime. Unless the soul has planned sequential lives, reincarnation does not immediately follow death with an instant rebirth. The soul experiences a resting point, a spiritual plane, "a heaven" until its next life. During the time between rebirths, the soul engages in planning the map, a layout of what will take place next. **The objective is growth, and at times, evolution of the soul.** Exploring past lives provides a different perspective on life and death. Additionally, it becomes a discovery of reoccurring patterns from one life to another, healing the unresolved matters.

In addition to Mary Magdalene's great sadness embodying me, the internal slaughter by the soul demons resurfaced for one grueling episode. Imagine you are alone, fully naked. Your wrists are strapped with iron chains to a cement wall. Dangling, you feel the slashing of sharp, animal-like claws unrelentingly piercing through your flesh. I experienced this when my mother and I paid a visit to her niece and one of my father's relatives in the city of Homs. We took an hour and half long taxi ride there. The moment I stepped out of the cab, I felt uneasy. It was like landing and walking on polluted ground. I knew immediately I was in for it. With these two obligations, there was no turning back. I stayed quiet, barring it like a bird stained by an oil spill.

As veiled as my mother was, she saw the dark oil. While sitting at her niece's house, she asked me what was wrong. Knowing nothing could be done, I told her I was just feeling unwell.

She took a look at me, the ego mask came back on, and she turned her head away. Hours went by and we were now at my father's relative's house. I found this relative very sweet and kind. She immediately had a special place in my heart. Still stained with this dense oil, this pure drop or any amount of clear liquid could not wash it away.

As we were sitting in the relative's living room, the covering came off my mother again.

She stopped talking and said, "You look like you're dying."

She stared a few seconds longer and returned to the chit chat. I wish there was a way to explain exactly what came over my mother. I can only refer back to the black veil of ego. Due to her "blindness," she became, at times, a burden to carry through the coiling darkness.

When the sun was almost completely set, my father's relative offered to take us to the oldest church in the area. I had enough energy to nod my head and verbalize, "Please, yes."

We walked down the old chunky stone roads and approached the church. We entered to find they converted the back section into a museum. I knew I had to set foot in this room alone. So, I gathered the last bit of energy and paced ahead. When I stepped in, there was an immediate knowing something was waiting. Strolling down the long wall, I turned the corner. A gravitational pull had me skip over the next panel of displays. I tilted my head upward to meet a huge dark-wood framed portrait. The massive painting depicted a man suited in armor, on a white horse, holding a staff dagger. This weapon was aimed down toward what resembled a monster dragon. In that very moment, it was as if something submerged me in a tub of water and scrubbed me with soap. The dark oil was cleansed away.

The city of Homs turned out to be one of the first central areas where the future Syrian War started. It took me seven years after the war began to recognize what was actually playing out during the Homs visit. That sick paralyzing feeling was in truth, my soul digging into the extensively toxic soil. Sifting through the poisonous layers to plant seeds of light, deep enough where it was safe, where they had a chance to grow. Maybe even sprout fully one day.

While this dark passage faded, my mother's ego got even bigger. Already born into a family of large egos, a dangerous aggressive aspect of her character was now heightened. **We are more energetically tied to our mothers, no matter who or what they are.** This is because we were once attached to them through an umbilical cord, a physical life line. She was my mother, and this made me susceptible to her. Her turbulent and sometimes destructive storm of painful words and actions went back many years. Only the current setting was different, as I was confined to her on this Syrian land.

My mother's ability to ignore common sense rose to a level of ridiculousness. This can be illustrated within this scenario: A person reads a random magazine article. They take it as total fact and the best information. It becomes the lens they look through. They never for a moment stop to look at the source, or decipher the validity. It limits their perception and hence their stance. That is exactly what occurred with my mother, as I endeavored to save her from paying the price for her narrow field of vision.

We were driving back to the village up the mountainous pathway in a taxi cab. My mother and the driver were in a conversation. After telling her he was from a certain village area, where the majority of people are Catholic, she started nit-picking Orthodox Christians. Mind you, this is a very religiously sensitive country. It turned out he was neither of the Christianities, and his whole demeanor changed. Then the subject turned to the cost of the ride.

I knew he could not understand a word of English. So, I expressed to my mother, "You shouldn't tell a taxi driver you haven't returned to Syria for twenty years and don't know the value of things."

From her view, I was mistaken and her tongue gave me a lashing for it. Weeks after, she was speaking to my uncle about the cost of taxis and out loud stated, "I paid almost four times as much in the last taxi cab."

Near the end of our stay in Syria, my mother asked a cousin, "Why do the taxi drivers always take me on a longer drive when there is a shorter way to the destination?"

What more can I say?

Two of my cousins, on my mother's side, took us to their best friend's jewelry shop. We had a gold ring and four heavy gold necklaces we wanted to exchange for new pieces. I watched and listened as the man gave my mother the swap prices. I cannot understand high numbers in Arabic, but I had a solid knowing the gentleman was not giving the correct value for the gold.

I still asked, "Mom, is he giving you the right price?"

There was a glazed look in her eyes. She replied, "Yes."

When he continued rambling numbers off, I disagreed and pulled my mother to the side.

I told her, "We are getting ripped off, Mom. I don't want anything and I don't care about gold. Let's just take everything back. That gold ring means something to you."

She retorted, "No. We can't do that! They will think we are cheap!"

"Who cares if they think we're cheap."

"Shut your mouth! They heard you!"

I replied, "I don't care if they heard me. We're not getting ripped off!"

We got swindled. My mother figured it out for herself a month later when she asked my eldest sister about the gold currency exchange. But we did not get fully duped. Thankfully, higher forces swooped in. I was urged to grab back one of the pieces of jewelry off the counter. It was a gold cross necklace I paid Grace to purchase two years prior, when she was visiting Syria. There was a purpose in saving this necklace and it would unfold the day before we left the country.

I advised my mother, "Stop going around the village drinking coffee and believing everything these people say."

I was ignored. These were the same people who thought my cousin's fiancée could not conceive because she had small breasts, and my mother completely believed them. In addition, these village members persuaded my mother the fiancée was not worthy of my cousin.

As a result, she persistently attempted to instill doubt in his mind by saying, "It's not too late. Even if it's one day before the wedding, you can stop it."

I repeatedly explained to my mother the fiancée was not the negative portrait everyone was painting her out to be, and to stop believing in the rumors.

The day of the departure, my mother finally saw the proof of the fiancée, commenting, "She's so sweet and soft. I don't know what everyone was talking about."

I had to go through a test of my will as well as hers. Many things during this Syria trip, could not be realistically changed or controlled, like my mother. Laughing at life's hiccups and continuous gratitude, kept everything from really effecting my personality, and response. Why let something negatively influence you, when it is out of your hands?

My intent to make the best of the circumstances was unwavering. I searched for, even fought for, opportunities to experience the true Syria I knew to exist. As a child there, I was told stories about the beasts that dwelled in the woods but still wandered alone feeling protected. I came across snake eggs and their skins, tarantulas too. Now as an adult, I attempted to escape into the wilderness again. I walked up the dirt path that led to the area roamed during childhood. I was met with attached town homes, that were like a wall blocking the distance. There were other areas of nature uninhabited nearby my grandparent's home. However, each time I tried to venture out, I would get instinctive warnings not to go. I tried to ignore these foreboding signs, but my mind could not convince my body to simply step forward into the landscape. That was how powerful the block was. I could not even return to the nature that once revived me.

"My People"

Often, the things we favor and find beauty in are a reflection of ourselves. The graceful weeping willow tree grew to become, and has remained, my favorite tree. The open crown of its low-hanging, pendulous branches cascade down to create a tearful canopy. Very adaptive to their environment, its assertive and shallow roots form a network, extending out much further than the tree itself. As a result, this resilient tree is able to survive in a wide range of conditions, including various types of soil. The beauty of its wispy branches, covered with delicate leaves, do not allow us the opportunity to appreciate the adaptiveness and exquisiteness of the roots themselves.

Much like the clandestine roots of the weeping willow tree, countries and even cities have roots, but of energetic composition. Each land contains its own active and powerful formation, which unknowingly effects its people. The roots of Syria provided a dark mirror image of the beautiful and complex roots of the weeping willow tree. They were dense, black, and anchored deep below the surface of the land. These dark foundations thrive and gravitate toward any flicker of light.

Uprooted from the United States and taken halfway around the world, I found myself replanted in toxic soil. There were only two ways to conquer the coiling of the draining Syrian roots— either by completely removing the source of light, or by allowing the light to be so radiant the suffocating grasp is pierced. We all have a unique energetic signature, a certain presence about us. Our intuition and essence compose and create this distinct vibrational imprint. Our vibration grounds us to the roots of anywhere we go. For this reason, intertwined in the dark roots of Syria, my intuition had to be shut off. Intuition, the channel between the soul and the mind, was suddenly a tightened and immovable faucet. Not even one drop of light could trickle out and alert the dark roots. I was in one of two states: intellect form with the light off, or complete divine form with the light radiating. There was no in between. It was the sole method for keeping the body and soul together.

The Syrian people, members of my family and village, presented a strikingly different experience from childhood to adulthood. Growing up with my cousins involved many adventures; we stomped through the dirt, played soccer, climbed trees, and went on hiking excursions. We set up fires, brewed tea, and picked fruit. Now in my mid-twenties, the playful connections turned into intentions for marriage. They no longer spent time doing those enjoyable activities. Instead, they sat in their front yard, compulsively drinking cannister packaged tea, turning the rumor mill.

I longed to see my three uncles who looked after us as children, they were like parents at times. Amid youth, my uncle Sharif paraded me around on his shoulders, while the village adored me for my light-colored features. Present day was not so sunny. I was scorned and dissected. Now, one uncle was a puppet to the female neighbor. The second uncle was part of the fueling of false tales. The third uncle was the only ray of sunshine during this visit. He stayed unscathed by the negativity and did not change for the worse like the others. I rarely saw him as a child, he was serving his mandatory time in the military. I only had fond memories of him and twenty years later, his good was preserved.

My families' houses stood side by side, attached by a cement staircase. As you walk up the staircase, you are met with three options. To the right was my uncle's home, to the left was my parent's, and straight ahead were cream-painted, metal doors with glass windows. Through this set of doors, you enter a hallway containing another stairwell. This would lead you to the grape vine covered rooftops. To the furthest end of these two joined pavilions was the white stone barn of my deceased grandparents. The closeness of everyone's home made it nearly impossible to be alone.

After the first sunrise in Syria, I awoke almost every single morning to my sixteen-year-old cousin, Halim. Scrawny, petite, and fair-skinned with glasses, Halim's unpretentious exterior was deceiving. Initially, he hovered around like an annoying yet harmless insect. He drove up the dirt road to stand under the fig tree which was directly in front of the home. It was understood for safety, as well as cultural reasons, I would generally be accompanied by a male relative. I anticipated it would be a positive bonding experience, rather, I was "supervised" by a teenage boy. I allowed it; He knew more English than everyone else, seemed innocent enough, and thankfully was much younger. Eventually, Halim resembled more of a leeching spider. I did not recognize the web he was spinning to keep me close to his side until the end of my visit.

Every time I stepped out of the bedroom, Halim would adhere to my side. Except for the few days ventured outside the village, I had no transportation without him. When I rode behind on his motorcycle, he grabbed my arms and placed them firmly around his waist. When we hugged, he began to embrace and pull me in closer, pushing his chest against mine. My confinement to the village did not help the situation, nor the parasite he was becoming. Any time I tried to sneak away, he roamed around looking for me. I slept for over twelve hours every night, and as hard as I tried, could not wake up any sooner. If Halim was not under the tree when I finally awoke, he left frustrated, tired of waiting. When I awoke, uncle Sharif would summon Halim. Uncle Sharif was fairer than his four olive-skinned brothers, had little blue-eyes slightly close together, and spoke with a lisp. He tended to uncontrollably repeat questions, like an animated Syrian cartoon.

With a lisp, Sharif asked, "You want me to call Halim?? I can call him, and he can come right now. He can be here in two minutes. You want me to call Halim?? He has been waiting for you."

I was never able to decide who was more bothersome, Halim or Uncle Sharif.

The homes were staggered so closely on the steep hillside, you could climb across from one house to the next. One day by chance, another male cousin found I was not being looked after by Halim or uncle Sharif. I hopped on this cousin's motorcycle, riding down to his house directly below mine. Lounging on his rooftop, we watched Halim arrive on his motorcycle at my higher-tiered house. He did not find me, so he left, only to return a few minutes later. This time we shouted for him to come down. Halim just stared, stomped his feet, yelled gibberish, and rode off. Something was not right with him. Halim ran to my mother and complained about my "disobedience." She, in turn, pushed me to stay with him.

My mother said, "Why didn't you wait for him or go to his house today? He got upset and started crying. He is sensitive, Jasmine."

I thought to myself, *"Sensitive?"*

Sick was a better word. I wished there was a way to leave this place.

On a random mid-afternoon, my mother, uncle Sharif, and I visited the city of Tartous. Walking through the markets, we stumbled upon an archaeological site. We stepped in the doorless building and found scientists examining artifacts from the Assyrian Empire. They gave us permission to fully enter and look at the ancient stone carved pieces. Many of them resembled pieces found in Ancient Egypt except with softer outlining. After taking a short tour of the sculptures, we went outside to eat fruit purchased from a nearby market. We discovered more works of art in the courtyard of the building. Uncle Sharif chose to sit on a historical wheel-sized stone, embedded with a ceramic mosaic, which dated back thousands of years. In disbelief, I watched him begin to stuff his face with food while sitting on this ancient stone.

After the shock of his ignorance passed, I asserted, "Mom, tell him to get off that artifact."

"Sharif, you should move to the bench."

"No," he replied.

I explained to my mother, "We saw security officials inside, if they come out here and see him, we will have to deal with the consequences. Please tell him again."

"Sharif, can you please get off so she can be quiet?" my mother requested.

"No. What is she going to do, call the FBI?"

I laughed to myself, thinking, *"Maybe... he's a Syrian with no U.S. citizenship, perfect."*

I do not know how he was aware of the FBI. This was the same person who knew one word of English—woman—which he misused as "come on."

Anything was better than watching him disrespect a priceless piece of history. I responded, "Yes, I will call the FBI," chuckling at the twinge of fear in his eyes.

"Woohweee," he responded, while making sure he did not move one inch.

His ignorance drove me crazy. The rest of the family members were from the same cloth but cut differently. Out of ten male cousins, more than half had the agenda of marriage to me on their minds. Though mostly an extinct practice, the idea of marrying your cousin is not an abnormality in many cultures. It dates back to a time when families wanted to maintain property rights. In a culture where a woman's eligibility for marriage diminished around her mid- twenties, I found it somewhat humorous, since some cousins were younger. This did not matter to them, I looked youthful and was a United States citizen. As a result, a slight feud occurred between the two aunts, trickling down to their children. Halim fed both factions.

During the last days in Syria, I finally told them, "Halim is telling you untrue things to purposefully divide and set you against each other."

They responded, "No, he is the son of our uncle George who is an honorable man. He would not do such a thing."

Just because you are blood does not mean you are of similar character. This was their world, and they could live with the consequences. I would be gone soon. The suffocating roots, negative experiences, and the intense episode with the soul demons took a toll. I was bed-ridden for three days from the disturbance to my mind, body, and soul. A trio we will call the dynamic triangle; a symbol of the need for healthy well-being not limited to one area, but rather, a balance between all. The workings of the mind affect the actions of the body, which impact the seeking of the soul. You can mix and match this order, but, they are cohesive.

My mother planned to get dental work done due to the cost being much lower in Syria than in the United States. Even though all the necessary work had to be completed within the forty days, she did not schedule it until the last minute. After each appointment, she would come home from the dentist and disappear until nightfall, lost amongst the village houses. I did not come halfway across the world to spend time with a sixteen- year-old all day. Desperately needing to leave the village environment, the opportunity arose with the quest to find the lost love of Mahir. I called Reema, Sabah's niece who was a lawyer. We spoke over the phone and decided to visit for the day, then Reema would let me know what she discovered. The next thing to tackle became who was going to drive me to her house, thirty minutes away. I went outside to find my mother and tell her the plan.

With Halim present, my mother said, "Let Nizar drive you and take Halim with you."

My eyes were on fire. You would think my mother would have asked herself what two grown women were going to do with a teenage boy. She wore the black veil of ego which blocked her from any degree of common sense.

When we reached the destination, Halim decided not to get out of the car. He had sensed my inner frustrations. With overwhelming relief, I greeted Reema. I thanked the angels for providing someone who wanted nothing but company. Reema found only one thing about Mahir's love; She did not live in the city of Sophita, but in one of the suburbs. With this new information and after getting a few male cousins involved, the search dried up. Despite being disappointed to hear this news, I savored this brief taste of freedom.

Reema asked several questions, "Why does your family tell me you are not there, when I hear your voice in the background?" "Why does your mother keep you with a sixteen year old boy all of the time?" "You have barely gone anywhere, and your trip is almost over? You didn't come here to be trapped in a village."

My eyes fell to the ground. I shrugged my shoulders and changed the subject. I was content having someone simply acknowledge what went on. A time without someone putting me down, lying, deceiving, having selfish intentions, or telling me to shut my mouth. She was a witness, the crumb of replenishment needed. Before I got into the car to return to the village, I gratefully took a deep breath and relished in this divine-sent solace. Without the gifts I needed to deliver to Reema from the States, and the search for someone else's love, this moment would not have occurred. I traveled back downhill to the dark valley.

Though life may present a flurry of negative experiences, gratitude is a necessity in these times so we are not swallowed in the negativity. When speaking of gratitude, it is an appreciation on a soul level, a true feeling for whatever is in reach. There are two different forms of gratitude, neither is right or wrong. However, one is lasting, and one is fleeting. The fleeting type of gratitude is an auto-response from the mind, and many times becomes a limiting excuse. We think we are not allowed to be frustrated with certain aspects of our life and grateful at the same time. This keeps us wedged, preventing us from moving forward. It takes a bird's eye view to access the lasting type of gratitude; A self-awareness of pausing, taking a breath, and redirecting your focus on or doing something else. In this space, the chaos is outside of you, and a sweet peace is within you. Making a conscious effort to direct your attention to the things you are grateful for, starts the momentum. You feel stronger, the daily stresses become less overwhelming, and harsh circumstances are not debilitating. You are simply feeling through matters, instead of your emotions taking over.

Lasting gratitude started at around six-years-old when I was still living in Syria. I walked up to my aunt's house to pay them a visit. I observed my female cousins setting up a gigantic metal pan in their bedroom, which was also their living room, and filling it with water. The floor was made from cement with a bare drain in the middle. I offered to help, but they told me I was too small. All four sisters bathed in the metal pan, using the same water. My siblings and I had one of the only running showers in the village.

I was thankful for a cousin's wife for providing a rare chance for communication. She spoke English well enough to translate my words. I had no control over my surroundings, but I was determined to find the means to disable a young boy who was set on his own selfish needs. I transcended being trapped, and eventually the time came to break free from this entanglement. With only five days left, I asked the cousin's wife for clarification on certain events and timing, and the strings of falsehood came undone. Halim spoke fabrications about himself and others, falsified stories to my family, and used manipulation to gain my approval. From the beginning, I was aware the uncle Tony with the disabled leg, was Halim's confidant. With verification of this knowledge, there was recognition of a contributor to the spider's web. Uncle Tony was fully conscious of everyone's selfish intentions and the wrong-doings of Halim. This uncle did not interfere to protect the niece he helped raise, whom he had not seen for twenty years. He chose to watch her like a fresh piece of entertainment.

The cousins sat around, asking me what I thought of inter-religious marriage. I replied with limited vocabulary, fully aware of their intentions. The questions were a plot to twist my words, and feed the gossip monster. We attended a high school graduation celebration at a neighbor's house. The cousins watched and inquired several times where I learned to dance like that. Later, the true reason they were prompted to ask was revealed. Someone told them about seeing me dance at the hookah lounge. There was always an underlying motive, never an innocent question.

Thoughts of the near escape from this land enthralled all my senses. I removed Halim's fangs and dusted off the web. What my mother and his parents said had no relevance anymore. The main reason I continued to tolerate Halim was due to the great admiration and respect for uncle George, his father. At this point, I was finished with the deceit and cut all ties with the family. That was when the uncles Tony and Sharif decided to get involved and attempt to resolve the split.

Uncle Tony asked, "Why are you mad at Halim?"

Without flinching, I pronounced, "You know why."

His mouth was open prepared to speak again, but my response immobilized him. He was silenced by the power of the words, knowing I was now aware of Halim's intentions and what he had been up to. While uncle Tony left me as a sacrifice to Medusa's caretakers, there was a strong connection between us which we were both aware of. He dared not contest my words and counter with an untruth. My icy look was more paralyzing than Medusa's glare. Ten minutes later, Uncle Sharif took his turn. He was a puppet to Halim's aunt and mother. The women pulled his strings as they added a boulder on his shoulders due to my stand against Halim.

Uncle Sharif demanded, "Jasmine, come inside the house."

Sternly, I replied, "No."

Flustered, he persisted, "Listen to me and go in the house."

"No. Why?"

"Because I'm asking you to."

"No."

He asked me why I was upset with Halim and pleaded for me to make amends.

I responded, "You know the answer why."

Uncle Sharif just said, "You are going to leave like this?"

"Yes." When he began to weep pathetically, I gave him a blank stare. This was an act with no real feeling behind the tears. Just fear of Halim's aunt's wrath.

I hold sadness for the family members who prepared me as a feast. They fed me to

the polluted atmosphere of contrived gossip and rumors. How did my own blood contribute to the shunning? I can only give you a partial answer, just what I can surmise. They simply had way too much time on their hands. Though ill-intentioned, the family taught me a very important lesson. Their opinions and esteem were worthless. They would no longer be part of my consideration, dishonorable in their eyes or not.

While the family created these ordeals as a welcoming, the village members shunned my presence. The cause of this behavior was gossip repeated by a few individuals from the Syrian goon squad. They were present one night at the hookah lounge and were the initial source of the rumors. They happened to be visiting Syria during this exact same time. These goon squad members rehashed and dispatched the gossip to people willing to believe anything about a girl who grew up in America. One rumor stated I did not understand Arabic. Some people believed this, and thus had the courage to speak disrespectful words right to my face.

They would say, as they scanned me up and down, "There goes the American, look at her." Their facial expressions explained the rest of their distaste.

Most of the village people did not speak or associate themselves with me. As I took strolls through the area, they would stare like I was a dirty creature. They labeled me a "Muslim lover," a disgrace to this Christian village. As the dream foretold, "my people" turned against me with little persuasion, believing the dishonesty. I braved the effects of their intense dislike, only when it was brought up by my mother.

Masked by her ego, she spoke, "Everyone keeps saying…" "They think…" and "They keep telling me…."

I heatedly responded, "I don't care. I live my life by what I feel is right, not by what people say. I don't harm anyone. I try to be a better person every day. Keep living your life this way and see what it keeps bringing you. You never learn…"

Stone-like for twenty years, the village community was accustomed to spiteful manners and indifferent to divine principle, ironically to which they professed honor. I presented to them we are human beings with a basic need for love, shelter, food, and dreams. The disposition of religion, country, color, and gender come later. They are merely descriptions that label a person, but do not define their true character. Neither the family nor the village members could comprehend how I could think in that manner, or why I did not judge a person on their outward traits. Maybe they would understand if they saw, once a person removed those layers, we were essentially the same. Universal truth is worldwide and applicable to all. One instance is the human condition. On a basic level, we all need food and water. On a higher level, we are faced with two main questions: What is my purpose? Is there something greater than myself?

There was a difference between the Syria I experienced as a child and the Syria I found as an adult. It had nothing to do with the age of the eyes I was looking through. Externally, besides a few more home developments, the landscape barely changed. Something within the people shifted, and not for the better. Materialism was more prominent. They substituted the replenishment they received from their faith with attachments to things. I witnessed a culture that was disconnected from its true roots and coiled in dark ones.

Zenobia's Illustrious Golden Chains

Transformed over time, the modern region of Syria contained many ancient empires and kingdoms. One of the most remarkable is Queen Zenobia's Palmyrene Empire. This third-century queen's husband and only remaining son were killed. Unlike other rulers, she made the choice to continue their legacy instead of seeking vengeance for their deaths. In honor of them, she spread her territorial claim from Roman trade routes to the conquest of Egypt. Though short-lived, Queen Zenobia gained the title of "warrior queen," due to her dual prowess as a ruler and a soldier. Her downfall came at the hands of the Roman Emperor Aurelian. After her capture, the fate of Queen Zenobia is not definitively known. Theories range from death to release. Personally, I prefer to believe she was granted freedom by her captor. Almost as a reflection of Queen Zenobia, the universe was molding me to encompass both the solidity of a warrior, and the regality of a queen.

Syria was movie-like, I was watching things happen as an observer, while experiencing it in its totality. During the time in Syria and Lebanon, I took almost every photograph placed within this testament before any thoughts of writing. Taking pictures became my means of expression, a means of encapsulating the smell of the orchard, the sights of the people, the hillsides, and the night sky. I could escape all that was happening to me, around me, and to an extent, within me. The camera clicked, and the world seemed to pause for those few seconds. It let me capture things unperceived to most human eyes, and savor what my senses delightfully came upon, even if only momentarily. When it was later decided to include some of these pictures to visually go along with the journey, it was amazing what appeared. The random snapshots correlated directly to these chapter titles, and to the content of this book.

A very long time ago, I came to understand **life brings unexpected things, and the only part we can control is how we respond to them.** Honoring this lesson, I used humor and humbleness to survive and transcend the difficult circumstances, especially in this country. My sister's mother-in-law wanted us to visit her in Lebanon. My mother committed us and called the taxi company at 11:00 P.M. to find out the cab was scheduled to pick us up at 3:00 A.M. I sat by her as I watched her facial expression turn from cheerful to astonished. I just shook my head, unsurprised. My mother was afraid to cancel with my sister's mother-in-law for fear she would "talk badly about us." I was forced to wake up at 2:30 A.M. after getting only two hours of sleep. One hour into the roller coaster-like taxi ride, we came to a sudden stop. The driver asked everyone to make sure they had their Syrian visas on hand. My mother opened her purse to find she forgot hers. This meant we had to turn around and back track to the village. The entire drive back to the house involved her blaming me for this occurrence. We returned to the village at 4:00 A.M., tired to say the least. I tried to crawl into bed, and was literally dragged back to the cab by my uncle.

Restarting the drive to the Syrian-Lebanese border proved to be as rocky as the first attempt. There were bouts of nausea, dizziness, and heavy sleepiness. As terrible as I felt physically, there was a lifting of some sort that occurred when we crossed into Lebanon. It was like the dark roots encompassing me retracted. This newfound sense of freedom was interrupted when we were left stranded, with no phone, baking in the afternoon sun. My mother could not recall the city we were supposed to be in, only remembering bits and pieces of landmarks. We carried two big suitcases while dodging heavy, flying traffic in one-hundred-plus-degree temperatures. I looked around, trying to figure out how to navigate our way out of this situation. I honed in on a glass-paneled pastry shop, told my mother to stay put, and headed in. Luckily, not only did they speak English, they also had a phone.

Shortly after settling into Lebanon, my mother became physically ill, while I felt free as a bird. Within the three day stay there, I effortlessly lost weight, dropping almost two inches on my waist. Despite the fact of eating sweets every night. It was as if my mother could not handle the transition from the entangled dark roots of Syria to the more liberated Lebanon. The veil of ego that covered her since the onset of soul demons, made thicker when we arrived on Syrian soil, suddenly dropped. All the negativity produced by the veil was like a parasite, attaching itself to her. Stepping into Lebanon was the first chance her soul had to fight it off. This was so powerful it caused a physical reaction. My mother was depleted and child-like, refusing to go anywhere.

I visited the ancient archaeological site called Baalbek. During the Roman times it was called Heliopolis, or City of the Sun. The structure brought to life my desire to see and feel ancient history. As we left the space, there was a considerably sized white tent propped up outside. I decided to enter and was met with images of violence and weapons. Although not disturbed or shocked by the pictures, it rattled something inside. I was reminded Lebanon might not have the same dark roots as Syria, but at one point it did. Within a few moments of recognizing this, my sister's mother-in-law and daughter came into the tent to pull me out. I was not with people I felt connected to, but their courtesy was an unexpected gift. Their genuine kindness was a stark contrast to the Syrian family members whom I oddly and actually had a connection to.

I took a deep breath as we crossed the border back into Syria. I was recharged and was able to reclaim the two main desires for this trip. One was to see the Mediterranean Sea, the second was to visit Damascus, the capital of Syria. It is the oldest self-sufficient, continuously thriving, capital in the world. What got me to the Mediterranean destination was a gentleman, who was Reema's first cousin. Although he had romantic interest in me, there was a purity to him and I knew no lines would be crossed. I took the opportunity to visit when Reema called and invited me. I met them in the city of Sophita and we drove from there. When we reached the Mediterranean coast, I asked him to pull over so I could get a good view. I exited the car, walked over to the huge boulders, and climbed on top. I witnessed an overdeveloped, polluted, and under construction area. It was disappointing and sad to see the water was stripped of its natural beauty. I found the gentleman driver standing next to me speaking and marveling at what he saw as beautiful. I turned to him puzzled, wondering if he was seeing the same sight. I turned around, hopped down to the road side, and back in the car. I focused on being grateful to get out of the village, and the hospitality of him and Reema to drive all the way there.

After four weeks of pleading, I managed a trip to Damascus. I awoke at 5:30 A.M. to the blaring horn of the village taxi driver and his long white van. Our group consisted of myself, my mother, and nine other relatives. The original plan was to head to the capital, however the excursion began with a stop in Maalula. It is one of the last remaining Aramaic-speaking villages on earth, the language of Jesus Christ. The vibes exuding from the people there were very unwelcoming. I came to find out they perceived and felt everyone outside of the area was an intruder on their sacred land. They put up with tourism because of the influx of income it gave their village. I understood and respected all of this, so I requested for us not to stick around. That was ignored.

In the vastness of this isolated desert land, there stood a structure made up of massive grey boulders. These boulders paved a stone pathway, which we entered. When I started to take snapshots, the camera began to filter the photographs in a green hue, returning to normal once we exited the stone monument. We continued to the neighboring building that was built around a small ancient church. Before stepping through the open archway, I was stopped by a solid arm of a nun and handed a shawl to cover my shoulders. There was a nun sitting in the old pews by herself. She looked like a crumbling statue, absent of color and life. Her deep religious devotion seemed to drain her spiritual essence.

After we drove two hours to Maalula, took pictures, and left, we immediately got lost for an hour.

Innocently, I asked, "Mom, I thought this taxi driver knew where everything was?"

My mother shrugged her shoulders and replied, "That's what they told me."

A sense of impending doom began to loom over the day. After driving an additional hour, we visited another church and I got more great pictures. We drove two more hours in the sweltering heat, with a broken air conditioner, sticky leather seats, and packed into the van like sardines. We reached the next destination and somehow got off course again. This time, for only thirty minutes. The village taxi driver found his way back to the highway and after an hour of driving, abruptly veered off an exit. We traveled down the bumpy, empty road, as the heat radiated off the leather seats and our bodies bounced around. I looked out the window, bewildered as I stared at the desolate, dry landscape. I wondered where we were headed. Soon we all found out it was a seminary, a place where people went to become a priest or nun. It sat in the middle of nowhere, with nothing in sight for over fifty miles. I encountered a nun there who embodied an energetic spunk, that had nothing to do with her personality. She spoke, and the moment she met my eyes, she stopped. There was an acknowledgment, a connection of who she was and who I was. She was the only person to recognize it. This nun was quite a contrast to the statue-like nun at Maalula.

We drove another two hours to get lost once more. After stopping three times to ask for directions, we found the exit for the next destination. On the gravel vacant road, all of a sudden

massive sand dunes filled our entire vicinity. After twenty more minutes, the taxi guide pulled in the only existent shaded spot, told us to get out, and went to sleep. At the height of the afternoon sun heat, we stepped out of the vehicle to find ourselves in front of the stairs of Saint Moses. I stood stunned, staring at the outdoor monument with over a thousand carved stone steps. It was yet another place where you could become a priest or a nun.

If it were not such a scorching hot day to the point of making someone sick, on top of the nauseating driving skills of the cab driver, I would have gone right up those steps. My adventurous personality and curiosity were lost for the first time. There was no Damascus in sight, and I had hit my breaking point. I refused to walk the steps and sat next to the van. I lost it.

I exploded, "Is he crazy?! He drops us off in the middle of the afternoon during the hottest time of the day! What is wrong with him? Does anyone have any common sense in this village?! Yes, it would definitely take a crazy person to do this."

My mother lashed back, "Shut your mouth!!"

"What! Do you understand this man decided to drop us off to walk these steps, when it's over a hundred degrees in the middle of a desert?!"

She responded only with a crippling look. I grew silent. I knew it was useless to keep repeating the obvious. Astonishingly, no one else saw anything wrong with this situation. I leaned against the stone archway, staring at what seemed like countless steps. I watched Halim's mother put a grocery bag over her head, and sit on the stone landing before the staircase began. The female cousins ran ahead, with the male cousins slowly following behind. With the exception of one cousin, we saw them return in less than ten minutes, ready to go. At this point, I wanted a reminder of why I decided to come to Syria in the first place. I started to plan an escape.

My thoughts raced, *"Maybe I could move up the date of the return flight without telling my mother, get a cab to Damascus, and never return to this country. Yes, I think if there was a contest to name the place closest to hell on earth, this would rank in the top ten."*

Apparently, the ticking time bomb in my mind just exploded. After a few more of my inflammatory thoughts passed, it finally dawned on everyone, walking up those steps under these circumstances was not a good idea. We staggered back to the van and waited for the final female cousin to come back down the stone staircase. She was the one who was passionate about becoming a nun.

My irritation blasted, "Thank you, Mom. Now I know exactly where to come to become a nun or priest. I came all the way from America just to see this. If one day I decide to become a nun, I'll travel here, halfway around the world to convert."

I was on fire from the frustration of living through yet another scenario, where so many things went south.

Oblivious to the cause of the flames, my mother replied, "I didn't know this was going to happen…where do you want to go?"

After almost a month of begging to visit Damascus and hiring this taxi driver specifically to take us there, how could she not know? I figured her mind fried in the heat, along with the rest of the brains in this village. She listened to the villagers' high praises about the taxi driver knowledge of navigating Syria, especially in Damascus. This was why we were in this situation to begin with. I did not allow my current feelings of disappointment to destroy the original objective and desire to visit the capital.

I answered, "I want to go where we were supposed to go from the beginning…Damascus."

My mother asked, "What's in Damascus?"

"Mom, it's the oldest capital city in the world. I'm assuming there must be something there. You know, many tourists do come to Syria just to visit Damascus."

When she finally told the driver to head toward this city, he replied, "Why didn't you say you wanted to go there from the beginning?"

I was in shock. I needed to get out of this country. Little did we know, by law, a permit was needed to drive in Damascus. Of course, our driver did not have one. We became aware of this very quickly when he shoved us out of the van in the middle of traffic, and abruptly drove away. I could not believe this was happening. I was in the center of the oldest capital city in the world with nine other people who had no clue where any of the sites were. The reckless maneuvering of the absent-minded driver, the long hours on the road, and the unbearable heat in the van took a toll on everyone. Unable to take any more, we rested on the nearest shaded benches. After cooling down for an hour, we took the public bus to the market, the only place my Uncle George knew how to get to. Friday is a Muslim holy day and is observed by closing businesses. It happened to be Friday. When we arrived at the market, we found all the shops were closed except two.

There was still hope and time to salvage the day. A male cousin worked in Damascus and knew all of the sites to visit and experience. We waited for an hour and a half for him to get out of work, but he could not make it in time to meet us. To lighten the mood, I bought everyone chilled fruit smoothies from one of the only open stands. With home as our last destination, we vanished from Damascus just as quickly as we appeared.

About a week later, another male cousin who once worked in the capital, took pity on me. We planned another trip there without my mother and the large group. To no surprise, this visit also entailed quite a few frustrating hiccups. In spite of this, I stumbled upon a special gold bracelet in the bustling market arena. I knew it was meant for me. However, I was unable to purchase it due to an insufficient amount of Syrian currency. So, I requested one thing from my mother the day before our departure back to the States. I asked her to take me to the city of Homs where I knew I would find the same gold bracelet I saw in Damascus. Everywhere in Syria, handling and retail of gold jewelry is utterly disorganized. The odds of finding exactly

the same bracelet was in no way in my favor. Even so I forged ahead, solely based on a divine knowing.

I entered the city of Homs accompanied by my mother, four male cousins, and one female cousin. In the intense afternoon humidity, amidst a large crowd, the search for the gold bracelet began. Again, the van escort was not licensed to drive around the city. Therefore, we were left in the same predicament as before.

He stopped in the middle of a high-traffic area and announced, "The shops are down that road and only ten minutes away."

In actuality, he had dropped us off thirty minutes away from the market location. This made everyone miserable and irritable. My mother was bathed in sweat by the time we reached the shopping district. They followed my lead as we scoured and weaved throughout jewelry shops. Frustration levels were high by the time we entered what seemed like the tenth store. After three more shops, the tension was somewhat eased when we found a small version of the Damascus bracelet. One of the male cousins took a picture of the bracelet on his cell phone, and the other cousins divided up to continue the hunt. While they were flying in and out of the over forty-plus jewelry shops left, I went to search on my own. This was mostly to avoid the rising impatience of my mother. My cousins independently assumed this piece of jewelry was for my brother, and it became their motivation to help. Unbeknown to them, my intentions for this search were not clear in my mind. My soul however, knew there was a divine purpose.

They all put the pressure on to buy a different bracelet, but I refused to settle. They complained about the heat and the heavily crowded area, but I would not stop in my quest. They may have buckled to the unfavorable circumstances, but I trusted the divine insight. When another hour of searching passed, my mother went off like a fire cracker. We all watched her frantic display.

I immediately stopped what I was doing and sternly stressed, "No. Do not even begin to do this again."

Whatever came through my voice penetrated through her veil of ego, and became a mirror for her behavior. She backed down. Shocked and amazed, I only had time to quickly thank the angels and continue the mission.

One of the last untapped gold retail owners saw the photograph of the bracelet and said, "This is old gold. You won't be able to find it. If you do, it will be very used and worthless."

With the words of this shop keeper echoing in my ears, I persisted onto the three stores left. The next boutique offered nothing except the return of my mother's irritated voice. I overlooked her presence, determined to not let it discourage me.

In the very next moment, a female cousin came into the shop screaming, "The store next door might have it!!"

I ran over with the necklace that I saved from when we got swindled and planned to exchange it. I gripped the box tightly in my hand and flew through the mass of people. My mother stood to my left and my five cousins stood around us, huddled in the cramped shop area. We all watched the owner turn to the wall, grab a green velvet case, untie the ribbon knot, and unfold the contents on the glass counter.

"Yes! This is the exact one!" I rejoiced.

We paid for the bracelet and exited the shop as a group. While walking through the doorway, I found one of the younger male cousins on my right-hand side. Before I knew it, he took my hand and interlocked his fingers with mine. Startled, this snapped me back into a more grounded state. The uplifted feeling experienced from finding the piece of gold jewelry opened me up to anything fully entering, which included the dark roots of this land.

Afraid it was going to somehow disappear, I held the Damascus bracelet during the entire drive back. I admired the design sliding my fingertips over the grainy textured surface. Holding something that was at first so intangible was an affirmation of divine power. I found closure to the forty days and forty nights. Nostalgia of my childhood left a bittersweet taste in my mouth after this visit. The village people and family members became a distant memory I chewed up and spit out. Ultimately, I left knowing I loved my native country more than it would ever love me.

The constant disagreements between my mother and I persisted when we returned to the States. At the Chicago airport, she began her charge in front of twenty-five people, as I sank deeper into my chair.

Blinded by her ego, she erratically spoke, "Something is wrong with you!"

Worn down from the tribulations experienced in Syria, I weakly replied, "Mom, stop before you start. I just want this nightmare to be over. You did enough damage in Syria. Can you please just give me some peace? That's all I ask for…"

She exclaimed, "Look at yourself! You are so sad. I hate seeing you like this!"

"I'm tired…you have no clue what really took place in Syria. Again, I just want peace. Can you give me that one simple thing?"

My mother paused for a few seconds and then spoke of what was really on her mind. "You're in love with him, aren't you?! Everyone kept telling me, 'Look at her. She is in love with someone from America.'"

Calmly, I answered, "No mom, for the millionth time, stop worrying if I'll ever get married. Let me ask you something. How could I be in love with him or anyone else, when I don't even know how to love?"

From as early as I can remember, my ability to bond with others was disabled by watching my parents bicker, fight, and intentionally hurt each other. My mother was an independent woman with a job at Ford. She thought differently than other ethnic women of her time. When my father arrived fresh off the boat from Syria, he asked for my mother's hand in marriage. Instead of saying yes, my mother decided to, in her words, "See how his mind works." She went on a dinner date with my father and brought along her first cousin who was also her best friend. Not only did he argue with her, but also made her pay for the meal. Back then this was unheard of, and even now, most cultured Middle Eastern men generously pay for everything.

She came home telling her mother she refused to see him again, let alone marry him. Her mother would not have it and my mother did what was expected of her. She justified her decision to marry him in order to maintain the family's honor. The marriage resulted in an environment where every day yelling and arguing was the norm. Both individuals refused to stop the negativity and change.

Repeatedly, I instructed her, "Fighting on a daily basis is not normal mom. You need to back down. Let things go."

My suggestions were going against thirty-years of ingrained behavior and stubbornness. In Syria, I found it ironic how my mother wanted me to fall into the same trap she did; Making a major life decision based on false pride.

I brought this up to her once and she replied, "I learned from my mistake. I know more now. I know what's good for you."

My mother knew better than to force my hand in marriage, so she attempted to get me to meet someone in Syria. She pressured me to go to weddings and church functions.

Once, as I left one of the weddings early, she brutally shouted, "This is unacceptable!"

"Mom, go back inside and enjoy the wedding. I sat, ate, and paid my respects. What is so wrong with leaving early?"

She insisted, "No! No! Why should I go back inside!"

I just looked at her and thought to myself, *"To give me peace…for once."*

She yelled, "You know what?!?"

"What Mom?"

She said curtly, "I don't care if you die right now!!"

How do you say that to a daughter for leaving a wedding early? My mother made sure to tell my father, four aunts, and one uncle, the story of my 'crazy' departure from the wedding. Those are the only relatives I knew of. My mother had to appease her ego. And me? I confided in one person, Maya.

Back in the United States, my mother targeted her cannons with better aim and power. The conversations began in a calm-enough state, but within a few minutes the heat rose. Cannon balls of assault discharged from my mother's mouth while I held my tongue. Her anger was fueled by my unwillingness to meet someone in Syria, and her various self-created beliefs. Not everyone is meant to be married, and maybe I was one of those people.

After she told me of a relative who was getting their second divorce, I commented, "See, mom. I'm glad I'm waiting and being patient for the right person, instead of going through a divorce."

Her ego took offense and fired back, "I would rather see you get three divorces than be like this!"

Every opportunity she had with me was shrouded in the black veil of ego.

Not long ago, she screamed, "If someone else had you as a daughter, they would have cut you up into a thousand pieces."

"What happened to you, mom? You listened to those village people who told you negative things, and you believed every single word."

The astonished look on her face showed a momentary openness. For a few split seconds, I saw a flash of light in her eyes. The look disappeared before I knew it, and was replaced by her becoming defensive and retaliating with hurtful words. Clearly my mother lived in the shadows of others' approval, with her ego as her guide. During this time period, I was weakened, and my protective shield was worn down. She would drain me to the point I could not sleep and would elevate my anxiety to volatile levels. My mother was caught in reverse as I endeavored to help her move forward.

Queen Zenobia was captured in the end, like her, I was also captured. The difference between our chains was that mine were of illustrious gold, molded from divine composition. Detainment is not necessarily looked at as positive, but when serving the soul, it is. This somehow made what happened, and what was to come, worth it.

The Chariot of Revelation

The spindle of life continues to spin, even when the laborer lets go of the pedal. I returned to the states drained and exhausted. From the time we landed home, there were a few more days left in summer before graduate school was to begin again. I awoke at 7:00 A.M., went downstairs, and settled on the leather couch. I turned on the television and the Syrian channel was on. Synchronistically, the first thing I heard was a quote by the Syrian president speaking about regaining the Golan Heights sector. It was an angelic reminder of the connection to the plight of these people.

Golan Heights was once a Syrian territory, then fell under Israeli occupation. Israel attempted to persuade the people of Golan Heights to take on Israeli residency. The Golan Heights community decided to execute an open strike and fight for preservation of their Syrian identity. They were met by the powerful hand of Israel, which included the deployment of thousands of soldiers. After five months and six days of resistance and combat, they bargained to not take Israeli citizenship, only an identification card that showed Israeli residency. Thus, the identity of the Golan Heights people to this day, is listed as "undefined" with no nationality of origin. They are like children without a home. I can attribute the connection to the Golan Heights natives to my Syrian ancestry and their courageous actions. While I was on the ancient Syrian land, I internally called out for the people of Golan Heights for forty days. Now I prayed at home, a and where hopes and dreams can turn into reality.

With a full load of courses, and writing this book, there was no time left to watch television. I stood in the kitchen which opened to the family room, and waited for the coffee to brew. Listening to my father ask me if I started applying for jobs yet, my ears perked upon hearing the name of Golan Heights come from the television. Written Arabic has a different sound than spoken Arabic. Since I was unable to understand the newscaster's Arabic, my father translated it. "The United Nations voted again on the dispute over Golan Heights. I think they said one-hundred-and-sixty-nine nations voted for their return, which is almost all the nations except Israel, who voted against them, and the United States, who voted neutral."

The timing of the coffee and my father being there to translate was not coincidental. These synchronized happenings are a form of communication from a higher source. In this instance, the vessel was the television. **The monotony of day to day living can prevent us from taking notice of these extraordinary tidbits.**

There are other means of communication we experience and are not always aware of. One of the most prevalent, we will call invisible energetic cords. Has someone in particular came to your mind and just a few moments later they contact you? **Everything including our thoughts and intentions are energy.** A person's objective to communicate with you is sent out through the invisible energetic cord. It reaches you before actual physical evidence shows up like a message, phone call, or email. **Even when two people separate or lose track of each other, energy fibers remain attached and so does the line.**

These cords have existed since the beginning of life. In ancient times, they were actually used to their fullest capability. **The moment you make eye contact with a person, this cord is instantly created and activated between the two receivers. Some cords are a thread, others are a rope, and a few are umbilical cord-like.** The size and strength of the cable depends on many factors such as time, state of mind, and the type of connection shared. Without any prior knowledge, I knew this was possible. My mind decided to put it to the test. Through the soul connection, I sent a mental message, letting Hisham know I returned. Within five minutes, I received a phone message asking me if I was back. Hisham and I planned to meet before he had to go to work. We both ended up running late.

Hisham called. "Jasmine look in your rear-view mirror. I'm right behind you."

He drove behind my car to an indoor lot, where we parked on the same level, at opposite ends. We greeted one another with a casual hug and then we headed to a coffee shop. I told some stories about Syria, leaving out the details and cutting them as short as possible. I showed him some pictures taken, skipping through them at a quick pace. What should have been an enjoyable time of sharing, turned out to be dull. After less than two hours, I wanted to leave and reminded him of his work schedule. The connection we shared went from soul level to complete surface level.

I felt different that day, more serene. The heaviness of all I went through was lifted. There was a sense of being in control from within. Something not experienced for over half a year. I soon discovered this was only a temporary reprieve. It served as reassurance everything challenging is not permanent, whether it is on the realistic or soul grounds. There is always an end.

We walked back to the cars. He asked me to sit in the passenger seat of his car, so we could finish the conversation. Soon after, I pulled out a jewelry box from my purse.

I said, "I have something for you..." I handed him the blue magnetic box and watched him open it. Sincerely, I spoke, "The bracelet has special energies, you know...it will bring you good luck."

He responded, "I don't doubt that. You shouldn't have...I can't accept this."

"There are also three shells in there that I picked off the shore of Tartous because I know how much you love the beach."

Hisham smiled and said, "The shells are the real gift, but because it's from you, I will accept the bracelet."

I softly said to him, "Now you have something to remember me by."

I held back tears, I was saying goodbye. We knew each other only for a short while, but time was irrelevant. This connection was much deeper. I was losing a very old friend.

Sitting in the car, I watched and took notice of a person who completely reverted back to his lower self. I reminisced for a few moments about past memories when his higher self was active. That person was no longer present. This meeting was one of the last times I witnessed Hisham in his true form, not immersed completely in doubt or fear. Like a ghost, he disappeared into the reality of his domain.

Hisham was given a mirror to see his disorder. It showed him he compromised himself and strayed from what he was supposed to accomplish. **We tend to choose the less painful path.** We do not want to hurt or feel down. It was far less uncomfortable and wounding to separate. **Although we are disengaged from our feelings, they are still there, in the depths of the trunks.** When we try to reconnect, there is a rush of intensity that is overwhelming and aided with a vulnerability. Hence, Hisham chose the option of retracting.

I prayed every single day to disconnect from whatever bound me, but the connection refused to break. When I landed on United States soil the solitude compounded for the next thirty days. As alone as I was in life, this was a new depth. Fatima called when I returned from Syria and asked how it was. Before I could finish one sentence, she cut me off to go on for twenty-five minutes about her husband's crazy family. These stories truly had nothing to do with her. I debated staying on the line, but after feeling immense draining, I hung up on her. I wished she would learn to stop taking on other people's problems as her own. I worked so hard with her for four years only to find for every step she took forward, she went three steps back. I prayed for the higher powers that be to help her find and grant her peace within herself. I had no one left.

Mercifully, fate brought Maya to revitalize me. She was a light worker who came in these hard times of need. A healer who mended the wounds inflicted by the dark entities. Maya provided a respite from their attacks, if only for an hour. She became a confidant at a time where the truth of this world was disorienting my mind, body, and soul. The immediate trust between us allowed me to share my visions, sensing, and deep knowing without judgment. She was a rare treasure that reminded me of my true calling. I set up an appointment with Maya to find answers to the things I did not understand and end the confusion.

Maya asked, "Tell me what you need, and I will focus on just that."

I replied, "I want to figure out why I can't break this connection. Why am I stuck in this place? What is the purpose of all of this? Why is there this level of connection to someone I barely respect? Is it because he filled a void, a friendship, or provided comfort? I'm trying to realistically evaluate this situation and find an answer, but I can't seem to accomplish that. In all of this, I feel like everything inside of me is saying I am on the right path."

Maya replied, "Okay. I understand completely. You want the understanding of what and who Hisham is to you?"

"Yes. No more puzzles," I pleaded. "I just want the truth, no matter how odd it is. I can handle it. What I can't handle any longer is the confusion."

I needed answers. Maya guided me through a meditative trance to a place of clarity, where the verity is untainted by reality. For this to happen, she had to open the heart chakra. Every person has seven main chakras, or seven energy centers that flow through in the body. However, there are numerous of chakras, thousands of spinning wheels of light all around the body. **Just as the physical body has major and minor organs with blood vessels that keep blood flowing, the energetic body has major and minor chakras with meridian lines that carry the energy throughout.** The main difference is, one is visible and the other is invisible to the human eye.

A vision emerged of Hisham in Syria with three versions of me: My present-self, seven-year-old me, and three-year-old me. On the front cement steps of my parents green crumbling home, Hisham rested with my younger selves in his lap. The toddler on his left and the child on his right. Adult me sat to the left of them. As the house sat on a high point of the mountain side, I watched them play with him. I took in the scenic view, listened to the innocent giggles and smiled at the delightful sight. Within a few moments, the two girls hopped off his lap, taking each other's hands. The two carefully made their way down the steps, with the older child guiding the toddler. After reaching the gravel pavement, they took five steps forward then turned back around toward Hisham and me.

In unison, they said, "He is A truth. YOUR ultimate truth is destined to capture the hearts of many and forever change the world. Believe, trust, and have faith in what we tell you, for we are you."

They hovered in the air and suddenly turned into shooting stars to join the night sky.

When I awoke from the meditation, the questions were answered. I discovered he was a character, playing his role. Everyone in our life has a part to perform. It could be for a couple days or until the end of our years. Hisham was a slice of the pie in the creation of this book. Now I understood the overwhelming visitation from the angels when they surrounded me, three days before the departure from Syria. As simple as this was, there was more to be revealed. I kept writing and moving forward. I did not know the purpose, why I was doing this, or of the outcome.

As the message of the vision was conveyed to Maya, there was denial that more was still in store to experience. My mind rejected this knowing and started to run away. I wanted the peaceful ending with this newfound understanding finally reached. This brought on the same type of tender pains experienced the times I tried to break away from the fated steps. My breathing became difficult, I placed one hand on my heart to try to control the intense feeling. I placed my other hand on the Reiki table to support my body.

I pronounced, "I don't know what is happening to me right now. I'm trying to control this reaction, but I really can't. It must look crazy to you."

Maya explained, "Jasmine, you have to tell Hisham your truth. I opened your heart chakra just for this purpose."

"Are you kidding me? He's going to misinterpret it. He seems to think most women he interacts with want him. He'll think I'm trying to win him over, and I'm like other girls who throw themselves at him. I have none of those intentions."

The throbbing burst forth again, cutting my breath short.

Maya said, "He knows you're not like them."

"Maybe…but his ego is huge, he'll assume something I don't mean…"

She asked, "Do you really think so?"

"Yes. I know and I'm certain…you don't need a gift for that."

"I don't believe he would do that to you. He cherishes your friendship."

I knew him for both his genuine soul and his controlling mind. Within the mess since meeting Hisham, I found a companionship. A kind that was new. A mutual support, some sort of balance of give and take. It was granted for six months and stripped away. I continued, "You know… he barely calls anymore. To be honest with you, I think he is afraid of me. Can you believe that? Scared of little Jasmine?"

She smiled, remarking, "He's afraid of his truth."

"…Besides knowing he's part of my path and caring about him, I don't feel anything else."

She said, "That is enough. You caring for him is your truth, and he needs to hear it."

I questioned what there was to gain from this. I knew where he was at and how he would receive it, without any assumptions. The fear of disappointment and backlash entered. "What happens if he doesn't respond well?…says hurtful things…turns his back."

"He won't do that to you."

He was still somewhat of a friend, at the same time, not really. **I returned, as I always do, to what was ultimately right.** Following the instructions of Maya was the next step.

With every part of me not wanting to do it, I asked, "Is this really necessary?"

Maya responded, "Yes! You have to speak up, for him to hear it. After he hears your words, he can't pretend. Right now he has minimized the true feelings he has, and is able to detach from it."

Maya was now playing her role in instigating the continuation of these chapters. I let her take the wheel, not knowing what turns were coming. For better or for worse, they would be just the right ones.

I processed out loud, "You are right…no regrets. This is so difficult. I have never done this before."

Maya replied, "Well, now with your heart chakra open, it's your best time. This opening is giving you courage. It is something you need to take advantage of. Jasmine, I know you are feeling a lot, but do not lose focus of what you have to do."

"Yes… I have lost much in this lifetime…. **All I have is truth.**"

Departing Maya's office, I placed a call to Hisham. It went to voicemail and I left a message to call me back as soon as possible. I had lost my mind. This approaching interaction was going to be a disaster. I knew this with my whole essence. Yet, I trusted Maya's guidance. Ten minutes later, Hisham returned the call. There was a strong inkling present we needed to talk in person. In my mind, I saw a flash of a location that held a labyrinth in its backyard and suggested it as the meeting spot. It was a place I previously and randomly came across when I got a nudge to turn into a parking lot. After my recommendation, I recognized the reason for the vision. The labyrinth was a tangible exhibit. The labyrinth originates from Greek mythology. It was a complex structure built for King Minos to hold the Minotaur, a monster half man, half bull. It was made so elaborately even the creator could barely escape it. The minotaur was eventually killed by Theseus; a hero who personified intelligence and wisdom, in addition to the typical traits of strength and courage found in other mythological heroes. The final meeting point, **the modern-day labyrinth, reflected a place whichever direction chosen, the seeker arrives at the core.**

We met at a bank, right down the street, just a two-minute drive. Also, this happened to be the same bank location which led to the attendance of the February 14th wedding. We proceeded to the labyrinth. It was almost a script being followed, while not knowing any of the lines, actions, or outcome. My mind did not want to go forward, while my soul knew there were higher motives playing out. To counteract the resistance, the soul began to convince the mind through realistic points. I would not look back and say, I should have done that, or be a person who let their fears control their actions. I would know I fulfilled my part and that was more than enough. That is all we can do. There would be no question of 'what ifs,' or 'maybes.' **The skillful soul knew exactly what it was doing.**

We should embrace moments like these. This is an opportunity to grow. We put ourselves in a box even though it is a limiting confinement. It seems safe and falsely comfortable. How does this happen? Society projects the image of how we should look and what we should have. Family demonstrate the ways of behaving. We might believe the box is the best place for us. These all become sources of programming and we end up in this container. If we step outside, we think something will be lost. However, we are not losing anything, we are gaining ourselves. True living is beyond this box.

I prayed the labyrinth was not in use and no one was in the vicinity. As we parked and walked toward the area, the place was clear. After Hisham asked, I explained a labyrinth is like a maze, but no matter which path you choose, you end up in the center.

He inquired, "What's the point?"

I elaborated, "To clear your mind, hear your soul, and find answers without thinking of your destination. This is already guaranteed. No distractions exist except within your own self."

The circular area of the labyrinth is blanketed with white stones. The frame of the structure itself is outlined with bricks. The center contains the seven colored chakras in stained glass, embedded in cement stones. We settled on one of the four surrounding wooden benches. It seemed like he had no care in the world. As for me, the uneasiness was rising.

He spoke, "Tell me what's going on."

I replied, "I don't know where to begin..."

The reason I was there was missing. I pushed myself to connect to the purpose, and shared, "I know you are afraid to see and speak to me because I remind you of something, and it makes you feel uncomfortable."

Light tears started flowing, and simultaneously confusion as to why I was shedding them. It took me several years and writing this account to understand the reason. I knew I did all I could, and the rest was up to him at this point. The program was so ingrained, it was going to take his soul to reverse this. The problem was, his mind was still so overpowering. **A sacredness, not a weakness is found in tears. They are a form of release, a token of power.** During a particular emotion being felt, a chemical is released by the brain, then broken down by the body, and finally expelled through tears. In this process, certain emotions produce waste in the mind and body. **Tears are the liberation of this waste. Sometimes tears speak more than the tongue can express.**

He began to pat my shoulder, saying, "Be strong."

"No. This has nothing to do with being strong, Hisham. There is nothing wrong with crying, or being vulnerable at times."

"Yes... I guess you can't be strong all the time. If you don't have times of weakness, then something is wrong with you."

It is also not weakness, but for him that is how he understood it.

His ego perked up, "Jasmine, I wish I could sugar-coat everything and tell you something different, but I can't. It's been really hard for me to focus and do even the simplest of things. Even when it comes to practicing music with Fadel, I can't wait until we finish. I don't know what else to say."

I was not sure why he was saying this. I replied, "You don't need to explain yourself. That's what I meant to say in the beginning, I just need you to listen, and you don't need to say anything."

Relieved, he said, "Thanks…"

I swallowed my reservations. "I care about you, Hisham."

He responded, "I care about you, too, and I know you care about me."

I learned not to assume a person knows or will figure out how we feel. I regarded, "But I want you to hear it from me. It's nice to hear things like that out loud."

He answered back, "Yes, it is."

He disengaged, pronouncing, "I'm a full grown man and overnight I had to sell my house, sell my car, lost my studio, and became a fugitive. I have to deal with this, when I should be so much farther along in my life."

That was the "reality" he chose. In the clearer perspective, he sold his house in less than a month, and had a free place to eat and sleep. He bought an almost new luxury car, and the studio was relocated to another friend's basement.

The angels encouraged, "Follow through."

I kept moving forward, "Remember when I told you my cousin said 'those are foreign men and all they want is one thing'?"

"Yes."

"Now, reality tells me I should believe my cousin who I grew up with and who is looking out for me, correct?"

When he responded with a yes, I looked into his eyes to see his mind take a back seat and his soul began to steer. I had not seen him in this state since the immigration chaos.

The angels tapped in, "His core is unlocked. Take advantage of this rare opportunity."

I spoke, "But even though I got scared and confused, I looked back at you and my intuition told me you weren't like that with me. Now that truth proved to be right, correct?"

Again, without fear he answered, "Yes."

"Now remember the time when my other cousin, Othman called, and told me about your reputation as a player with women?"

He nodded yes.

I explained, "Again, reality told me to listen to Othman, who is my blood, who stayed numerous times at my apartment, who I cooked for, and who's trying to protect me. This was weighed against someone I've only known for a few months. But when I looked at you making sandwiches, the same feeling told me you were to be trusted. Now that feeling was right, correct?"

"Yes," he responded.

"See, Hisham. I went against everything reality told me and listened to that inner voice, which as you see is always right. I am here to tell you, I'm never going to stop listening to what this divine voice tells me."

"I understand that, Jasmine, but I believe I'm doing the right thing at this time in my life. Now I sleep better than I ever have."

I became a burden to his mind.

I responded, "That's what your mind thinks is the right thing, but that doesn't mean it is."

"Yes. That doesn't matter now, as long as I think and believe I'm doing the right thing."

"Remember, Hisham, just because reality gives you all these justifications, does not mean it is the ultimate truth."

With a smirk, he replied, "Okay, for now it is the truth to me."

I had no clue why he grinned. I elaborated, "Hisham, we are connected. I don't want you to get the wrong idea. I never even thought beyond a friendship. I couldn't discount this connection, something else was in charge and kept pushing me…"

I continued to steer the soul and make sure my intentions were clear. At the end, Hisham shared, "You're actually one of my best friends."

I cannot tell you why, but I knew in that very moment, somehow he gave himself permission to return to his old pirate ways. I would no longer hear from him. A pirate's ways are foul, but he does not perceive it as such. Could one persuade him otherwise? I never tried.

Throughout the entire conversation, Hisham kept his face turned away from mine and never looked in my eyes. It was easier for him that way.

His phone rang. "Excuse me for a second."

When he began speaking on the phone, my eyes were drawn to the necklace he always wore. It contained a prayer from his birth and for whatever reason, I was intrigued by it. As I went to touch it, I unconsciously began humming the two-note melody that kept returning during those initial months of us meeting.

Hisham ended his phone conversation and remarked, "There goes those two notes again."

"Yes. They always come back. I've tried to figure out the third and fourth notes, but I can't."

He pronounced, "It's because there is no third or fourth note. Those two notes stand alone, repeat, then a third note begins the next part which leads into the fourth."

He was right. I was astonished. I thought I was the one who was supposed to know that knowledge.

The angels' whispered, "Remember what we advised you to do with those notes."

I figured, why not. He can think whatever he wants. If unfavorable judgment is the price for helping him return to his passion, then so be it.

I said, "Hisham, you should take those two notes and create a song. I know you will produce something very beautiful by starting with them."

"You think so?"

"I know so. For the whole past week, my intuition has been telling me those notes are meant to be turned into a song and it's for you to create. Begin with those two notes and the rest will naturally come to you."

He accepted my words, and we departed the labyrinth.

Driving home from a class, something came over me. It was set off by a conversation with a friend, Sarah. She professed she was used by a man and after I told her about the labyrinth meet up, she projected I was too. I completely and totally went against my free-will for six months. I was left empty handed. All that following higher guidance did not change or help anything. No purpose seemed to be served. What resulted was chaos. The shallow cousins had new contrived fuel to use. The Syrian goons had manipulated material to feed on. When before, both had nothing on me. This poured into the Syria visit. Family and village members were vultures picking at my flesh. My mother's pressing amplified ten folds. All of these revelations presented a dilemma to my mind and soul. I entered into a string of inquiries, addressing the angels...

> You have led me this far and now you remain silent. Why? Offer me the reasons for the demons which torment me every day. Give me justification for the onslaught. What have I done to attract such intruders into my mind and soul?

This was a time of weakness, therefore an opportunity. The dark voices entered. **"Just take your car and ram it into the concrete. It will be quick and painless. Press on the gas! Faster! The faster you go, the more certainty there is of instant death."**

Instead of going home, I decided to visit the labyrinth again. I walked into the arena and settled on the bench. The combat continued.

> I do not understand. Make me understand your reasons. I faithfully bowed to your guidance and here I am being attacked. I have nothing left to say to you. I come here for understanding as to why you have led me astray. Do you know what it feels like to have your own truth paralyze the very essence of yourself? I do not think you are aware to what extent I have gone in order to do what I was commanded against my will. I hear no response…Why? Why can't you give me an answer? That is all I ask. Abiding by your every word, I did not falter. But now I am like a lamb left to the wolves. I am a loyal disciple of the Truth, but my own truth has failed me. Do you understand what it feels like to be

taken against your own will into the depths of darkness? I want peace. I demand PEACE. It is the only thing I ask of you.

The dark voices re-entered, **"When you get home, find the most potent pills and take them all, making sure there is no chance for revival. This is your chance at peace!"**

I ignored them and persisted with the angels as I trudged on, bypassing the gladiators of darkness.

Who can stand even one moment of this internal torment without speaking blasphemy to you? How can you fail me when I have not failed you? I have nothing left except an assault to my soul from my mother and disappointment. I come to you in hopes that you can provide answers as to your purpose. Who can truly know what I have done? I live as a profiler, witness, and seeker of truth. Yet, I hear no answers to my words. I beg of you, please have mercy on my soul for I can no longer defy a reality without its truth. Give me an answer and I will be revived a stronger person to the light, dispelling the darkness to oblivion. My angels, my comrades, my loyal allies, answer this one request.

The angels answered, "Believe in the impossible for ultimate truth supersedes this reality allowing things to become possible."

Whatever came over me, lifted. I gathered enough energy to stand. Trying to keep my balance, I took each step with caution. There were two light beings, one on each shoulder. They held me up and assisted the trail back to the car. **There was no win or lose to be had on this account. Rather, there was the need to submit, process through, and purge the underlying feelings there. We typically have an undercurrent of feelings we suppress, ignore, and/or neglect. We just want to get through. Yet, this disregarding leads us to disconnect and not be in tune. We end up living a falsehood, that robs us of the beauty and jewels of life.**

Lost is a good word to describe how I felt. Lost to the past. Lost to the present. Lost to the future. What helped me get through? **Trust and confidence in the soul. The mind might lack understanding of what, why, how, or become bitter.** However, when you replenish from deep within, the will is recharged and your ability to recover from any challenge is quicker. If only as a tiny light in complete darkness, the soul never failed to sparkle.

The Telling of the Sacred Rose

Our five senses and our conscious mind do not pick up on certain things. The mind cannot always comprehend mystical happenings that surround us. Like a computer program trying to download a large file, the mind fruitlessly grinds to process through. It tries to categorize extraordinary experiences as coincidence or imaginary. These special files do not fall into its frame of reference. The next time something like this transpires, it becomes an automatic response, and is filed in the wrong place. This conceals and at times loses the beautiful things that come from the soul. For eight months, this rose sat on a mirrored dresser, next to my bed. As I routinely lit candles, wax ended up dripping on it. I decided to cover the rest of the rose with wax. To my surprise, it preserved the rose. It was the same rose I placed in my hair at the February 14th wedding where the first spark ignited and began to create what is now inscribed. I never understood why I kept the rose and why it seemed magical, until one late September day.

In the present moment, when I looked at the dried rose it reminded me of a time when things were simpler, and confusion did not consume daily life. I needed to focus on making it through with no additional remembrances of the difficult realities of the past. I had to remove the rose from my sight. As I extended my hand toward the bud, my fingertips froze. My hand began to tremble. Each attempt to touch the rose was resisted. It was simply a dried, wax covered rose that was falling apart. Why could I not just grab it and throw it away?

My intuition intervened, *"Do not dare think of tossing this precious rose away. It holds magical memories and mystical energy, extracted from your inner being. Once you accept these facts, follow the instructions."*

The rose had an impression, suddenly was like an ancient object. Just as these artifacts have a feeling of their own, which seem to tell a story, so did this rose. The energy imprint of the flower unraveled. *"There is a special message here."* I was compelled to sit in the center of the bed next to my pillow, light a white candle, and place the rose in front of me. I continued to follow my instincts, I quieted my mind and sat peacefully.

The divine voice went on, *"Take three deep breaths. Hold the rose in your right palm and cup the rose with your other palm. Do not doubt or question what you hear. Just listen to what unfolds."*

I began to tune into a conversation between two individuals, identified by higher guidance as Samir and Hisham.

Samir spoke, "Hisham, how is Jasmine doing? How come we haven't seen her?"

Hisham replied, "It's a long story. I don't want to talk about it right now."

Samir said, "You know what, Hisham?? I know you, and I know what you're doing."

Hisham gave no response and stayed silent.

"I want you to tell me yourself what you did and why."

"Samir, you know why. So, don't ask me that question. You, of all people, understand the situation. Don't play stupid."

"Okay! Hisham. Why don't you tell me how you're never going to find another girl like her, she has everything you want? She's sweet, honest, smart, and beautiful. What more can you ask for? You're an idiot."

"How am I an idiot? I'm doing what I have to do."

"You can stop pushing her away and have her in your life again. Is that so hard for you, Hisham?!"

"Come on, Samir. Give it up."

"No! You're making a big mistake and I can't sit here and watch you do it. Let me call her and talk to her?"

"No. You will in no way do that."

"How would you feel if you saw her with another guy? You think you would be okay with that?"

"Yeah, why not? We are just friends. Why would I have a problem with that?"

"Really, Hisham? Really? Give me a break. Now I want you to really think about what I just asked you and then give me the answer."

Hisham quieted his mind just enough for the soul to share its communication.

"It doesn't matter, Samir. Can we stop talking about this?"

Samir insisted, "No, you have to face how much of an idiot you are for giving up the perfect girl for you. You know what?...I hope she does find someone else, then maybe you will wake up and realize what you lost. Man, Hisham. If I were you, I would never let her go. Do you understand how lucky you are? You are such an idiot...It's not too late, Hisham. Call her. Talk to her like you always do. Don't be short or cold with her. Let her feel comfortable with you again."

After the conversation ended, Samir continued to contemplate calling me, but because of his extreme loyalty and respect for Hisham, he dared not go against his cousin's wishes.

Although the sacred rose provided insight, it had no effect on my mind. They validated the sense I had about the situation and then I filed them away. With time, the realness of this revealed itself. The first segment unwrapped when I received a random phone call from Hisham. I have not heard from him since the meeting at the labyrinth. Oddly, the twenty-minute conversation was pleasant. Since I returned from Syria, I did not hear of or see Hisham without some awkward and distant behavior. During this particular phone call, he was acting like himself, telling me what he did since we last spoke, the events that took place, and how his day went.

Suddenly shifting the subject, he randomly brought up Samir, "I spoke to Samir yesterday…" He paused for a long moment before he continued speaking. "He came over to make soup."

The only thing I could think of was to ask, "Did it taste good?"

The inner voice imposed, *"Is it not obvious Hisham is following Samir's advice? The rose's message is slowly shaping into realistic evidence."*

The interpretations of the mind and soul ignited.

The Soul attested, *"True. This was part of the telling of the rose. He acknowledged speaking to Samir on the phone and now he was taking Samir's advice to act natural again."*

The Mind rationalized, *"Maybe… or maybe it's just a coincidence."*

The completion to the rose's story showed me even more, there are no such things as coincidences, only synchronicities.

It had been three weeks since my late August return from Syria. Since then, I began to connect the dots of the many unconventional experiences, which Maya encouraged me to write down. Now there were pages full of foretelling dreams and unusual occurrences involving the inner knowing. I still had no clue these inscriptions would become a book. As I kept writing, an awareness grew that these stories should be heard by others and not hidden. Maya and I discovered a house we wanted to develop into a sanctuary; a place where we could help others to heal and find their own truth. This is when the writing took on more significance. Turning the pages into an entire book, would have two benefits: Inspire others and fund the sanctuary. Here lay the foundations of why this inscription is in front of you.

The sacred rose reaffirmed its power by allowing Samir's words to be heard again. This time by my human ear. Three days later, after the phone conversation where the rose's impressions began to unwind in reality, I dragged my cousin Anastasia out for a night on the town. Having her as my partner in crime, I made arrangements to meet a distant cousin who had VIP access at a downtown club. As I was getting ready to go out, I started to feel a light pull to stop at the hookah lounge. I resisted and ignored the magnetic force.

The inner guidance set forth, *"Go to the required location. Let go of the past remnants."*

I drove while Anastasia sat in the passenger seat. I held onto my stomach, attempting to tame the odd increasing anxiousness. It felt like hundreds of butterflies were fluttering inside me.

Anastasia asked, "Jasmine, are you okay?"

"Yes. I just have a strange feeling."

She said, "You know, it's weird, so do I."

Next thing I knew, I was exiting off the highway in the direction of the hookah lounge with no safe place to turn around. As Anastasia followed me into the hookah lounge, there was much activity and a large crowd. Stopping at the hostess desk, I scanned the room through the doorway and saw a sign for a twenty-dollar cover charge. I refused to pay a dime. It was time to turn around.

The inner voice reminded, *"Remember the communication from the rose."*

The loyalty to the soul placed me in some very uncomfortable situations. Even so, I follow, informing the hostesses, "I'm just here to say hi to Hisham and leaving right after."

With strained fake smiles, the two women nodded their heads, "Go ahead."

I took a couple steps forward and froze before we merged into the mass of people. There was no direction to this book or even a notation to how I was to accomplish it. Still lost to it all, my eyes drooped to the ground.

The inner voice prevailed over the despair. *"Through higher truth. You cannot ignore this statement. This is part of your makeup."*

Raising my eyes, I ignored the numerous stares, and looked over toward the right, in search of any familiar face. I wanted to break away. The urge to run is from the fight or flight response of the mind. It is designed to alert us of danger. Yet, the majority of fight or flight is fear based and wrongly perceived by the brain. Identify the fear, stabilize it, then view the situation with a clear lens without the emotions involved. The soul force's magnitude and the physical discomfort increased. There was a push to persevere and stay on course to attain validation of the rose's message. I gave in and sent Hisham a message, asking where he was. After I sent it, I looked up from the phone, and caught a familiar face standing next to the bar. Without hesitation, I walked over with Anastasia and gave Jalal a hug.

He asked, "How have you been, Jasmine? You just came back from Syria??"

I gave him snippets of the events in Syria and told him I would not go back unless the president himself asked me to. He laughed heartily about the crazy experiences. Despite the fact Syria was unpleasant, I laughed about the entrapping events. With what you have read so far, it might be hard to believe, but I laugh quite often. Even if life serves you its worst, do not take yourself too seriously. Easier said than done? Yes, but just as a Vietnam veteran once told me he played games with his comrades in the trenches of war. I affirm to you, it is contingent on you.

Jalal asked, "Who did you come here with?"

I answered, "With my cousin, Anastasia." I introduced her to Jalal and stated, "I'm not here to stay. I just wanted to say hi to Hisham and leave."

"Why?"

I tried to hide my feelings by remaining silent, but my eyes gave everything away. Hisham distanced himself and at this point, fully let go of the friendship.

As Jalal sensed the answer to his question, I said, "I respect his decision. He thinks he's doing the right thing."

Jalal pronounced, "It doesn't matter what he thinks. He's wrong."

I slowly blinked and nodded in acknowledgment, replying, "It doesn't matter what we both think, it is his choice."

I looked a few feet in front of me, to spot Samir with his back turned. I sensed he was patiently waiting for me to see him. In that very instant, Samir turned around to face me. I broke away from Jalal and took a few steps toward Samir. He threw his arms around me, embracing me with joy and comfort. During this reunion, the room and the crowd were blurry except for Samir and Jalal. I could sense the negative vibes of the space rising.

Excitedly, Samir blurted, "Jasmine!! How have you been? Long time no see! How was Syria?"

"I'm good. I know. I haven't seen you guys in over two months! I missed all of you. Syria was a challenge."

"Tell me about it!"

"I don't even know where to start…"

With smiles, the conversation continued about my time in Syria as he added in, "You can speak Arabic! Now you're really one of us!"

Shifting the subject away from Syria, Samir asked, "Why did you come here so late?"

I replied, "I didn't even know this was going on. I just came here to say hi to Hisham and leave. Anastasia and I are actually on our way to another club, but since we had to pass right by here, we stopped in for just a minute. I wasn't expecting such a party."

"Hisham didn't tell you?"

I shook my head indicating no.

"Jasmine, he's an idiot. I keep asking him about you. He told me a little about what happened in Syria."

Smiling, I said, "I ask him about you, too."

He hugged me again and said, "Jasmine, you're the best! We need to talk. You don't know a lot of things. Just three days ago, I asked Hisham to let me call you, but he wouldn't. I asked him before then, too. We really need to get together. I need to tell you something."

I was shocked. **Here was the complete verification of the sacred rose's illumination. It served as an oracle** of the conversation between Samir and Hisham. Can you believe a dried up rose, falling apart that sat on a dresser for eight months—could be such a vessel? I never thought so myself. It was magic. Circumstances and events convince most of us that magic does not exist and that miracles do not happen. I can now show you, with great certainty, magic absolutely does exist and, in good time, miracles absolutely do happen. Magic is a naturally occurring energy that surrounds us. For example, the alignment of the moon and sun are not coincidental but created by a supernatural art. As no tides exist without the moon and no pollination occurs devoid of the wind, this orchestration is nature, but also evidence of magic. **Our disbelief and/or scientific rationalization minimize the beauty and wonder. An inanimate object, a rose plucked from a bouquet, covered in wax, was able to transmit a conversation between two people. Magic lives and thrives all around us.**

Like a guard protecting a fort, Samir took me over to where Hisham was seated. As I followed him, I checked the time on my cell phone and saw I had an unread text message. It was Hisham's response that read: "At the hookah lounge. Why?" After I shut my phone, I looked up to meet Hisham's stunned face. The greeting with him lasted only a few minutes. Samir waited for me to finish, then walked us outside. I was content in that something magical and beyond reality was proven true. Most of all, I was thrilled I could finally leave.

Outside, Samir asked, "Jasmine, why don't you stay?"

"Samir, you know why. I really don't care to stay."

Not commenting on Hisham's manners, he said, "This was a social media invite. Everyone was invited. Just come back in."

"Well, I don't have any social media accounts and Hisham knows that. Honestly, I wouldn't have come, anyway. I can't stand this place. Let's end this conversation. No point in continuing this discussion further."

Before Samir could reply, a young man ungracefully came through the nearby doorway. From the corner of my eye, I saw him stop in his tracks and gawk at us.

"Hey! What's up, man??" Samir and I turned toward the voice and stared at the young man. In the next movement, he slung his arm around Samir's shoulder. I laughed on the inside about the entertaining scene and Samir's uncomfortable facial expression. I guess he knew Samir, but Samir did not like him.

"I have to go, Samir. I just received a text message from the friend we are about to meet up with. Remember, you have the choice to call me."

Samir responded, "I will call you."

I walked away knowing Samir's words were empty, but that was irrelevant. What mattered was the magical communication of the rose, coming to life before my eyes and ears. I drove to the club and the rest of the night involved dancing and more smiling with great company.

The next day, I awoke nauseous and exhausted, as if I ran a marathon and was hungover without drinking a drop of alcohol. The rest of the day and the following six days brought forth a recurring battle of doubt and fear. I felt as though something grabbed me by my throat and held me underwater. I was suffocating on the inside, with neither hands, nor a weapon to fight off the affliction. After completing my own assessment, I knew I was weakened from that night at the hookah lounge. The openness and lack of defenses made me an easy target. I called Maya to help lift me out of the dark waters.

Maya told me, "It was like moths attracted to a flame."

The negativity that exuded from the people that night latched onto me, fueling the soul demons. Already in a place of rawness, I became a sort of open passageway. I was more susceptible to environmental negativity, when before it had little effect on me. The demons used this, in turn, flooding me with insecurities. I was immobilized during this time period. Unable to read, write, or even taste the flavor of food. While my experience is an extreme example, the effects of people's negative vibrations can be felt by anyone.

I came to understand **we usually process these vibrations in two ways, we ignore them completely or are overloaded by them.** Neither of these really work well for our makeup. The alternative is to adapt like a chameleon. This lizard has the ability to change colors. It does this to warm up or cool down, as well as to communicate. **We can adjust to the degrees of negativity, not by reacting, but by responding. A reaction is driven by emotions and defenses. A response is driven by awareness and being in the present. If we do not take on the negativity, we can change the direction of the environment and situations.** The lizard changing its color is not deliberate, it is a skillful evolution.

A sacred rose was provided to support the fact magical experiences happen. The night its magic unfolded, I became keenly aware I was serving something higher than myself. It was like standing outside peering through a window, witnessing all the happenings. At the same time, I saw myself on the inside and part of the scene. Through this window, I was to observe and write down the events transpiring.

Dream: Old Friend

The foretelling dreams continued to intertwine with reality. I call this one, Old Friend, and originally dreamt it at the age of sixteen. A month after I returned from Syria, the recall of it was brought back by the arrival of Spring. I parked my car on a side street, walked down the sidewalk to a relative's corner house, entering through the backyard pathway. For some reason, I paused before stepping on the first stone which led to the sun room. The flowers were in full bloom, the grass was a vibrant green, and the sun was brightly shining. I visited this relative's house several times prior, but it was during late autumn, and winter months, usually at nightfall. I never saw it during spring time, and now in this season it looked so familiar. As I stared at the backyard garden, it hit me. I had seen this place long ago...

I glided across meadow hills made up of soft green grass, speckled with wild flowers, and stopped at a peak. I saw in front of me what looked like an ancient ruin of stones. It was forbidden to cross into the area. Yet, I was internally compelled to go anyway. From behind, a male's voice came through, telling me to not walk any further. Unaffected by this young man's pleading, I proceeded.

"Jasmine, I'm begging you not to do this. You don't understand how difficult it's going to be. You cannot do this to yourself. As your friend, I cannot allow you to take on such an endeavor. Many people have attempted this terrain. They either failed completely or were lost. Are you listening to me?"

We passed old stone remnants that once looked like they were standing structures. He paced behind still. Without turning around, I responded to the unseen companion, "I am listening. I need to do this. I am meant to do this. I want you to come with me, but I know you are afraid. I know many people have tried and failed, but this time will be different. You fear the end, I know the end. We will succeed. I have courage and I will continue on, with or without you."

He continued to beg. I kept going. Only a few feet remained to the destination. The breeze lifted my long locks, gracing me with its comforting whispers. I reached the edge of the cliff, and he halted. At that pause, all was silenced. I looked out over various landscapes before us. The vast scenery below presented segmented areas of rugged forest, scorching desert, and icy snow.

"Look at the reality of it, Jasmine. Look at the facts in front of you. No one has been able to make it to the end. I know we have both gone through training and are very strong, but this is impossible. How can I let you make such a crazy choice when the probability of defeat is so obvious and likely?"

I responded, "I have always listened to you, old friend, but I must do this and now is the time. We have been through much, with and without each other. We have grown and developed ourselves from every challenge faced. I am here to brave this trial and because the truth is with me, I will triumph."

"Let's just go back," he replied, "You do not need to put yourself through this. You have everything going for you. You are very young, one of the most skilled students and warriors."

"No. I want to do this. I have to do this. I know it will be worth it."

As I finished the declaration, I sensed him drawing closer. He took a few steps forward, moved to my left side, and took my hand.

He leaned over and whispered, "Jasmine, I am not letting you do this alone. I am coming with you."

I knew he was meant to come along to play his part.

He asked, "So what do you think is truly at the end?"

I raised my hand and pointed to the magical site. "Just look over there."

He followed the direction of my gaze. There lay, at the furthest point the eye could reach, a shooting rainbow that poured into a pot of gold.

The dream fast-forwarded to the closing stage. Foothills were wrapped in dark grey fog swirled with a reddish haze. Our eyes watched iridescent, human-sized spheres bouncing across the terrain. The winds emitted a high-pitched, whistling sound.

He asked, "How do we know which one to take?"

I scanned the area. "That one!"

"Do not let go of my hand!" he told me, as we ran toward the chosen sphere.

Without hesitation, we threw our bodies into the mass of energy. Our circular vessel entered into a tube-like path, and launched forward. While being transported, I began hearing a disembodied voice tell me about premonitions of the future.

You will arrive in a faraway land full of advancements where the least expected became reality. Though technology took a launch forward, the people failed to know and see the truth of life. So, the truth came to teach them a lesson. It showed them the worth of money is nothing in comparison to the rewards of their inner truth. Though money provides materialistic clutter, truth provides treasured jewels which fill the voids of their minds and souls. Through a story you will courageously live and tell, the rain cloud will lift, and the sun of inner truth will shine. Do not forget our message. You are gifted beyond your knowing and chosen to relay this truth.

In the sphere, through the tunnel, I landed by myself in an unknown backyard of a brick home. Small in size, the yard included fresh cut grass and high stemmed sunflowers that were encircled by various other flowers. A narrow, cement pathway split into two divergent paths. Despite the beautiful sunlit scenery I was in, there was a strange heaviness. I sensed something financially grave had taken place and depressed many people. This could not be possible to me. I lived in a time where opportunity was widespread, the economy was strong, and no such conditions existed.

The voice returned, "Yes. This dream possibility is not in your time, but the future."

I realized the man in the dream was Hisham. Another validation, this alignment was predestined. The dream Old Friend came to reveal its prophecies ten years later. I was amazed at its coming together in real life. The brick house was the first glimpse into the foretelling of the dream. One day, Fatima and I were searching for a seamstress to alter her engagement dress I gifted her. My mother suggested a distant relative, Sabah, whom at the time never crossed paths with before. Sabah lived fifteen minutes away and when we first met, we had an immediate connection. Our relationship grew even after the alteration of Fatima's dress. When I stood there, and a flashback of the dream came through for the first time, I recognized her home. The brick house was identical to the one in the dream Old Friend. Sabah revealed a story where she did not listen to her family or friends and things went terribly wrong. After she spoke of her tale, I dug deep inside to decipher if I was headed in the right direction.

The angels divulged, You show no fear in the name of truth. You hold on to what is rightfully yours. She may speak of truth, but it is not yours she speaks of. We come as milestones in your life and tell you, it is your ultimate truth which acknowledges the confidence you exude. Have faith, we cannot fail, for the truth binds you to a destiny that can no longer be denied to you. The path is difficult we warn, but reaching the destination is worth the price, as well as the many sacrifices you will endure in these coming months. The shadows will follow, but the sword of light will conquer these dark beings that plague your every move. This is a promise for your eternal service to truth and light for humanity's evolution.

Even with the angelic replenishment, the seeds of doubt were planted in my mind from hearing Sabah's saddening life mistake. Many months after, the seeds remained, becoming a buried gem trunk. Sabah called me, inquired about updates, inadvertently releasing the gems. Her question struck a cord and the tears flowed. I did not realize how much things hurt. The soul demons were at my back and surviving them took precedence. My humanity took a back seat, but was very much there.

The next day I sat in class and attempted to listen to the professor's story about his trip to Thailand. Instead, I laughed on the inside about how he really needed to retire. I felt my phone vibrate in my pocket, grabbed it to find Hisham's name flashing on the caller ID. While walking to my car, I returned missed phone calls, with the last one being Hisham's.

He said, "I swear there's something in the air. Everyone is going through something; Fadel lost his job, a friend might be getting a divorce, and another friend is dealing with her parents' split."

I reflected, "Yes…everyone is going through their own challenge. Things change. People go in and out of your life. You can't do much about it except focus on the blessings and goods things."

Hisham questioned, "Are you talking about us?"

"No, Hisham. I wasn't referring to anything about our friendship but obviously something is on your mind and you want to talk about it."

"Yes…I have been avoiding it. You know, I don't like to open up. You will always be one of my best friends."

The time came to gather courage to speak. The mind did not want to ask. The soul demanded an answer. I swallowed the resistance and spit out the words. "Can I ask you a question?"

Relieved from addressing his behavior of avoidance and disconnect, he replied, "Sure."

I asked, "Why did you let go of our friendship?"

His voice scrambled to answer. "I didn't let go."

I started to doubt what I just said. By this time period, I knew I was supposed to bear witness to the scenes and live through them. I could not explain it, although it was unlike me to confront anyone, it needed to be expressed. There was a higher motive, I was planting some kind of seeds.

The string of questioning went from the bigger, divine picture to the smaller, lower picture. What is the purpose of continuing on this path? What could possibly be the reason for still being chained to this? I was bewildered as to why Hisham possessed such little courage. I was confused by how I was even in this situation to begin with. The soul demons capitalized on the doubting, intensifying their lashings. It was as if I was in a maze trying to find my way out and at the same time I was being slammed against its walls.

I had a conversation with the angels that night. What prompted it was simple, but deep enough to bring another gem trunk of baggage to the surface. It was a crisis of faith.

> I fall unto you in this time of need. Where is the justice in this case? How am I bound to this? Forgive me for my weakness. I can no longer follow when the answers completely evade me. I come to you in a time where I fail to see the light in this tunnel of darkness. Where is the truth of this matter? Offer me, once again, validation to a cause which currently seems in vain. I keep bleeding truth, but no bandage is available to heal and recoup the loss. Others have evidence while I have nothing, but pain. The soul demons' voices penetrate my being. I cannot shut them off for they feel they are right and I am wrong. How can the piercing sound of a mother be silenced? She tears into me and walks away with clean hands. All I ask is for the re-balancing of my foundations...please.

I found the answers were within me, as they are for all of us. The people, places, and things we are exposed to on a daily basis influence how we view things. It can be related back to a muscle. This mind muscle is worked out, growing stronger with each passing day. The soul muscle is unexercised, developing no strength. The mind overpowers the soul, and we become firmly fixed in our five senses. Our ability to feel and connect to our higher parts is hindered. Insights to what is beyond our perceptions are limited and restricted.

I came to understand more of the symbolism contained within the dream. The three landscapes, forest, desert, and winter beyond the stone cliff, communicated the undertaking of large feats. The forest represents deep roots and potential for growth. In addition, it denotes older relationships, specifically Fatima in this case. Like any tree, the relationship with Fatima took decades of growth. The forest is life, even as it is decaying, it is creating life.

The desert and tundra encompass the abstinence of comfort, and sometimes loneliness. They are hostile environments and to survive, one must protect themselves from outside forces. It is a land of nomads, wanderers who bring everything with them and must adapt in order to survive. The desert portrays my family circle and the years in the job industry. Most are trying to get out of the desert, not remain.

The winter expresses casting off the old, preparing for the new, and ending of cycles. The white frozen water solidifies our inner workings and braces us for introspection. The embodiment of snow is found in baring witness and experiencing these testaments. The transformation of water to snow does not change its nature, but merely modifies its form, a reinvention of itself.

All these terrains can be light, safe, or inspiring. Other times they can be dark, dangerous, or frightening. They are all significantly beautiful and serving their divine design for us. We must get through them and make it to the rainbow and pot of gold.

Sanctuary of Dreams

What was in store for Maya and I went beyond our perceptions and intuitions. We were guided to find a place of considerable significance to our future. It seemed to be a perfect setting for a sanctuary where our individual callings to help and heal others could merge to make a glorious dream come true. The angels encouraged me to allow Maya to provide some relief from writing about all these experiences, so for a while, I will let Maya tell the story…

In late September, I attended an amazing Tibetan singing bowl ceremony. The peaceful sound lifted my spirit, carrying me across its harmonious melody. Afterward, it felt as if I was crawling back into my body, regaining my normal senses. It was then that Jasmine text messaged about having something important to share. Upon returning to my establishment and a few moments of déjà vu, I took refuge in my Reiki room and called her. She began to describe a dream about a sacred structure with much excitement. Somehow, I felt connected to it. I internally knew this would be created in reality.

Jasmine went on to describe the house was owned by philanthropists and guarded by dogs. The owner's children inherited the house and did not care about the inherent value. Jasmine told me about her ascent through the two floors of the house and the very meaningful spiral staircases. They represent a journey through the years. Through her mind, through her fate, only to reach the top when the vision met its completion into reality. Beautiful landscaping surrounded this stellar house, along with a magnificent balcony. It was unlike the typical Cleveland architectural standard.

As she retold the dream to me, she went from a child-like wonder of reliving and exploring the house to a tone of determination. "Maya, I am going to buy this house! I told my mom in the dream I would buy it," she stated.

As her voice continued, my mind suddenly drifted to a recent dream of my own. "Jasmine! I have been in this house! It is a palace for the work of light."

This type of work involved the cultivation of raising consciousness, healing, and guiding others on their path. I then went on to depict my dream.

My father, who was a great spiritual medium when he was alive, had led me through an extraordinary house. Through each room we traveled, he explained every detail as it went along. The rooms were glorious and filled with an indigo light, which represented higher vibration energy at work. The ceilings were bathed in gold and when we finished, the individual spaces were illuminated by a decadent chandelier.

My father said, "Maya, you and others will do great work in this palace. This is not a home but a sacred space for you to do what you were born to do. When the right person comes along, you will be certain."

Jasmine and I found our roads intertwined more than we first thought. This was just the beginning in our journey to find this house and make it reality. Jasmine would certainly be put to the test. The angels placed the pavement for our first footsteps to walk fearlessly forward. The passage to this sanctuary began with a simple phone call. I knew Jasmine was working with her aunt, a realtor. She provided her with details about the house based on pieces from the dream. Higher guidance would soon supersede.

I asked, "Jasmine, what do you think about going to the east side of Cleveland, where we are both drawn to, and allowing the angelic energies to guide us the rest of the way?"

"Yes!" she responded, "My aunt forgot what the house even looks like. Let's meet and follow our intuition."

We decided to meet on a beautiful autumn day with brilliant rays of sun shining down. As I pulled up to a coffee shop, our meeting point, I felt a pull of sorts. I turned my head and there she was. Jasmine was waiting outside, leaning her shoulder on a column of the building. She had an exceptional glow, an aura about her that day. The aura is the energy field that surrounds every living thing. You can picture it like a white gold dome-shaped shield, that extends three to five feet around the body of a healthy person.

We sat down and talked about recent occurrences. Hearing about the trials Jasmine was experiencing, the two parts of me, the higher and lower aspects, evaluated the right advice she needed to hear. I wanted to protect the nature of Jasmine. Someone who would put her heart and soul on paper, expecting nothing in return, except for a person to flourish, for other people to benefit. **As we reincarnate data or memory cells, self-awareness and compassionate understanding build into one's soul. Consequently, an individual becomes a more awakened and evolved human being by remaining in touch with this higher self. The balance between the higher self soul with the lower self mind is a union all individuals, who desire to live in an authentic way, should strive for.** My higher self understood Jasmine decided long ago to swallow the sometimes bitter pill of truth.

After the initial conversation over coffee, the drive began. We started off and in the first mile had an immediate sense of being in the area before. Jasmine experienced sharp headaches. This is a forced turning off of the mind scanner. The information goes straight to the soul, not as copy but as original document. The head pains went on for miles of driving. It is said patience is a virtue; Well this became a true test of that adage. From the time we left the coffee shop, five hours passed.

All good things come to those who wait. We needed to gather ourselves and connect again to deeper guidance. I sensed there was an article or something tangible that would lead us to the house. We decided to go to the library to search the internet. Word searches, such as "philanthropist," "death notice of," and "estate," resulted in thousands of articles. Nothing was resonating. We looked at each other's faces for answers.

I asked Jasmine, "Do you feel like we should stop for today?"

She replied, "I can't. I want to, but I am glued to this chair. I can't move my body to leave even if I wanted to."

I understood.

She continued. "I want you to get back to your life, but I simply cannot stop."

I knew this was significant for the both of us. I affirmed, "This IS my life."

The quest resumed, but with a home-for-sale database search instead. After countless city-wide searches in two different counties, she typed in one last city.

"One final try," she said.

There it was no address or price, only a street name. Agreeing to follow this last attempt, we headed out the door with clear intentions.

As we reached the street name, Jasmine asked, "Left or right?"

"What do you feel?" I replied.

"Right it is," she said.

A quarter of a mile down, we encountered a home-for-sale sign and pulled into the driveway. With two cars lining the driveway and the sign listing a real estate company that suggested an extremely expensive home, Jasmine began to back out.

I recognized the treasure being revealed, and suggested, "Wait, they're backing out and leaving. Let's pull in!"

As the cars left, we drove up the drive and were struck with a sense of awe. There was a majestic lion statue we noticed as we coasted to the front door. This represented protection and determination of true pride. The energy increased as we drove through what apparently became a complex of sorts, certainly no ordinary house. Beyond the elaborate exterior, the familiar essence of the house could not be denied. Within the coming weeks, a particular call from Jasmine validated the recognition of the house and our connection to the owner of the house.

Jasmine said, "Maya, we have been in that house, in the art studio to be specific!"

She explained the dream, "Our spirits transported there. You were being playful inside, but I felt you were misusing your powers, so I told you not to disturb the owner with your energy. A movement in the entrance of the room caught my eye and I told you to follow me. I stood in front of the door, a grey and blue mist formed and took the shape of a pyramid with an eye on the upper region. It then cracked open like a treasure box as dollar bills sprang forth. I heard footsteps coming, to the back of us, a portal opened. You told me, 'Come on Jasmine!' and I told you 'no!' I made myself invisible just for a brief moment to get a glimpse of the owner walking in. I felt the entrance to this portal shrinking. I turned back to face it, knowing this was my last chance to follow you. I took a glance back at him to see his face as a 'reminder.' I then leapt in the portal. The dream didn't go further than that, but somehow I know we jumped backwards in time."

After she verbally played back the dream to me, I responded, "I think the rest of the dream will uncover itself to me. If it is a part of this ongoing journey, I have faith it will come."

I requested to the angels that the rest be discovered quickly. I had a dream that night which answered the questions of not only where we went in Jasmine's prior vision, but also where we came from. I knew from the first time of meeting Jasmine, we knew each other before. There was a familiarity to her face and within her eyes. I knew she was a kindred soul and now, the reasons began manifesting themselves.

In the dream, I was transported to a past life, where I was a prince and Jasmine was a queen. She summoned me to her palace through telepathic means. We had a connection that allowed us to communicate with our minds, without verbal words. This portrayed only a snapshot of our abilities. Our deep bond and masterful gifts made us a powerful union and threat.

The impact of this past life did not diminish or fade. It was born into this lifetime as well, waiting for our meeting once again. My allegiance to Jasmine is now in a different form but does not stray away from its origin. In this lifetime, a sanctuary from both our dreams is to be created.

A week or so later, I was led to re-enter the area of this sanctuary. It began with a gentle nudge, followed by a magnetic push. I took along a different travel companion, someone else who was very close to me. We drove down the now recognized eastern road, finding the house with much more ease, compared to the initial journey with Jasmine.

"There's the hand shaped mailbox," I thought, *"Where is the for-sale sign? It's gone."*

For just an instant my heart sank.

My companion's words became important. "This house is incredible. It has such a strong energy! It's almost like someone famous lives here. I think he's trying to hide from the public."

Those words resonated, "Yes!"

He was simply tired of the intrusion. I remembered his private nature and how Jasmine reminded me in the dream not to disturb this or his way. As I stared down the occupied driveway, I knew this was true.

An angelic being exuded, *"You will have a sanctuary and a trusted relationship will form between you and Jasmine."*

Ringing in my ears, these words had multilayered reasoning, as did everything within this true odyssey. Dark and light struggled equally to emerge. The truth shall prevail, and much shall be set free.

> I am grateful and honored to have Maya carry the weight for a short time and write this chapter. Before this sanctuary of dreams could manifest, the palace within would need to shatter.

Shattered Palace

I was constantly being pushed to decipher, build up muscles but not of the physical body. It was of the soul form. Trusting the knowing and practicing inner guidance was a daily exercise. The challenge was the presence and programming of the mind and its want for control. The reason for this can be summed up in one word, security. On the surface, there is not a problem with wanting this. The dilemma is in the deeper layers. This core strength of the mind takes over, at times completely. The mind scrambles, you come to question everything, even things you were once certain about. It sends the whole system into a tailspin. Because the soul muscle was not strong enough yet, I was wobbly. I was alert to everything that was going on but my mind's old impulses were still there. The knowing and my logic were both speaking at the same time and I did not know which to trust at this point. Add in the soul demons that surfaced because of the clashing noise, and everything was bleeding together.

I found solace in the clockwork of life. Everything was still moving along outside of me, and somehow that was comforting. The old rumor mill was still turning but no new gossip was circulating. This allowed my mother to be somewhat pleasant, softening my awareness. Then out of nowhere, she would pounce. I never knew what I was walking into. The soul demons used her like a toy in the onslaught of their game, playing on her inflated ego. I wanted her to stop, and just be there. Her attacks struck me to the core. You would think after awhile, I would see it coming. When it comes to our mothers, that is not the case. It was like the deepest and most aching wound. The laceration would begin to heal only to be gashed open again.

Even though this book was divinely driven, it brought so much painful commotion into my world. Circumstances conspire to align individuals together, and coordinate events meant to happen. I was not fully aware at the time, but these kinds of things are opportunities for growth, learning more about ourselves, and strengthening our connection to our divinity. It is easy to lose sight of this, because people's actions or behaviors can leave a negative impact on our mind and soul.

We cross paths with numerous souls, each one leaves an imprint on us, some deeper than others. A person can appear in your life, without notice, and change you even when you are resistant to change. I chose to not let the turmoil set into my system and kept rooted in my core values. I wondered what I could give Hisham for his birthday despite what transpired in the last four months. This is where I stood, untainted by the outer circumstances that occurred.

I thought, *"He needs more lyrics for the music album he is working on."*

While waiting for this thought to form, the angels suggested, "Write him some!"

I shrugged off the idea and the angelic encouragement. The pendulum began to sway back and forth between the mind and soul.

The Mind asserted, *"No. I know him and how he will react. He'll think I'm doing this for some self-motivated reason."*

The Soul contended, "It is difficult for one to believe someone will give without wanting anything in return except for you to be happy and fulfill your dreams, but that's how I am, and who I am."

The Mind countered, *"I reject the idea. Only negative things will result. It is hard enough maintaining this path without real verification. I can't allow opportunities for disappointment anymore."*

The Soul maintained, "I want to give him something in return for the birthday celebration he put together. I don't bitterly hold onto the past. Whatever course of action he takes is not mine, but his, to decide. I have always stayed true to the core so why should I change because of disappointment and fear of the way he will react?"

Throughout the rest of the day, the angels kept up a constant stream of support for the writing process, while the consciousness of the mind and knowing of the soul moved back and forth. I laid in bed wide awake, unable to fall asleep until three o'clock in the morning. I could not handle it anymore. The pendulum stopped at the side of the soul. I lit a candle and began writing some lyrics. The words flowed onto the paper as if they were waiting to be discovered. In less than thirty minutes, I had one complete lyric. It brought forth the story of a gift given by divinity and returned because the person it was for feared the magnitude of the gift.

The next problem? I needed it translated into Arabic. This required finding a person with a solid and flexible English and Arabic vocabulary. In my head, I examined the people I knew who had this ability. I remembered Othman, my cousin once converted a prayer into Arabic for me. It was to assist his sister in conceiving. The translation was effective, and his sister got pregnant. The second matter was convincing Othman to assist me again. I reached out and after much back and forth he agreed to meet.

The translation turned into three hours of struggling with Othman. He repeatedly lost his focus, sang randomly, told me how boring it was, refused to translate certain lines correctly, answered phone calls, and then, got in a huge argument with his brother over the phone. His behavior resulted in us being asked to leave the coffee shop. In spite of all of this, the mind was happy with the final product and the soul was ecstatic with the creation. When I held the pieces of paper in my hand, my body wanted to jump up and down for joy. I kept my excitement hidden, fearing the papers would somehow fly away. I knew the lyrics needed immediate delivery, so they could be used for the album still being produced. I folded the papers in thirds, placed them in a white envelope, and drove straight to where Hisham was staying.

Unable to recall the street name, I had to focus a little extra. As I parked my car on the road in front of the house, I started to hesitate. I knew deep down something unpleasant would result from handing over these lyrics. Looking out the driver side window, I watched the streams of rain slither down. In attempt to calm the nerves, the focus switched to how effortlessly and naturally these lyrics revealed themselves. When things come so easily, there is a higher purpose at play. I felt Maya would help ease the nervousness.

When I called, I conveyed, "I'm sitting in my car with the translated lyrics."

Relieved, Maya replied, "So you got it done?!"

"Yes, but I'm so nervous…I don't know why…"

"Those papers have a piece of you in them. You're exposing part of yourself. That's why you're nervous."

"Right….I'm just afraid of how he will react."

"Jasmine, that doesn't matter. What does matter is that you followed your truth and that took courage. I'm very proud of you."

"Thank you…It's time to get this over with."

I hung up, placed the envelope inside of my shirt to keep it safe from the downpour, and started toward the house. I was still not sure why I was doing this, but figured, here goes nothing. I ran through the rain and up the steps to the door. I knocked three times with no response, deciding to leave it in the mailbox. This action left a part of me concerned. Before starting to drive, I called him, but he did not pick up. In a last ditch effort, I gathered the courage to send a text message explaining I wrote lyrics as an early birthday gift and they were in the mailbox. He did not reply and I did not hear anything until ten days later when divine timing coordinated accordingly.

While continuing to write this book, I decided to go type at a coffee shop further away from home, but closer to the highway entrance of graduate school. I walked into the café with a laptop briefcase slung over my shoulder and a crystal box in my right hand. I imagine I looked strange to onlookers carrying around a container with a dried rose in it. This was the same rose that was the magical messenger of a discussion, where I was able to overhear without being physically present. I could not recall or capture the conversation to write it down without the rose.

I found a table in the back corner of the coffee shop. I set up my laptop and just when I began to tune into the sacred rose, a high-pitched voice interrupted my focus. I drew my head up to find a young woman talking loudly on the phone. You would think my stare would have been enough to quiet her, but no. I decided to drive to another café, hoping there was an outside patio with outlets to charge the laptop. In spite of having less than an hour and a half before class, I drove with no clear destination. The energy in the car shifted, the magnetic force surfaced, and a sudden vision of the coffee shop located next to the lake flashed in my mind. It had an outside plug and was right next to a highway, leaving me with only a twelve-minute drive to school.

With butterflies in my stomach and an uneasiness something was going to happen, I arrived and parked in the back cement lot.

While I collected my belongings, the divine guidance directed, "Leave the rose in the car."

Although unclear how I was supposed to write the story without it, I left it behind. With only the briefcase slung over my shoulder, I walked down the wooden steps that connected the parking lot to the shop. When I breezed through the front parking lot, I felt a nudge to turn to the right. As I did, I saw a familiar car backing out to the side street. I could not make out who was in the vehicle. These times reminded me of how I needed to start wearing my glasses. I turned back around and continued walking over to the outside sitting area, where I met a well-known face a few feet away.

I called out Khalil's name, as he stood staring.

"It's me, Jasmine."

"Jasmine!" Khalil replied enthusiastically.

He gave me a hug and checked me out again, stating, "I didn't recognize you. It's your hair. Hisham and Samir literally just left, come sit down."

My nerves began to take over. "Um…It's okay…I don't think that's a good idea."

"Why?? Come on, sit down over here. They will be back."

The angels assured, "Ease your mind. The soul knows what is the necessary step. Truth can be found even when it eludes the holder of its knowledge. Gain comfort with this fact."

I was absolutely uncomfortable. Yet with the angelic guidance, I gave into Khalil's friendliness and sat down. He introduced me to his friend Simeon, the journalist Hisham mentioned to me a few months back. A frail physique, his long face and shaved bald head, was accented with thick bushy eyebrows. Within five minutes of settling into the cold iron chair, my phone started ringing. I grabbed my purse, searched for it, and saw Hisham's name on the screen. It was almost two weeks since the lyrics were delivered. I did not meet any higher source pressure to answer, so I ignored and silenced the phone. After my cell displayed missed call, Khalil's phone rang.

Khalil verbally acknowledged, "It's Hisham," and he answered the call.

The urge to escape came rushing over me.

The angels returned, "You were brought here for a purpose, do not feel confined."

He announced, "Hisham said he's coming back in a short while. He took Fadel to the mechanic shop right around the corner."

I responded, "I should get going. This whole thing is awkward."

"No, it's not! Just stay."

The discomfort in the air was so thick you could slice through it.

Khalil asked, "What do you want to drink?"

"Nothing, thank you."

When Khalil returned, he went through the same questions as Samir; "When did you get back?" "How was Syria?" "How long has it been since you left?" However, he did ask one question Samir did not. "You have been back for two months now. Why haven't we seen you?"

Without hesitation, I answered, "Hisham is scared of me."

A huge smile came over Khalil's face. He tried to distract himself with the objects on the table to avoid laughing out loud from my answer. At least I was free to express myself with him. Khalil is a person who you meet and there is an automatic understanding. You do not question his intention. He is pure of judgement, and settled in himself.

I elaborated, "It's gotten even worse since I wrote lyrics for him and left it in his mailbox. I wanted to explain it to him, but never heard from him until now."

Khalil seemed embarrassed by Hisham's behavior. The conversation got interrupted by a new visitor.

Relieved, Khalil smiled, "Come join us."

The man looked at my face, appeared apprehensive, and switched to Arabic. He did not sit down.

As this behavior was replicated two more times with two different men, I remarked, "Why is everyone scared to sit down with us?"

Khalil assured me, "They're not scared, just shy."

"Shy of what?" I thought.

I looked over at Simeon for verification. Evidently, his mind was occupied with something else.

When Khalil excused himself to leave and run an errand, the angels hinted to me, "Find the purpose to your lock down. You were brought here for a reason."

I focused on trying to lift the low spirit of Simeon. While I observed his negative attitude, Simeon confided in me about his situation. He was set on getting out of Cleveland, a place he called a "shit hole" and what I titled the Trojan City in this book. Before I knew it, over an hour passed. Out of respect, I figured I should call Hisham back before I drove to class.

When Hisham answered, he first spoke to the background voices. "Okay. Okay, give me a second." Then he shifted to me. "Hello, Jasmine. Let me call you back later. Okay?"

I doubted he would but cared less if he did. I left the coffee shop and drove downtown to school. In the middle of class, I left to use the restroom and received the phone call from Hisham.

Hisham said, "I saw Khalil saying hi to someone and I was like, 'WHO is that?' Then I saw it was you. As you were arriving, I was backing out to leave."

When I walked out of the car, headed into the coffee shop, and felt something nudge me to look to the right, it was toward the vehicle Hisham was in. The conversation began with him complimenting me several times on the new hair color. It is funny how changing a physical attribute brings out a new side to people.

Out of nowhere, Hisham admitted what I told him in the labyrinth was true. "You know how you told me to take those two notes you always hummed and write a song with them?... Well, I did. I created an amazing piece of music."

What compelled him to listen? I did not know. Maybe each time he recognized the accuracy of my words helped him realize there was truth in the suggestion to utilize the notes. He was regaining his passion for music, and that was something to be grateful about.

I replied, "Really?!"

"Yes. The thing is, it sounds so familiar to me. It's like I've heard it before."

Without any doubt, I asserted, "No, you haven't Hisham."

"Are you sure...? Every time I replay the recording, I try to figure out where I have heard it...maybe it came from another song?"

"Not at all. It sounds familiar because it was meant to be. How do you think I felt humming it when we just met. It feels so familiar to me too, but it came out of nowhere."

Hisham stated, "I'm not impressed by my work and I'm critical about everything I produce. For me to say this song is good tells you how great it really is."

I agreed, "I have no doubt in that."

He went into detail about his ordeal with finding the right vocals and instruments for this new song, offering to let me hear a sample and see if I could give an opinion. The conversation wound down which provided me a tunnel to the confirmation I sought.

I asked, "What did you think of those lyrics I wrote?"

Seeming prepared, he responded, "I haven't gone past the third line. I haven't been in the right state of mind to read it. I carry it around in my laptop briefcase. Anytime I get a chance, like when I take a cigarette break in my car, I begin to read and stop at the third line.

I want to read it in the right state of mind it deserves."

Would you believe a musician in need of lyrics, would not quench his thirst from a free well?

I described the coffee shop episode to Hisham and all I went through with Othman to get the lyrics translated from English to Arabic.

He asked, "Can you give me the original copy? I want to see it for myself and make my own twist on it?"

"I was going to include it in the envelope, but it was a mess from all of Othman's writing. I went straight to your house, so I didn't have time to rewrite it. I didn't want to give you a destroyed copy."

With extreme hesitation, I revealed, "Hisham…I wrote another complete lyric after that one."

"Really?"

"Yes, but Othman's been avoiding me, so I haven't been able to translate it into Arabic."

"Don't worry about getting it translated. Just give me the original copies and I'll take it from there."

"…I wrote a third one."

"Wow. Listen, get those copies together and call or text before this weekend. We'll meet up."

He probably thought he hit the jackpot with three complete sets of lyrics to utilize. I was aware his attentiveness was self-driven, and he just wanted to get his raccoon hands on them. At this point, I was at full service to the soul and had to follow through as a participant. Sometimes the purpose of things is not apparent, until you finish the course.

Two days later, mid-afternoon, I polished the drafts and sent a text message to Hisham with the update they were ready. He immediately responded he was practicing music at Fadel's house and wanted to meet early the next day.

The final text I sent him read: "This time do not think about throwing the words away… Please title the one you have, The Gift."

He replied with only: "Okay, text me tomorrow."

Most likely, Hisham tried to logically determine how I knew he wanted to throw the lyrics away. Reality distracted him, his pirate ship became his comfort. The unexplainable feeling of foreboding in the pit of my stomach, transmitted a sense trouble was up ahead. It did not subside until 4:00 A.M. when sleep finally played its hand. I awoke at 10:00 A.M., with the same unsettled feeling that kept me up all night. I sent a text message to Hisham asking for an exact time to meet. Instead of responding with a text, he called.

Speaking to another person, he said, "turn right over here…"

"Who are you with?..." I asked.

"Fadel. I have so much to do I can't be long."

Trust me, I understood this meeting needed to be very short for him. He wanted to take and run.

Pushing aside self-resentment for why I even agreed to any of this, I inquired, "Which coffee shop?"

The angels sounded, "Stay focused and confront what is going to transpire without fear."

My mind did not enjoy receiving these imprints. It was an overload of knowledge. I took a deep breath, reminding myself it was going to be okay, one way or another. When I arrived, Hisham's face shone in the atmosphere of uneasiness. His soul was there but disengaged now. The truth of what he became over this time was crystal clear. I was saddened to see him like this, but it was his choice to walk down this path. It is hard to see a person drowning in their own struggles. I greeted the both of them with a smile and hug. I took the closest seat next to Fadel, the piano player in the band. Hisham sat across from both of us. When he and I made eye contact, he became vulnerable suddenly. His body language expressed his discomfort.

Hisham's phone started ringing and when he went to answer it, I turned my attention to Fadel, saying, "So you guys have had a full day of errands to run and things to do?"

He replied, "Actually, we haven't even started yet. I just picked up Hisham."

Fadel looked particularly uneasy. I presumed it must have been because he recently lost his job.

Fadel asked, "I heard you're writing a book?"

I responded, "Yes. But before I forget, I wanted to show you parts of the introduction and conclusion. I think you can create something with the concept. It's a conversation between the Mind and the Soul, then it reverses to the Soul and the Mind."

I pulled out the laptop, quickly scrolled to the entrance, and pointed where he should start reading.

When Hisham got off the phone, he immediately asked for the three lyrics. "Do you have them?"

I answered, "Yes, of course. They are right here." I handed him the white envelope, saying, "I placed the songs in the order in which I wrote them."

I watched him pull out *The Gift* lyrics, unfold the packet, and read the first page to himself. When he finished, his eyes returned to mine, and became those of an old friend lost to his old ways. Within a moment, the feelings were replaced by a panicked look on his face. The truth has that effect on Hisham. He immediately stood up, asked if I wanted a coffee, and walked away from the table. Thankful, I said no, but he brought one back anyway. He sat down as I kept speaking to Fadel. I stopped mid-sentence as I sensed the frailty in Hisham again. I looked over at him to see a vulnerable boy.

I said, "Hisham, come here and read this, too."

"No, it's okay…"

"Just come, please. I want to show you the part you didn't read."

As he made his way over, I continued, "Remember when I let you read the conversation between the Mind and the Soul from a dream journal?"

"Yes, I remember."

I mentioned, "I wrote another entry, but where the Mind and Soul switch roles."

"I didn't think you were going to put it in the book," he said.

"I didn't either, but it worked out very well. Here take my seat."

"No, I'll just stand…"

"I don't need to read my own writing again, Hisham. Just sit down. I'll grab another chair."

He relaxed, took a seat, and read. Moving away from the computer to make room for him, Fadel blankly stared at the surface of the table.

Hisham commented, "Wow, that's interesting. You're telling the story through the perspective of the mind and soul."

I replied, "Kind of."

Throughout this interaction with Hisham, I noticed Fadel's withdrawn behavior. I supposed the material did not interest him. As Hisham read through the second segment, Fadel's cell phone rang. I watched his body language ease. It must have been some call for him to finally relax. I heard him softly mumble a few words and he hurriedly ended the conversation.

Seeming in sequence, Fadel said, "Hish—."

"Give me a few seconds!" Hisham quickly reacted, cutting him off.

I wondered why the abruptness? Fadel hardly moved a muscle. It was as if Hisham knew Fadel was going to interrupt him. I reasoned Fadel was probably trying to remind him that they had a lot to do and needed to go. The thoughts rushed in and just as rapidly slipped away.

Hisham said, "We have to go. Fadel's wife is waiting for him."

How could Fadel's wife be waiting if he just picked up Hisham fifteen minutes prior to meeting me? Why would Fadel pick up Hisham, to drive twenty-five minutes, and return home in less than an hour? On top of it, Hisham could have driven himself in the first place. Fadel did not sound like he was talking to his wife on the phone.

Hisham stood up and continued, "Jasmine, this is beautiful. Why don't you email the Entrance to me? We know this Moroccan chick—I mean girl—who writes poetry and can change the words around to fit what we're looking for."

Why did he flinch and look nervous for a second there? I did not know someone else was going to take the lyrics and change them. What was going on here? Again, the questions formed and disappeared so rapidly I did not have time to express them out loud.

"Are you going to stay here and write?" Hisham asked.

"No, I don't like this location. I'm going to head to the one by my house."

Walking toward the doorway, he stopped. "Okay Jasmine. Don't forget to email that to me. I'll call you soon."

For some reason, I sensed it made him feel better to say that. When I placed the laptop in my briefcase, I caught sight of the two pomegranates I packed for them. I scooped them up in my hands, ran to catch Hisham and Fadel, but was halted.

"Do not go any further!" the angels commanded.

I followed orders. Disappointed, I watched them through the glass doors as they backed out of the parking lot and drove away.

The angels returned, "Do not worry. They do not deserve the pomegranates from you. You will see for yourself why."

I collected my belongings, walked to the car, and headed home. Relieved my apprehensive inklings were wrong, I focused on the part of the book that needed to be worked on. I tried to concentrate, but something started tugging for my attention. I was suddenly tuned into a conversation between Fadel and Hisham. It was as if I became an antenna and started picking up a channel. This was not the first occurrence, the ability to "overhear" discussions began when I was twenty-one years old.

I denied what was being channeled in, reasoning I was overly sensitive due to the uneasiness experienced before the meeting. I attempted to get back to business and tried to ignore the signals. They did not silence. I rejected what was taking place. I begged the words to stop. There was no stopping the flood. In the same manner the rose allowed me to hear the conversation between Hisham and Samir, it was intuition presenting the dialogue this time…

Fadel said, "Hisham, we should not have done that to her. Why did you do that? She didn't deserve it. I feel so bad for what we just did…"

"It's fine. Don't worry about it."

"No, man, that was wrong. I feel horrible. She's such a nice girl. I don't understand you sometimes. How could you even think of doing that to someone, especially a person like her? I would have never done it in the first place if I had known I was going to feel this bad."

"Forget it. She'll be fine," Hisham responded.

The interaction continued to pour through my mind as it concurrently resonated with my soul. I started to recall my quick thoughts and their behavior at the coffee shop. My eyes swelled when the puzzle pieces clicked together. They planned the whole thing out: The phone call. The excuse to leave. The entire thing was a ploy. He brought a friend to assist in his objective to take the songs and run. Their odd conduct caught my attention, and gave my mind just enough hints as evidence to what came through the intuitive channel. The pain of being deceived was overwhelming. I gave the lyrics freely, as an offering, but began to feel that it was a mistake.

There are casualties walking this path, at times they are major ones. Now there was another unsavory experience in the murky waters, and a testament to behold about the lighthouse. The ruse Hisham and Fadel used in the coffee shop brought me to one remaining conclusion. You cannot control what people say, how they react, or what they do. Yet, you can still speak your truth, when the time is right. You become a mirror to reflect. A text message was sent to force him to face his mean spirited behavior. He took a soul connection, a person who only showed him kindness and support, and twisted it. My normal caution in sharing the knowledge obtained from intuition was overridden. Without making a conscious decision about it, the text messages seemed to write themselves. Before my fingers pressed the keys, it was almost as if they knew which words to type. Courage was still required to press send. Hisham responded and the exchange of words ended with him seeing a reflection of the person he became.

I reached to the heavens for restoration. I called upon the angels many times to answer: How can such a person be a part of my truth of any sorts? I was a wanderer in unknown territory where greed was upright, and ego controlled the actions. I gave him an offering, but he choose to corrupt it within a lie. Droplets poured from my eyes. The mind punished me while the soul attempted to soothe the hurt. This meant to be encounter launched the last blow. The foundations crumbled, and my palace shattered. A floodlight covered a room full of shards of broken mirror and suspended particles of truth.

Many times, you follow what feels right, then a person acts in a way that shows you otherwise. It starts you in the direction of doubt, second-guessing decisions, and/or loss of trust in yourself. These discouraging occurrences undermine your confidence, spilling into your professional arena, daily routine, and relationships with others, yourself, and the world at large. Even when we experience disappointment, pain, or let down from others, we should not let that become our steering wheel. It locks us into the fear-based mind, separating us further from the soul.

It was time to stop diving into the dark waters. Hisham's direct role was completed. The testaments were not finished just yet. Now, I chose to withdraw from the waters, get on the shore, and be the lighthouse. If it was not for the lyric incident yesterday, this would not be shared. The relevance was not apparent until now. I learned about this theme through my sister, Rena.

Similarities between our experiences show we have certain themes that get repeated with different characters, circumstances, and timing. Life themes are an underlying current that run through our journey, honing in on necessary lessons. There is no dodging life themes, you might as well try to dodge your shadow. They are the interweaving of who we are, and mainly occur through interactions with people. These threads reoccur as cycles as a way to see if we truly grasped and extracted the lesson.

When we do not learn the theme fully, it is not the type of test we typically think of. It is an encouragement to know yourself, and for that person to find themselves as well. It is a need to respond to life in a manner that pierces through the emotional illusion and sheds light on the core, the most essential part of us. In addition, it allows you to access your highest potential, bringing you closer to fulfilling the purpose you are meant to accomplish.

I discovered one of my recurring themes is knowing where to draw the line between unconditional compassion and giving too much of myself to others. Once my sister, Rena, hit her teenage years, she became a tornado of worry for my mother and me. Her explosive nature climaxed when she attempted suicide at the age of sixteen. I will never forget the desperate, shrieking sound of my mother's voice, shouting up the stairs.

"Jasmine! Jasmine! Wake up!! Rena tried to kill herself!!"

I shot out of bed and scrambled to the stairwell.

My mother yelled, "Something woke me up and told me to look for Rena."

I stayed collected, replying, "I'm coming."

I ran down the stairs listening to her frantic words, recalling the empty and mischievous look on Rena's face from the previous night. I needed to start using my car which Rena claimed as hers. My parents took the car keys after days of her refusing to return them and not coming home until late in the night when everyone was asleep.

"Jasmine! Oh my God! I found all the pill bottles lying next to her and they're empty! Her skin is yellow and she peed on herself because she couldn't get up from all the medicine she swallowed! She's in the basement and won't listen to me!"

Calmly, but rapidly, I reassured her, "Mom, it's going to be okay. Call for an ambulance Nabeel and I will carry her up."

I woke up my brother, telling him, "Rena tried to kill herself. You need to help me carry her upstairs from the basement."

While Nabeel took her arms and I took her legs, every step of the way, she kicked and screamed for us to let her go. Where she got the strength to fight us, I do not know. When we finally got her up the stairs and through the door, she spoke the words which scarred me for many years to come.

Rena shouted at me, "This is your fault! I tried to kill myself because of you!"

It felt like I was punched in the stomach. I was left winded from those words. The angels were waiting by my side. They declared Rena's accusation to be untrue. However, the heavy impact those words from a person you love and deeply care about was unavoidable, no matter how false.

While I went to work at my parents' business to cover the shifts, my mother and sisters went to the hospital. On her first day there, Rena refused to let my mother and my older sister, Genevieve, enter the room. She only allowed her friends and our younger sister, Ameera, to see her. However, at the next visitation, Rena permitted them to see her.

Genevieve told me, "All Rena spoke of was getting a car and how our parents shouldn't have taken the car keys from her. I can't believe how a person who just tried to take her own life would talk about materialistic things."

Rena's state of mind and perception was explained in her diary. My mother handed the journal to me to read out loud for her, as she could not read English well. In the few entries written, my sister spoke of how our mother hated her, looked at her shamefully, and shunned her. None of this was true. Rena was unscathed by my father and received true affection from my mother. Rena created her own story to affirm her false beliefs. Before and after this incident, the whole family walked on egg shells with Rena and gave her everything they could. Growing up, my mother enforced her power with my father, making sure he did not upset Rena. More so after this attempted suicide as she feared Rena would try it again. All of this broke down my mother.

In the years that followed, my mother and I tried to get Rena help. I would set up the psychologist appointments, but Rena refused to go. When my mother found the courage to push for my sister's attendance, she made up an excuse about not being able to find the place. It was less than ten minutes from our house, with a clear sign out front.

When she began college, Rena came to visit me in Columbus which was a forty-five minute drive from her campus. My internal radar detected a warning of the emerging tornado. Rena asked for my advice: I guided her, "He's using you, Rena. You have to stop running away from your family and who you truly are. Let me help you."

"You don't know me! You're just jealous!"

Completely baffled by the remark, I responded, "Jealous? Of what?"

Rena lashed back, "I have friends, unlike you. All you have is Grace and she's a cousin. That's the only reason she's your friend. You have never even had a boyfriend! I'm calling my friends to pick me up right now!"

My jaw dropped in shock with the words that came out of her mouth. Each word was like a dagger.

"Rena, calm down. They drove you all the way here and left less than an hour ago."

"I don't care! They'll do anything I want!"

Grace came home while Rena waited outside for her friends to pick her up. I leaned on the sofa, looking out the wide glass windows, crying my soul out. When Grace could no longer stand to see me in such a low state, she snapped me back to life.

Grace stated, "Jasmine, stop this! You can't do this to yourself anymore. You have to accept that those are your sister's life decisions. Even though she is your sister, you need to step away and just be there for her when she needs you."

A lesson was learned with Rena. Later, she returned, knowing she would be received with open arms and unconditional love. She came forth admitting I was right about the male acquaintance, he was using her. Rena continued to lose herself. She attempted to fill the denial, guilt, and low self-worth with material things and men.

Worried about Rena's activities, one of her college friends confided in me. "Every day I see a new shopping bag in her room. I come from parents who are well-off, but I don't waste nearly that amount of money. I think the guy she's with is using her, but I don't dare say anything to her."

Gently, I said, "I know…I'm glad she has a friend like you."

"Please, don't speak a word to her about what I told you. I don't understand why she doesn't trust you. You're so nice and patient with her."

Sadly for Rena, she ended up losing this friend. I endured many sleepless nights over her, frustrated that I could not help her. I wanted my true sister back. The little girl who once repaired my hurt during childhood.

After I received a harsh whipping from my father, Rena came to me and kissed me on the forehead, softly saying, "Jasmine, I love you. Don't worry. Everything is going to get better."

Then she walked away, and the angels whispered, "Remember this truth of a sister who will become long-lost to her own internal battles."

Nineteen years later, I am writing about this vivid memory. We all have a core to us which does not change. Many times, it gets buried and muddied by our interior strife and the outside world. This results in us being lost to the hardships. I do not make excuses for my sister's conduct, but I see and know her core.

Over the years, Rena's own behavior took a toll on her. She randomly called my mother crying. My mother, in turn, explained to me, "She's been like this for days and she has no clue why."

At this time, Rena began to somewhat admit something was wrong. By then, my parents no longer had health insurance. They dropped it due to the unaffordability of the high cost. I took matters into my own hands, got Rena health insurance, pretending I was her in order to do this. Later, I discovered Rena only went to the psychologist twice in six months. I terminated the policy, knowing there was no change in her, nor was she moving in that direction. Although I felt an immense amount of pain, I was aware that just because a person loses their way, does not mean you have to lose yourself, or walk away from them. Many cling to what prevents them from feeling. The presentation of the behavior we see on the surface is not personal and should not be taken that way. These distorted images are the projections of a person's own issues, turmoil, insecurities and disconnection from themselves.

When Rena was ready, I would be waiting for her on the shore. I accepted I did everything I could. I just needed to be the lighthouse, reminding her of who she really is. This valuable lesson played a part in keeping me strong and was, in itself, a testament. When a person is drowning, it is an automatic reaction for them to fight back against the person trying to aid them. Remember this when these kinds of situations arise. Know you are stepping into murky, dark waters and when attempting to help them, they are going to resist. You would better serve them and yourself, by getting out of the waters and back on dry shores. Following this, you can become the lighthouse, their pillar of strength and guiding tower of light.

Sometimes we are meant to be a catalyst for change within others. Other times, our purpose is to simply stand and be the lighthouse. When we learn the life theme, you gain strength and raw power, the good juicy kind. Instead of being in grey tones, we become jewel colored. When you come out on the other side of things, your reward will be greater than anything you could ever imagine.

The reins of reality are close, while the whispers of truth seem far away. This is the battle of the rational mind and the knowing of the soul. I had to continue following the inner knowing, and I would not be knocked down.

Surrender?

The spirit and reality worlds fusing together brought chaos to surround me. I shattered from the unrelenting obedience to follow the inner knowing. The whole situation was like falling down a spiral staircase, acquiring scratches and scars with each step. Eventually, I found myself at the bottom of the staircase, or so I thought. There was another stairwell hidden beyond anything I experienced. It started with Mansour, my cousin, asking me to go out with him for two nightly excursions, back to back. The first night, Mansour asked me to accompany him and his new love interest. He felt the presence of another woman would help her feel more comfortable. The second night involved a large gathering of familiar people and this apple of his eye.

Before stepping into one of my late night school courses, Mansour called. He asked, "Can you come?"

"Yes of course," I replied. "I assume the first night is at local bars. Where is the second night's location?"

"The hookah lounge," he responded.

I should have asked before I committed.

The inner voice interrupted, *"Though it is a place unpleasant to both your mind and soul, you must attend, there are higher purposes beyond the apparent reality."*

I asked, "Okay...if you sense awkwardness or discomfort from me, just ignore it. Remember the guy I introduced you to at the same lounge, Hisham?"

"Yes."

"We had a falling out...long story, but to quickly summarize, I wrote three lyrics that had Othman translate. Hisham pretty much ran off with them. So if he's there, you will understand the weird tension."

Without questioning, he said, "Got it."

The darkening clouds approached, and the weather outside reflected what was brewing. The spoken words from six months ago by Othman repeated compulsively in my head.

"How well do you know this guy?"

"Well enough."

How well do you know this guy?"

"Well enough."

"How well do you know this guy?"

"Well Enough."

The memory track kept playing those words over and over again, haunting the deepest recesses of my mind. Six months ago, I knew Hisham well enough. If Othman asked the same question now, what would the answer be? The possible stinging reply kept drilling in my head until I fell asleep. It was a night of raw awareness.

The sunshine of the morning eventually seeped through the window. It attempted to soothe the harsh reality. I laid in bed until I could muster up enough energy to rise and drag myself into the shower. The day's weather changed from snow in the morning to sunshine in the afternoon. Every cell of my body and soul was vibrating. It was pure organized chaos within my being. I wanted to relax, stay home, and recover from the intense experiences. I also disliked bars in general. I set out to send a message to Mansour, stating I did not want to go. I physically could not finish typing it. The magnetic force emerged with an elevated level of power. During this quarrel, I received a message from Mansour asking if I still wanted to go out. I made the strongest effort to respond no, but reluctantly said yes.

The Soul convinced the Mind to follow with obedience. I persuaded myself to go, thinking, *"Why not? It would be a much needed break from writing."*

In addition, I enjoyed the company of Mansour's friends. They were entertaining, laid back, and respectful of me.

As I drove to Mansour's house, the mind changed its assessment. It caught on to the soul's awareness of the trap that laid ahead. I did not want to go through with this anymore. I was still reassembling the fractured pieces. I latched onto the idea of escaping. However, at a red light, I could not compel my arms to maneuver the steering wheel and turn around completely. Confused, I took the opportunity to send Maya a message stating the presence of the soul force. Knowing what I was about to get into, I was unable to stop it. After acknowledging what I was in the middle of to Maya, I just let go and went with it.

The first local bar we went to provided a potential website developer for Just Beyond Dreams. Sitting on bar stools, I filled the developer in on the details. Distracted with explaining the design, I did not hear the incoming text message from Maya. When I eventually read it, I sensed her concern for me. The mind failed to remember why she was so worried and the soul stayed hushed.

After much wasted time trying to round up everyone, they started to wonder if we would even get to the second place. I remained quiet and watched. I knew we were destined to be at the downtown club. Finally, we assembled and took one vehicle. In a car with four guys, I tried to divert the conversation as they kept forgetting a lady was present. It was refreshing to be in the presence of individuals who offered the same respect I offer others. There was a mutual understanding, allowing everyone to freely be who they are. Lasting less than ten minutes, the rest of the ride involved me rolling my eyes, laughing, and putting one of them in his place for what came out of his mouth.

We arrived an hour before closing time. In the midst of socializing, three companions were lost. With one of Mansour's friends, Raphael, I stood and waited by the bar for everyone to reassemble. I looked around to a scene witnessed hundreds of times. People trying to loosen up, girls stumbling, guys chugging beer. All of a sudden, my peaceful eyes shifted to a look of despair. Raphael opened his mouth to verbalize his concern, only to close it and turn his face away as though he was told to do so. Standing there, exposed to these surroundings, brought out the feeling of making a huge mistake. A mistake on a soul level. It was paralyzing. There was no getting around it. What was once true, was now untrue. I already realized this, but now was unable to look away. It was in my face, in my mind, and in my entire being. The higher guidance was a waste, the entrustment placed in their hands was thrown away. I did not understand how such infliction could be presented after what happened just one week ago.

The raid by dark beings had begun. Like a surgeon they cut right into my core. It caused the sounds of the loud music and talking to drown out into a background hum.

This is what he was before you met him and what he is now. How did you convince yourself there was more to him? Look at what he has done to you! Is it not proof enough that your first mindful thoughts of him were true? He used you. He deceived you. There is no justification. Simply the knowledge that you are a fool! Look at what you know about him. You were fully conscious of his lifestyle so why do you deny who he truly is?! He is a con, a player, another abuser of your light. Now THAT is the truth! Open your eyes to the reality of who he is! We offer you the truth, right? So, do as you have always done. Testify to truth. You, yourself, cannot deny some of these statements because they hold validity. Is that why you are paralyzed, unable to hear your inner voice, or sense your inner knowing?

The dark voices were right. This lashing by reality brought my mind and soul to their knees, on the brink of submission.

"Give in! Give in! Give in!" they taunted, **"By the way, where are your high and mighty angels?? We know you are alone now. This is another fact we serve to you. You have nothing left!"**

This was also true. I did not just feel alone. I was alone. The angels disappeared, the divine voice vanished, and the soul force was nowhere to be found. The background hum was muted, everything went silent. I internally searched for replenishment from the divine source. I found no oasis. The deeper I went, the darker the surroundings became.

"*Has my truth, left me, too?...No. No. No. Is this a deception?!*" I screamed, as reality's whip continued to lash at my being, "*Please don't abandon me. I cannot survive without you.*"

The battle of dark and light escalated to a full-out war where resources were exhausted. Even the divine weapon of the soul's knowing, which contributed to previous victories, ceased to exist. Time had stopped. I stood completely frozen, my eyes shifted in absolute despair to the overwhelming army of darkness.

"*I have come too far! This cannot be!*"

I was in a desert solo without even the wind for company. On my knees, I scooped handfuls of white sand, and sifted for a small speck of light.

I internally cried out, "*I cannot take much more. Please help me!*"

I received no response. The soul, whom I sacrificed for, was silent. I was more alone than a person could be. Depleted of energy, I desperately rummaged through the endless stretch of grains. I went further than my own being was capable.

"*I chose not to surrender! How could this be happening??*"

Once more, no reply, and not even a speck in sight. On and on the chaos continued. I had no angels, no inner voice, nor soul force to subdue this anguish. I had only faith.

My palms shook, I screamed, "*Here it is!*" as I lifted my hands from the sand.

I snapped back to the bar atmosphere. The peace returned to my eyes. I was able to move again. That hour was the most frightful time of my life, even more so than other realistic experiences. At the age of nineteen, a semi-truck hit me on the highway. My small economy car flipped over two times across four lanes of oncoming traffic, to land back upright. Another night driving alone, I got lost in a very dangerous area of Cleveland. I paused at a stop sign to have a man jump in the passenger seat. He demanded I hand over all my things and commanded a sexual act. Both were very real, but somehow it still did not come close to the intensity of this night of surrender.

This was a war where I called out for help to the divine legions, but stood alone to face and fight the black army of darkness. The arena transformed into the deserts of time where God found me as a witness to His existence. God (Spirit, Source, Divine Being, whatever we may refer to him as) was the one who presided over the profound execution and ignited the end. Essentially, this was a rapid expansion of the soul. A transcending of it. Much, much later on

After this, I discovered what "God" truly is. God is one immense spherical soul. We, as souls, as pieces of divinity, are the small collective orbs that make up this pure globe. At this point, the realization came when stripped of everything else, all you have is a connection to the higher power. You cannot take that away, as you are a literal piece of it.

The sunflower is thought of as one large flower. However, it is hundreds of smaller flowers. The dark center is made up of disk flowers that are both male and female. The head is composed of yellow "petals" which are really individual ray flowers, and do not have gender parts. They are neutral. The yellow ray flowers' role is to attract pollinators and be aesthetically appealing, as is God's role of being a universal magnet and beautifully present. Like a sunflower and its seeds living within its disk, we are the makeup of God.

I went beyond my own essence in order to persevere. It was like a rebirth, a phoenix rising from its own ashes. The aftershock of the metamorphosis came during a phone conversation with Maya. With heavy flowing tears running down my face, I professed my disbelief of having to push myself the previous night. More than anything, I poured out my fears of failing this book. An ending seemed so far away and unattainable. I could not explain to Maya what exactly came to pass. The impact of the dark voices was so deep, they were blocked out and only impressions were left. The angels cautiously brought back the exact words of the dark voices for the purpose of writing this chapter.

Maya assured me in the face of these crushing circumstances, ultimate truth is not overruled. Ultimate truth is similar to destiny, a truth to be fulfilled which brings fulfillment. It pervades reality, while leading you to what you are meant to be. Ultimate truth is a seed growing, then unfolding into its true predestined nature; a rose is always meant to be a rose.

Maya continued, "Much will be revealed. No matter how the story ends, TRUTH is always simply itself. I believe in you."

I ignored the implications behind, 'much will be revealed.' I did not, and could not, fathom something that could compare to last night's war of surrender.

Ultimate Offering of Reality

Fate set up a stage where instincts and intents clashed behind the scenes. You are told the colors and stripes a person wears show who they are. You dress the part, you act the part, you play the part. **Who a person really is, is underneath their garments. Their intent is the driving force of their character, not what they display.** I thought I went as far as I could, but the divine was not finished.

It was the calm before the storm. Still recovering from the previous night's near surrender, I left home to go to a local café and redraw the website design. Later in the day, I received a text message from Maya. She asked how I was feeling. To sum it up, I was faithful. The magnetic-like force was on active duty once more, and a knowing surfaced. The butterflies in my stomach increased as the night drew closer. The Soul had a premonition. The Mind was in denial. With inner knowledge, and the thought why contest when failure is imminent, I chose not to challenge the magnetic force and submitted to its power.

Maya sent another text message stating undoubtedly the stage was being set for this outing with Mansour and it would be a struggle. I left the coffee shop, headed home, and rushed to get ready. Mansour and I had a miscommunication which brought worry I would have to go by myself. Yet, there was a knowing Mansour was to accompany me. Around 10:30 P.M., he finally called and said he was on his way to pick me up. Mansour also informed me that Grace would be meeting us there. I was surprised, having not seen her out for a very long time. It tugged at my heart, with reminiscence of when we used to go out every weekend and dance.

While in the car, Maya called, saying, "I had a strong thought of you…Then opened a draft of your book to this line…'Fear serves one main purpose and that is to keep us from actualizing our potential.'"

I responded, "Yes, a very true statement. The angels rejoiced when I wrote that. We are fifteen minutes away from the hookah lounge…very anxious."

"Remember those angels that held you up after the visit to the labyrinth? I will be with you supporting you in spirit," Maya replied.

The hookah lounge was the setting and all the characters were in place for the heralding storm. With Mansour by my side, I walked into the theatre not as a spectator, but as a participant. Through synchronicity, the people who came alive throughout this book, resurfaced this night. They played their roles and confirmed the power of the true source. The first face I met was Fadel, the piano player who accompanied Hisham at the coffee shop where I gave the lyrics. He completely avoided eye contact the full three hours I was there. A man of good character, he was embarrassed by what they did.

To my surprise and joy, Grace was already there. Many months passed since our paths last crossed. I felt an instant comfort, like no time elapsed. I settled next to her in the semi-circle booth and we started our chitter chatter. Thirty minutes passed when Grace noticed a large group of guys sitting at a booth, staring at us. When I turned to see what Grace was talking about, I caught them whispering and pointing at Grace and I. Almost like they were stirring the pot for the next installment.

She asked me, "Do you know those guys?"

I responded, "No, I recognize a couple of them from being around Hisham, but the rest of the group? I don't have a clue."

Grace nodded her head and started to laugh at my facial expressions. My eyes were drawn to a recognizable face, Johnny, Hisham's cousin and friend. After the first and only evening I met him, Hisham's behavior changed for the worse. Tracing the course of this change led me back to this encounter with Johnny.

When Maya and I were in her office and examined some of what I wrote for the book, the angels whispered, "Remember Hisham's cousin, Johnny. He was jealous and a manipulator in the weeks prior to your Syria journey. Please know you did bring truth and light to the area of Syria, trapped in its own fears of the unknown. We will never leave you in time of imminent need, but your journey was necessary."

With Maya, the blocks were removed, and I was surprised by this knowledge. We tapped into Johnny's jealousy. He planted the thoughts in Hisham's mind that I was "manipulative," "fake," and "sneaky." I saw a vision of Hisham sitting silent and searching his mind for his own proof of Johnny's words. Hisham discarded what he truly knew about me, believing what his cousin fed him. On the other hand, I remained, not wavering when Othman questioned Hisham's character. I belonged to the soul, Hisham belonged to the mind.

I sat in the hookah lounge booth with Grace by my side and composed a text message. The energy shifted around me, and there was a physical uneasiness. I stopped in the middle of typing, my head shot straight up to the booth parallel to us, separated by the stage. I saw a woman entering the seating are and instinctively knew this was "the Moroccan chick" whom Hisham mentioned he was going to give the lyrics. Then Hisham appeared next to her. The young woman looked a bit like Fatima. When I initially met Hisham, he hit on Fatima and now, here was a close copy of her. I found it quite amusing. He stepped into the booth, placing his arm around her. Unfortunately, I was witnessing the start of Hisham's tricky showmanship. He was like a magician and as we all know, this type of magic is all an illusion.

I was ready to go home from the moment I stepped foot into the hookah lounge. Grace was a distraction from this but after the chemistry between us dissipated, the urge to break out returned. With the mere thought of leaving this theatre, there was a physical lock-down to stay. There were divine plans and it was for good reason; the creation of this chapter. The constraints, the stage of people emerging, and the validation of past fears yielded escape mode. This in turn generated sudden discomfort of knowing. For the first time, I could not repress these bodily effects and hide them from the many people on all sides. There is a difference between anxiety or panic, and what I describe as the discomfort of knowing. It is one of the methods of communication by the universe, manifested on a physical level. A tangible level we cannot ignore as easily as our subtle intuition and instinct. I had no choice but to leave to the outdoors where I could better deal with them. I went outside, walked to the parking lot, and called Maya to help calm my nerves. As she attempted to console me, a rose bush illuminated from the dark setting. It was speckled with light-red roses against dark green foliage. The bush seized my mind's attention and soothed my soul. I picked a rose, tucked it behind my ear, and picked another one to give to Grace.

Within a few seconds, I turned to hear Grace's voice. "Where have you been?? I called you twice and texted you!"

Calmly, I replied, "Sorry, I had to get out of there and get some fresh air. I was having a hard time breathing inside. Here, I picked a rose for you. Put it in your hair."

Grace said, "Thank you. He said he didn't know you!!"

The inner voice shouted, *"That is NOT the truth of what took place!"*

"What?" I remarked, wondering who she was referring to.

"Yes! I went up to Hisham and asked him if he knew you and he said no!"

I did not say, "Why did you go up to him?" Rather, I asked, "Why would he do that? Okay, Grace. I never did anything wrong to him. I don't think he would do that."

Grace responded, "I don't know, but he just did!"

Internally, I sensed this was inaccurate. I have a tendency to not just forgive immediately but forget, until I am reminded. This was the reminder of Grace's flip side. As sweet as she is, she stirred the pot. A few months after this night, it was revealed Grace contributed to the family rumors about me. It was disheartening to know this fact. We used to be inseparable not so long ago, now I sat next to a different Grace, whom I saw maybe once every three months.

As we were walking to the patio entrance, I questioned, "Are you sure you're speaking of the right guy?"

In coordination, we spotted Hisham smoking. Grace darted her eyes at him.

"That's him with the dark jacket on!"

She identified the right person. The storm arrived with its thunder of arrows striking at my will. Now more than ever, my will was divine's will. The first arrow of his reality shot. Thoughts flashed back to my original judgments upon first meeting Hisham at the wedding. My

mind went into full throttle. More of those thoughts came crashing in. These were the reasons I did not want to pick up when he first called. It went against my mental instincts, and here they were on the big screen. What was I thinking? Why did I do what I did? Look at him. How was he worth divine involvement? The Mind punished the Soul.

I was the fool and looked like a fool in front of people who thought highly of me. The landslide of humiliation pulled me under. All I had was what was within. I honored it. I protected it. It was the same thing that brought me into this spectacle. Here was a person who I let in because of a higher power. Here was a person I spent time with because it was angelically guided. Here was a person I actually mentioned freely because of entrust in the divine compass that led me.

I stood at the edge of the booth, staring through the glass door. I wanted to be free of this whole production. I turned to see Jalal, who sat at a booth directly across from us, on the opposite end of the lounge. We were only separated by the band's stage. In the middle of this organized chaos, and to my astonishment, I watched him breeze through the same group of men that Grace and I noticed earlier. Their gabfest somehow created a territory wall where no one was to cross through. Jalal bypassed this barrier which no other person dared to do. He made it across, greeting me with his usual smile and embrace.

Jalal asked, "How's everything?"

I replied, "Good. I have been working on a book and finishing up my MBA classes. How about you?"

"Good to hear. I'm staying busy doing side jobs in construction. You're sitting at that table with all your cousins?" His eyes roamed to the booth packed with people behind me.

"Yes, but the majority of them are not my cousins."

I looked up at the performer on stage and asked, "Do you think the singer is Lebanese or Syrian?"

"I don't know. Why don't you ask Fadel?" Jalal responded.

Visibly, Jalal did not know what transpired less than two weeks ago.

I answered, "I can't…something very bad happened, Jalal…"

Immediately, his face fell. I named no names, nor spoke of any blame, but Jalal knew what his cousin was capable of and what my words entailed.

My interest in the singer was not for his nationality. After several songs, he received little enthusiasm from the crowd. At most, three people danced out of a lounge filled with over one-hundred people present. The overall mood of the crowd did not help the singer's situation, but he was patient and kept his cool. Instead of admitting defeat, he was able to eventually pull a packed crowd onto the dance floor. After Jalal and I caught up with each other some more, I thought he would walk back to his companions. I could feel and see them watching Jalal. Grace and Mansour approached the two of us. I introduced them all to each other. Jalal's eyes lit up like a Christmas tree when it was Grace's turn. He does admire the beauty of Syrian women. I heard his thoughts once again like the first night of our meeting. I wanted to say, "She is beautiful, isn't she?" but his eyes spoke enough for the both of us.

Like me, Grace loves to dance and so she initiated, "Mansour. Jasmine. Let's dance!"

I could not leave Jalal alone when he just went against the posse to greet me.

I asked, "Jalal, do you want to dance?"

Unpredictably, he said, "Yes," and followed us to an open space on the dance floor. Jalal and I found ourselves separated away from Grace and Mansour. I tried to get back through the crowd to find them, but we were blocked in.

Somehow, we got steered to the other side of the dance floor and were in view of Hisham's booth. Even though my back was turned against them, I could strongly sense the group was signaling for Jalal. Just to confirm my feelings, I turned around a couple of times to catch their hands waving in the air and aggravated faces. Jalal also took notice by looking up to see them. He returned them a clueless facial expression. Then reassured me with unspoken words that he did not care about their attempts and was enjoying my company. Though it was noticeable Hisham was extremely drunk by that point, his thoughts came clearly to me. I knew what he thought my intentions were, but he did not know I would never lower myself to his level and found no reason to do so.

The heat of the room was increasing from the bodies of the audience. The urgency of the angels arrived, "Go to the outside patio now. Timing is imperative to this occurrence."

I stared at the fogged-up glass door. I knew what awaited and it was not going to be pretty. I resisted, no more.

The angels insisted, "The truth will set you free, but you must follow through with the process to this release. We encourage you to see a truth and another testament."

If only my soul could refuse, but even my mind told me there was no turning back now. Raphael, who stood beside me during the night of surrender, became one of my dance partners for the night.

I said to him, "I'm sweating. You want to come outside with me? You need to smoke, right?"

"How lady like of you. Thanks for the information about your perspiration. Yes, let me find a lighter. I still have your phone in my pocket."

Laughing at his briefly disgusted face, I replied, "Anytime. Please don't let me forget to get it from you. Hurry up."

Raphael said, "Okay. I'm going to ask Michael to come with us."

"He smokes?"

"No, but I want to talk to him."

I led the way, coming in contact with Samir who looked distressed. Along with the rest of the crew, Samir did not acknowledge me.

While my two companions waited, I greeted him with a smile. "Hello, Samir."

Samir replied, "Jasmine, I saw you dancing. I wanted to say hi…"

"Oh, why didn't you say hello then?"

Uncomfortably, his eyes wandered away from mine. Sensing he was somewhat conflicted, I brushed his right cheek with my fingertips and relieved him of the need to answer.

"I know, Samir…I have to go…"

As a trio, we walked through the doorway and naturally into the sight of Hisham and his date. I sat outside at a metal table while my two companions discussed their friend's drama. I never realized how much men are like women. I had no clue who or what they were talking about, but it was almost like watching two women gossip. It was maybe worse in a way.

Bored with the conversation, my ear strayed to an almost squealing voice, that I soon discovered belonged to Hisham's date. It must have been like nails on a chalkboard, especially for a musician. When I turned to observe them, it appeared I was wrong as she giggled while he smiled and conversed with her. Despite this, I knew the interaction was an act. I kind of felt sorry for him. Karma has a way of entangling a person, like ivy growing on an untouched statue made of stone.

I asked, "You guys, can we go inside now?"

At that exact moment, the friend they were speaking of joined us. The situation was getting uncomfortable and these gentlemen would not stop talking. Ready to escort myself back in, I looked toward the doorway to spy another arrow of Hisham's reality coming at my will. There stood one of the goon squad members who took part in the trash talking.

Hisham raised his voice, and acted out an exaggerated handshake with him. "Hey! What's up, man?! You have my number. Give me a call and we'll hang out sometime!"

He concretely knew this was one of the men who spread the false rumors. In the midst of this showcase, Hisham wanted to upstage the other performers. Hisham viewed me as the highlight. He thought I was putting on a exhibit by coming out with two physically fit men. Unbeknown to him, my intentions were pure. A higher source than me guided me to step outside the lounge, to even be present. I now saw them standing together, a man who spoke ill of me, and Hisham, embracing like buddies. I looked up and saw everyone's eyes fixed on me. They searched for a reaction. I did not oblige. Something below the surface was happening, I was hurt. I did not think he would stoop that low, charging at my dignity. Now there was another chink in my armor. The arrow of his reality struck my will, pulsating through every millimeter of me.

I remained stoic as the shock wave immobilized my body, but I still had a voice, "I need to go inside."

Mansour's friends who accompanied me outside, followed me back in. I settled next to Grace and took refuge in her presence.

The angels spoke, "Look to the area of his occupancy."

When I followed the instruction, I saw Hisham handing his date a long-stemmed, red rose. It appeared this was not just for her, but his intent was for me to see it. Hisham knew roses meant something symbolic to me and always placed them in my hair. I currently had one positioned behind my ear, courtesy of the bush outside. Not only was my mind punishing my soul, Hisham continued working his magic tricks.

The inner voice shouted, *"HE PURPOSELY BOUGHT HER THE ROSE KNOWING YOU WOULD CATCH SIGHT OF IT."*

Grace asked, "Jasmine, what's wrong??"

I was speechless. Grace's eyes followed the path of my clouded ones.

"Jasmine, something just told me he bought the rose on purpose!"

I got external confirmation of my intuition, but I was done at this point. I did not have the energy to open my mouth and elaborate. All the arrows of embarrassment, disrespect, and powerlessness pierced my will. The will which survived six Gothic teenage years, a four-year challenge, and forty days and forty nights of unpleasant experiences. It was as if my will was lying broken, bleeding, and paralyzed on the ground. My heart went stiff. My eyes lost their glimmer. My body movements became mechanical. Yet, everything was still moving, voices speaking, commotion all around. I was surrounded by Mansour, Grace, and the three guys who were outside with me. Nobody had a clue what just happened. I watched them, telling myself it was going to be okay, but I needed to leave this burial ground.

Already thirty minutes past closing, we stood on the brim of the hardwood dance floor. I asked the companions to leave the lounge. They agreed but kept getting distracted. I made the decision to leave by myself and wait outside. I started walking toward the doorway alone. Within taking a few steps, something stopped me in my tracks, and required me to turn around. I halted at the perimeter of the stage, and followed the magnetic-like pull. At that moment, the angels came.

"Stop. Do not move. We have proof that he recognizes he was putting on a performance. Wait and see. Trust us."

I stood like a stone statue with my arms crossed over my chest. Only my eyes moved back and forth as the scene played out. On my right-hand side, ten feet away stood Hisham, talking with a group of people. On my left-hand side, also about ten feet away, was the owner of the lounge, talking to a woman, more like talking to her chest. He yelled Hisham's name three different times, but Hisham ignored him and pretended not to hear. Hisham's date decided to go over and introduce herself to the owner. She stumbled, drunkenly, to where the owner sat. She had to grab onto the table to keep from falling as she introduced herself. Again, Hisham ignored his name being called. Finally, the owner raised his voice even louder and Hisham could no longer act as if he did not hear. He knew exactly where I was and knew he would have to pass by me. He turned his back around to the owner's direction. His head immediately dropped to the ground. As he walked, he glanced at me out of the corner of his eye. It was like watching a little boy who felt he disappointed an elder. The curtain closed, and he took off his garments.

We all left in a big group, and walked to the back parking lot. Though I was lifeless sitting in Mansour's car, I saw a vision of a turquoise lagoon, surrounding my heart. The soothing water flowed through all my arteries, covering every nerve. My mind went back in time to the teenager inside who sincerely wanted to make a positive impact in the world, but felt like a failure to it and to herself. From school to home, my external environment was a reinforcement of that negative belief. One English teacher informed me I was one of the worst writers she ever saw and a lost cause for improvement. In her defense, even while absorbing her hurtful criticism, I admitted to myself this type of evaluation was not her usual behavior with students. Somehow, I knew it was a chosen obstacle to overcome in the future. I tried to find a tutor to help me with my writing skills but found little assistance.

The academics were not the only negative area of high school. While I walked to the next class, I watched the cruel behavior of other students. I saw the male athletes mocking and teasing the special education students. I wondered how they could do that and whether or not the whole world was like this. I found no answers for many years to come. My deep empathy and compassion for others seemed to be a curse. Aside from Fatima, I had no real friends during my high school years. Fatima was less than an ideal companion. She endlessly smoked cigarettes and retold the same negative stories. Sophomore year, my mother forbid me to hang out with any other friends. She allowed me to spend time with family members, adding to the physical disapproval. I came home to the never-ending feuding of parents and almost constant put-down from three sisters. The gloomy time period started at the age of fifteen and lasted seven years.

This book encapsulates a lifelong desire to help others. It rehabilitated my soul to fulfill the deeply embedded purpose. It reassured my mind of its potential. One person now stood in my path. Hisham may or may not deserve my friendship, but at this point he was an obstacle, halting the next segment from unfolding. He was a major character, unknowingly creating these chapters. My ability to conclude this portion of the book hung in the balance. This was the straw that broke the camel's back, the final arrow of reality to the will.

The next morning, I called Maya and poured out the night's theater-like events. "Maya, last night didn't go too well…He made me look like a fool…He embarrassed me in front of my family…He disrespected me. He took my name and dragged it through the mud, my reputation is ruined in this town. I have to live with it now. This is something I could never imagine someone would do, a line that should never be crossed…"

Maya stayed silent.

My words began to speak of despair, "I want to finish this book. I refuse to leave this world without fulfilling one of my ultimate purposes. After I accomplish this, I simply want peace and there is only one way I can attain it. I prided myself on my integrity and it was stolen. How could this happen? I have always served the truth. I have no faith left, and I don't want to go on…"

Faith is part of my DNA code. Scientifically, 'DNA is a molecule that transfers genetic messages to every cell of your body.' Without the strand of faith, my system would be in disorder.

Maya said, "Jasmine, you can't do that…Do you have faith in me?"

"…Yes…" I answered.

"Then let me help you regain your faith."

The wheels started turning. If I had faith in her, that meant I still had my faith. Yet, hopelessness swept me up again. "No you don't understand. I can't just get it back. It's completely broken. It was the only thing I always had no matter what I faced. I cannot survive without it. I fear I will have no light in my eyes and will walk around empty."

Concerned with what was coming out of my mouth, Maya said, desperately, "After what happened last night, I understand why you would feel this way, but you can come back from this, Jasmine!"

An epiphany from the angels came to disperse the darkness. "Your faith is not lost, although you feel martyred for truth's testament."

I explained to Maya the revelation that I did not lose my faith. My will broke, my dignity was tarnished. That was why after everything happened, during the drive home, I still sensed an immense pouring and flowing of truth through my system. Maya exhaled in confirmation and relief as she almost lost me there. I went on about two previous instances that reminded me of what just transpired with her over the phone. Once in Columbus with Grace and a second time in Cleveland with Fatima. Grace was standing in front of the mirror, putting her makeup on to go out. I laid on the bed positioned behind her. Noticing the difference in my voice, she turned from the mirror and stared at me. She said I did not look like myself and my eyes were almost all black. I told Grace to go so I could kill myself. These words caused her to instinctively realize it was not truly me speaking. She commanded the despair out and I returned.

With Fatima, we sat in my room across from each other, she told me I looked different and asked me what was wrong. Her instincts went into high gear when she looked at my eyes and saw the darkness.

She began to scream, "JASMINE! Don't do this! Snap out of it!" She moved to my side, overwhelmed with worry. She said, "Okay. I need to make you laugh." Then she showed me a video of a gym member dancing to old school hip-hop in front of her. She got me to laugh and I came back.

It is like falling down a black hole, and the light keeps getting smaller and smaller. In these times of weakness, the despair, fears, and negativity can take hold of any of us. How you respond allows it to either spiral you downwards or make you stronger. Do not give into the hopelessness, the darkness. The light is always there.

I would rather die than live without my faith, my connection to the divine, and that is what I candidly told Maya. Even the thought of losing it started my descent into a darker place. Our will is like the spine of the human body. If the spine is stripped from the body, then it definitively collapses. On that night, my will broke, the spine was dismantled. Yet, faith gave me wings to stay up.

Monday came and while I sat in my class, I focused on healing the damage done by the events of the weekend.

My attention returned to the professor's words which resonated within me, "What happens if hopes are higher?"

In unison, the Mind and Soul replied, *"The crash and despair is harder..."*

No one answered out loud, so the professor did, "The fall is harder."

This was the final course in the MBA curriculum to obtain your graduate school degree. The closing project involved teaming up with three other students and choosing a company to dissect and improve. I was placed with two men and a woman. When we met to choose the topic, my suggestions and opinions were ignored. They ended up picking a company that I instinctively knew was not a good idea. We met at various times at different locations, with the same cycle of interactions. They would discuss the breakdown and parts we need to work on, I would give my input and they would just move on. It came time to actually write the paper portion and put the presentation together. They gave me the task of giving the background information on the company. I know when I am beat and cannot change the outcome. So, I took it and thought, less work.

The presentation consisted of two segments, the group exhibition and a panel of professors cross-examination. The day of the presentation came and we all dressed in professional attire. I decided to put my hair up in a bun. Relieved I did not have to speak much, I stood silent, gave my part, and the other team members took over. Our professor asked about the company on an international level. The other team members were stumped, I stepped forth and provided the answer.

That was when the professor took her pen and lightly slammed it on the desk, and she began, "Every year I have one team that chooses this company. This is the worst company to pick and I do not understand why it happens every single year."

I knew I needed to speak up, not out of being right, it just did not sit well with me.

I said, "I did not want to do this company."

She inquired, "Jasmine, why do you think your team did not listen to you?"

There was a long pause. Everyone knew the answer. The professor, the other panel members, the team members. However, it was up to me to answer.

I replied, "Because of the way I look."

"Exactly," she proclaimed.

The room fell silent. It struck a cord. I was concerned how uncomfortable everyone else felt from the display. Next, she pointed out how I had my hair up, and how much more "professional" I looked. I walked out and immediately took my hair down, with the group behind me. It was time for the examination portion.

Many things continued to happen in every area of life. My mother sat on the couch and waited for my arrival home from school.

She immediately pounced, "You are crazy for listening to your angels! Thinking they are going to make things happen! You are crazy!!"

She never failed to release her inadequacies and launch her missiles. She wasted her time creating delusional stories of what I was up to. Sadly, I could not even tell my parents I was writing a book. They frowned upon anything outside the professions of doctor, lawyer, and corporate business.

When my mother overheard me mention the book to my youngest sister's boyfriend, my mother called me "crazy."

This was not a new phenomenon as she used every opportunity to state I was "crazy," attempting to tear me down. I would not respond and remained silent, until one day it was the right time to take a stand, and knew it would penetrate through her mind.

I told her firmly, "Mom, I want you to remove that word from your Arabic and English vocabulary. You tell me I'm crazy every chance you get. I think you have overused it."

She paused, her wheels started spinning, assessing the words.

The words weakened the attack for a few moments, my mother started laughing, "No, I'm not going to."

I insisted, "Mom, you have two options,"

I sensed she did not know the meaning, so I asked, "Do you know what options mean?"

"No," she replied.

"They are choices. You have two choices," I continued, "You can keep making this harder than it needs to be, or let everything fall into place."

Her silence was always a hopeful sign that the ego was not dominating her logic. I definitely caught her on a good day as she, once again, contemplated my words. **Truth's power illuminates the light in even the most dense, defiant, and shadowed individuals.** After all

...ese years, I have yet to be immune to her disabling words.

    The disappointment with what happened in the last few weeks cannot be understated. To a great personal extent, because it was safer, I wanted to keep these stories to myself. **Undoubtedly, it is easier to be yourself when there is no intimidation or judgment.** Who wants anyone to know they once had internalized soul demons? Who wants others to judge them for their truth? However, **a higher purpose carried me to face the difficulty of opening up, being exposed and vulnerable. Nothing within these chapters is truly about me. It is a collection of experiences provided for you to use in your own discoveries.**

Truth's Miracle and Resurrection

I could touch, but not hold the contents of what was just beyond dreams. I knew it would take a miracle to conclude this segment, and open up the next door for the ultimate ending. **Miracles seem more common to people who are committed to a certain belief system. It is not the devotion that allows this phenomenon to transpire. It is the element of faith, a type of openness, and it becomes a passageway for miracles to come through.**

We are born into this world with a seed of faith. As with any seed, it can either grow or stay dormant. Over the course of time, the mind carries in weeds, which are harmful to the faith seed. These mind weeds compete for and consume the light, overtaking the entire internal system. When we are filled with weeds, we live in a state of impairment, strength is reduced, and we are susceptible to suffering. If you nurture the faith seed and pull out the mind weeds, you become practically untouchable.

I speak not just from my experience but from many others. A co-worker, who is a single mother with two children is prime proof. She held minimal esteem for herself, had little to no support from family, encountered spousal betrayal, and battled constant financial poverty. Mind weeds would overgrow, and she would spiral into disarray. As she learned how to remove the weeds and develop the faith seed, she no longer suffered even though her circumstances heavily worsened. She could not understand how this was possible, but knew it was due to fostering the seed of faith. It radiated and made the world not just tolerable, but flourishing, both internally and externally.

A miracle is an event that is unexplainable by science, that challenges our basic human thinking. It is like we are looking through a very foggy glass. We can make out something is happening, something is in the making, but it is far too cloudy to discern. So instead, we revert back to what we can actually see, rather than staying with it until the fog clears.

I could not see where any of this was going. The MBA courses were ending in about a month with no plan ahead. All the money I saved was nearly drained. The only friend I had, Sarah, turned her back and walked away. Moreover, there was no completion in sight for this book. Although there was a deep seeded sense everything was going to work out, it was too thick and heavy. I regressed back to doubts, confusion, and questioning.

I found enough solace in the inner knowing which continued to profess the same messages: Keep going. Truth is truth, no more, no less. Faith in what cannot be seen is necessary. Live in the now. Survive the now. Time will unravel the rest for your surprise.

During a day of running errands, the magnetic-like force stepped in and took me on an amusement ride in and out of various stores. I landed at what was the ultimate destination. Standing in the retail store and debating over makeup colors, I got this notation to turned around. To my surprise, my eyes met a very familiar person from this book's past.

I removed my perplexed expression and greeted Jalal with a smile. "Hello there! What are you doing here in my neighborhood?" I asked.

Jalal responded, "I live up the street now."

"Right, Hisham told me you lived around here, but I didn't think so close…How is Hisham?"

"I'm not sure. I might see him once every two weeks. I thought you guys were good, but I see things have changed."

"Yes…after I gave him the lyrics, we stopped speaking. The last night I saw you was the last time I saw him."

Unexpectedly, Jalal remarked, "As long as I have known Hisham, since he was twenty-three years old, he's been running from the TRUTH."

Now almost ten years in the future, that has not changed for Hisham. I was baffled by where that statement came from. With all my thoughts, I managed to verbalize only one word. "What?"

Jalal replied, "Yes. Jasmine, it's like he is waiting for something."

"Waiting for what?" I inquired.

"I don't know. When I lived with him, I kept getting the feeling he was waiting. Maybe for something to happen and change his life?"

The conversation drifted to how Jalal was doing and other subjects. We said our good-byes.

Through the help of Maya, we recognized and came to understand that Hisham was a necessary component in finalizing this segment of the book. I was very much in the soul, and Hisham was very much in the mind. **This contrast was necessary to make these chapters come alive for you. His character embodied how the mind overtakes the soul, and steers all the parts. This deprives one of true magic, while trapping a person in a limbo of the mind's illusions.**

After the encounter with Jalal, the first tidal wave took me under. The obstacles of clinching this ending and resolving the higher guided connection, was more than discouraging. I was stuck in this situation against my better judgment. A major question in my mind was how did I get myself into this. Self punishment overtook my thought process. I began to accept there was no end. Everything was out of my control and in the hands of others.

Until the angels gave a little drop of reassurance and whispered, "Miracle."

I reached out to Maya. She verified and provided confirmation about the angelic message. With her certainty and clarity, I stopped the mind's frantic running thoughts. I could not give up.

I asked Maya, "What do you hear now?"

Maya replied, "Your heart beats for many. The angels have not deceived. I also heard a man's voice saying, 'Don't give in.'"

This was a spirit guide named Anthony. If you drop the "guide" portion, you are left with spirit. We have a mind, body, soul, and spirit. **The spirit is our personality and heart essence, changes from lifetime to lifetime. Taking on feminine and masculine traits, these spirit guides memorize our soul charts and assist us along the terrains of each lifetime. This is to complete our growth, and possibly evolution. We can picture spirit guides as human-figured holographs, next to our side at all times of the day. They persistently attempt to get our attention so their guidance can be discerned. If we listen quietly, the distant whisper will be heard. It is like pulling the drapes away from the window and allowing the light to shine in.**

Without any mindful awareness, this odyssey unexpectedly turned into proof of the significance of the soul. It led to many questions. Why? How? Am I dreaming? Can I wake up now? A miracle seemed like a pure fantasy, and the soul demons were at the height of their power. The heavy waste-filled waves pulled me under once again. This could not be happening. Where do I go from here? How do I overcome everything? My convictions seemed to sink to the bottom of the sea.

The angels expressed, "Go to a place where you held confidence when disappointed with a harsh reality which treated you unfairly. You will find asylum and regain the lost truth."

As a preteen, my mother's family convinced her to place the four younger children in a private Catholic school. I entered at the age of twelve, with the new classmates knowing each other since the age of five. My mother dressed me in a casual shirt with white ruffles running down the chest area and pants. This set me apart from the crowd of girls dressed in sharp collared shirts and pleated blue skirts. I was teased and sat as an outcast on the playground. Even though the conditions were unjust, I found beauty in the cathedral associated with the school.

I followed the angels' guidance and drove to this building. The cathedral was built during The Great Depression. Utilizing their minds, the parishioners strategized to take out mortgages on their homes to finance the building of this sanctuary. From there, their souls designed the structure with temple pillars imported from Sicily, painted inscriptions of the zodiac above the alter, and created exquisite stained-glass windows dominated by the color indigo blue. When divinely directed to visit, the history of the structure was not known. Yet, I

was in tuned to this historic essence. It was the replenishment and mirror I needed to surface my convictions.

Internally, I was in broken pieces glued together. It was a time of vulnerability and weakness. The demons took the opportunity. Incessant, their mayhem continued. My hands were bound to their chariot of darkness. My mind and soul dragged behind, shearing my body. I wanted this to end.

Maya begged me, "Always choose life, please! 'They need to go! Don't give up…keep your heart connected…I send light. The angels remind me to tell you to remember a distinct image on the church's wall or ceiling. It represents miracles…"

The following day, the soul demons took a mild break from imposing torment. Only to transform from pulsating thunder bolts, into sizzling molten lava. Soon after, the first miracle transpired through the assistance of Maya, alleviating the suffering. The very next day, my mother was different. This miraculously affected her, she saw me with healed eyes. This second miracle was temporary, but I savored every moment it lasted. The soul demons surfaced night before a final exam. The anxiety flooded my system.

Early winter, I visited a local bookstore. I glanced through the loaded shelves and nothing looked appealing, until right before I decided to head home. Then suddenly I was drawn to a particular book. I shrugged off even opening it due to personal feelings about the author. However, a higher urging pushed for me to read the table of contents. I came across a chapter title which, for some reason, intrigued me. Again, I resisted but that did not last long. I turned to a page and read the very short chapter. I found a mirror reflection. Every sentence flawlessly described me. Simply summarized, **a person enters into a soul agreement where they give up their free-will for the evolution of humanity.** Part of the contract includes coming face to face with dark entities. Mine happen to be soul demons. The author listed some well-known people of history who had these types of soul contracts. However, there are numerous others who remained under the radar of this world.

Before we are conceived our soul, in accordance with other souls, plans a chain of events and experiences. Within this blueprint scroll, each person "inscribes" an agreement where they profess the service they are meant to fulfill. Arrangements of time, places, and state of being are made. Just like a realistic construction contract, there are parameters such as the length of time, specific job positions, and materials. The time-span varies depending on if the lesson is learned, if the purpose was accomplished, and if the evolution developed. Everyone plays out their part, from the countless roles of different relationships such as teacher, friend, or family. The materials come together in these spiritual agreements as themes, learnings, and karmic balance rooted from unfinished business of past lives. Just as an actual contract has an ending, so do soul contracts.

On a November day, I drove to a restaurant for a class get-together to celebrate the presentations recently finalized. The angels paid a visit. The question that came months prior, returned and repeated.

Phrased and spoken in the exact same manner, the angels asked, "Do you love him?"

The first reply was, *"No. I only deeply care about him. How could I love a person who exhibited only short glimpses of his true self? Who believed and spoke false claims?"*

The angels disappeared following the answer and returned a second time. "Do you love him?"

Again, I responded with, *"I don't know. How can I love him, especially now, after what he did? How do you expect me to tell you I love him after he used and deceived?"*

On the third encounter, they inquired once more.

With more insight, I came back with, *"Maybe...But so much damage has been done. Any normal person would not forgive or understand one-third of what has happened."*

On this final class meetup, the angels asked for the fourth time, "Do you love him?"

I hesitated to speak what was now true. I answered, *"...yes...I have learned to love despite what was done. He was one of my truths, therefore a person I cannot refuse to love."*

They asked for love of truth, and the steel reality was bent, which even I thought was impermeable. To love someone when they are not lovable. **This is usually embodied in pets, they love us despite what we have done. They do not make excuses for our behavior, at the same time, they do not judge us. This gives way to healing and change.** Now, I loved during the darkest hour. However, falling in love is another story in itself, for another person, and a much brighter time. Through the love I acknowledged, this became a segue for a miracle to transpire.

Nearly two weeks later, the road to bringing resolution to this portion of the book took more turns and time than anticipated. The characters from the past came back to help. First, Maya and I came across a pointer of a significant date. It gave us a crumb of premonition but w held no expectation or attachment to it. The hinted day arrived. I knew contacting Jalal was a required step.

When I was about to take a second bite from dinner, the inner guidance presented itself, "Do not eat anymore. Save your appetite. Send Jalal a text message now."

Instead of responding with a text message, Jalal called, asking, "Did you eat yet?"

He extended an invite to a local restaurant and I obliged. He mentioned Simeon would be joining us. Simeon was an Arabic-language journalist. I encountered him previously at the coffee shop with Khalil.

As soon as I arrived at the restaurant, Simeon greeted me, "Jasmine! How are you?? How is the book?"

"I'm good. The book is close to being finished, but I am struggling with the outcome."

If only I had a camera to capture the look on their faces as if they just got ambushed.

With no comment, the subject changed. A few minutes passed on to other topics.

Unexpectedly, Simeon asked, "Jasmine what can I do to help you put an end to your book? Hisham respects and listens to me."

The angels stepped in, "Here is your opportunity and a prayer answered."

Completely without any answers, I responded, "I don't exactly know, Simeon…"

"Follow your truth," the angels requested.

I searched deep within myself, and pronounced, "I need him to first contact me on his own will."

"That is it?" Simeon replied.

"Yes."

While Simeon was confident he could convince Hisham to simply meet me, Jalal told him otherwise. He informed Simeon he knew Hisham better, as he lived with him. I voiced an agreement with Jalal, but Simeon disregarded the reality of Hisham's mannerisms.

Simeon starred at me with a solemn face for a few moments. He decided to verbalize what he was thinking and said, "Jasmine, can I ask you a question?"

"Sure."

"Do you think Hisham has any idea in his mind you want to meet him?"

"I don't know. I have not had any contact with him for almost three months now."

Simeon then implied Hisham thought I was in love and obsessed with him.

I laughed and said, "Are you serious?"

You do not communicate with someone for several months, and they think you are infatuated with them. Hisham's mind was more tangled than previously witnessed. It was simply sad. I tried to think of a source to this. Maybe he mistook my generosity? When I am driven to get or give a gift, I am compelled by something higher. I give with no strings or expectations. Material possessions and money are but a means to an end. I only value them as such.

The food arrived and the conversation took on a lighter tone. Afterward, we elected to watch a movie and continue the discussions at Jalal's new apartment. I drove to my house, picked up a movie, and then followed them back to their apartment. I gave Jalal his house warming gift which was in the back seat of my car for over six months. I had a few possessions in my purse that I requested Simeon give to Hisham. One was a gift for Hisham's birthday which passed and the other items were all the things he gave to me. The night carried on to many subjects such as religion, but always bounced back to finding an end to this writing section. I was going in circles trying to sum everything up in a way they could understand. I could not talk about this book anymore or the strange happenings. My head felt like bursting

and after several hours of trying to explain to Simeon why I needed this closure, the mission was completed.

Simeon confirmed, "Jasmine, I will do my best, but I make no promises. I do not know how it will be received,"

Two days passed, Simeon and I met at a coffee shop. He recounted what took place when he went to see Hisham.

"I handed Hisham the items and said, 'Hisham, I want you to cooperate with me. As a friend, Jasmine came to me. She explained she doesn't want anything from you. She simply needs to put an end to her story. This is a dream for her and so it is her right.' After I said this I was surprised by Hisham's reaction. He said, 'Simeon, this is a complicated issue. I don't want to offend you, but it is none of your business.' I told him, 'I am not asking to know the business. I am just delivering the message and want to help her to fulfill her dream.' Then Hisham did not say anything more and left, saying he would be back."

Five days later, Simeon and I met up again. We discussed current events going on in Syria, and the plight of the Golan Heights people. He gave me a first hand account of the impact of the Israeli government on his people. Before we parted ways, he advised me to call Hisham and leave a voice mail, stating how I simply wanted to have a conversation to finalize his role. Later that day, I took a moment, composed my thoughts, and reflected. I made the call, left the voice message, and hung up with relief. Night settled in, I was typing a text message to Maya, when I received another one which flashed Hisham's name. I went to check my inbox, the message read, "Hey Jasmine, sorry. I have been very busy. I'll call you tomorrow. Hope all is well." I took it for face value, and nothing in me felt a need to reply.

I was right there. This was the last chance for the soul demons to slow down the progress. I endured an entire night and morning of attack.

While I sat with Maya at a coffee shop, she asked, "So what happened last night?"

Weakly, I responded, "I don't really know, Maya…just sick of these demons…"

"Okay….what did you sense from the thoughts you 'heard'?" she inquired.

"I feel he wants to call but doesn't know how to approach the situation."

"Then help him."

"How can I do that?" I asked, looking for guidance.

"Open the door for him."

The only way he responds is via messaging. The communication was like a business transaction where we established time, day, and location. By chance, I had a scheduled Reiki appointment right before this meet. The day arrived, and as I laid on the Reiki bed, Maya nudged was time to head out. Before walking out the door, I paused for a minute, and affirmed being one step closer to the end. I called Hisham to inform him I lost track of time and was en route.

Upon answering my call he asked, "How are you?"

I responded, "I'm good, I will be there in three minutes."

Approaching the lounge, I called him again to tell of my eminent arrival. He explained there were no parking spots available, the area was packed with people. Somehow I overlooked it was Friday, one of their busiest nights of the week. I found him standing on the sidewalk of the corner local bar. I put the window down and we decided, because of the crowd, we would talk in the car. He insisted we use his car instead of mine so he could smoke. He climbed in my car and immediately began grumbling about how he had to rearrange his schedule in order to accommodate this meeting. Asking someone for five minutes of their time, evidently was too much. I wanted to give him a piece of my mind, but also knew I needed to bite my tongue. I parked on the side street, took a deep breath, and hopped in his vehicle.

The first thing Hisham did was say, "Here are the lyrics you gave me."

I watched him remove an item from his coat's interior pocket. He proceeded to dangle a familiar white envelope in front of me.

My eyes changed, and the only thing that came out of my mouth was, "I gave that to you."

"Yes, but you said these were your only copies and you wanted them back."

"I did say those were my only copies, but never said I wanted them back."

A deep sadness came over me, my eyes reflected it. At the same moment, a smirk came over his face from my response. I guess this was his form of payback for returning all the things he gave me. I sat in the passenger seat racking my brain to figure out what I was supposed to say or ask for this conclusion. The only thing that came to mind was a flashback of the last night I saw Hisham at the hookah lounge.

I uttered, "I have one question for you. The last time I went to the lounge, Grace came up to you and was looking for me. Did you tell her you didn't know who I was?"

"Yes," he replied, in a near robotic way.

The answer was unsettling, although it was true. At that moment, the energy shifted and the intensity increased in the car.

He began to speak again in a raised nervous voice, "BUT, let me explain. I had this feeling she purposely came up to me. She asked, Do you know Jasmine and I said, Jasmine who? Grace replied, Jasmine Jibrael. I said, No, I'm sorry. I know you have been through some shit and didn't want your family to know you're friends with a non-Christian. Any more questions?"

That is exactly what he said. His mind formulated my frantically worried cousin was up ill-intentions by asking him if he knew who I was.

I answered, "No. That was all."

Hisham then inserted, "I didn't see you that night."

Something snapped withing me, and to which my soul countered out loud, "You're a LIAR."

He had a look of shock on his face, as I was equally shocked at myself.

Hisham reacted, "You need to watch what you say before you speak. I mean, I did see you. My friend pointed you out. Did you think I was saying I didn't see you at ALL?"

I nodded my head as a response. His ego driven fabrications were reminiscent of when I first met him. I have to admit I was a bit amused by his back-pedaling.

He muttered, "Okay, okay, it was just a misunderstanding. Yes, that's all. Let's not do this again."

He was having this part of the conversation with himself. Throughout the discussion, we drove in circles, passing my car several times. I kept thinking Hisham was going to pull over, but he continued driving. The ride unexpectedly lasted thirty minutes. He finally decided to stop and pull next to my car. During the drive, I internally called out for guidance. I needed to secure and finalize his character's involvement in this book.

Now, the angels chimed in, "Speak the truth of the book. We will guide you to which of the truths need to be released. You are on the right track. Follow the truth which seems impossible, but which is possible."

I enlightened him, "You know Hisham, everything you 'heard' in your head and thought was my voice, was not your imagination but true and real…I mean everything. When you came to visit me in spirit and I told you to leave, that was real. When I walked you step-by-step to release 'them,' that was really me kneeling next to you and a friend standing behind us."

I watched his profile as he looked out the windshield. I could tell the words were sinking in. The last part referred to a night when Maya and I extracted his soul demons, the evolution with them was done for him.

"Continue, as his eyes show remembrance of these times. Speak of Johnny."

I knew this was going to cause him to lash out, but I obeyed. "I know Johnny spoke many wrong things about me."

Hisham shouted, "That's bullshit! I know I went through some things, but I don't remember them in that detail."

"Maybe one day you will," I responded.

He offered, "One day…"

"My door is open and if you need anything, I'm a phone call away. Hisham, I want you to be there in the good times of this book."

He offered, "I want to hear from you good or bad. If you ever need anything, I'm here."

As I opened the door to get out, I answered, "I don't need anything. Thank you."

Hisham said, "That's right, independent. This is a fresh page, right?"

I nodded, turned my head, opened the car door, and walked away.

It needed to end on neutral grounds, so the reflection of falsehood could be seen. I was there as a mirror for Hisham to look deeper within, to deconstruct the illusion of the version he created himself to be, and rediscover who he truly was. I became a catalyst for him to find his truth, and what he did with it afterward was his will. My role was served, my responsibility in this soul contract was complete.

We never spoke or saw each other again. It has been over eight years. **We have contracts with people, our soul makes them before entering this body. When soul contracts are done, they are done. We can choose to dwell or try to preserve the connection. However, we must let go of the mind's attempts to make sense of it, and follow the soul's predisposed mission.** The miracle happened, the block lifted, and the passageway to the rest of the book opened up. **We are programmed to believe miracles are rare, few, and far between. When the element and seed of faith is involved, miracles occur.**

As the sadness crept in, I was bombarded with memories of disappointment. Life can be symbolized by a table. It gets piled with a lot of murky, unpolished rocks and buried within, are clear shimmering crystals. In order to handle and balance the present and future, I needed an uncluttered surface on this table of life, a stable frame, and a strong foundation. I used to clear the entire table, scrapping both the dark and glistening gems. I did not stop to separate and pick out the precious jewels. I started to learn how to sift through, and not allow the scratches from the jagged, raw pieces to bother me in the process. The closer to making this book a reality, the more the darkness enveloped. This fated occurrence was an eclipse over my being, almost binding me to destiny.

Wounded Healer

The truth is always beautiful, but not necessarily pretty. Whirling around uncontrollably, were events from the past that came to haunt me. Soul contracts with people deeply connected to me, adding to the strength of this turmoil. I just wanted the world to stop, so I could breathe. What ensued in the next seven years was even more devastating than what previously came. The soul demons would lift, but all the while there were still inundations of trials. The ultimate duel of light and dark continued to spiral within this. I broke many times and equally as much, burned to nothing but ashes, repeatedly. Only having to put myself back together, and rise out of those ruins. This chaotic wind placed me in a process of supreme evolution. It was all for the greater good and the soul's mission.

The accumulation of more unusual occurrences was unabated. It slowly but surely ripped the key of faith, out of my hands on to the floor. This key is what kept me locked into divinity throughout the previous storms. I debated including this portion, but was inspired after watching a documentary that so elegantly broached the matter. I will not go into detail of what exactly happened or what caused it. I just want to impart on to you what I learned as a result. Previously, the following thoughts and feelings people expressed baffled me; "God hates me." "God has forgotten about me." "God does not exist." Until I ended up being confronted with them myself.

These statements are not true, but our minds justify them because of the unpleasant reality. **Before we arrive in this world, our soul plans and chooses the obstacles, hardships, and lessons. Our emotional capacity is taken into consideration only to an extent. The essential objective is to learn from, overcome, and conquer. We "hate" ourselves for designing such a difficult course. In actuality, we are divine, making us capable of successful fulfillment of these plans.**

"God" is all encompassing; he/she neither hates nor forsakes. Simply, we are contracted as divine beings, not necessarily as human beings. Our divine form is expansive, with no limits. Our human form is defined, with a contained shape. This does not mean we are not permitted to feeling pain, grief, or any emotion that arises. However, in seeing and knowing there is a grand plan behind it, we can navigate our way with more ease. We should release those toxic thoughts and feelings and embrace the inherent value of being here. So, accepting what we charted, forgiving ourselves, and loving ourselves beyond the turmoil is the secret key.

The aftermath of the book, mirrored the aftermath of a storm. Many things were torn apart, including the relationship with my family. The dysfunction between my mother and I became more intensified. She never stopped fueling the demons, taking any opportunity provided. I would go to my parent's house to do laundry and she would launch her verbal attacks. I would pick up her phone calls and she would start yelling. In person, over the phone, her hostility never faltered. She was an indentured servant, selling herself to the thoughts of others as the way to satisfy the ego. As time went on, I learned how toxic it was to be around my mother. This helped to prepare mentally and protect energetically, which minimized the impact.

In times of struggle with family, there is a point we reach. A threshold where we know if we continue in the same pattern, it will keep repeating. Whether we are aware of it or not, we have a choice to bring this to an end. It involves honoring one's self by establishing boundaries, letting go, or, in extreme cases, cutting ties all together. This seems simple, but it is very hard to do. We know their behavior is detrimental to themselves and everyone else, however, we think being there will help them change. We think we are the problem, we are the source of what is causing the pain. If we keep feeding into these ingrained beliefs, the cycle of dysfunction continues. **Someone brave enough, must place the spoke in the wheel.**

For a number of years, I endured my mother's berating. The strikes weakened my system. The impact lingered, leaving me more vulnerable to darkness. A breaking point was reached when I realized this was never going to stop if I kept listening, trying to get her to understand, and open her mind. I sadly, had to cut the cord. The unconditional love for my mother remains, and always will. Sometimes we have to choose what is healthy for ourselves, over what is expected of us. It is okay to let go. They are separate souls. They have their own individual paths and lessons. When you give that space, you provide an opportunity. **You take your power back and they are given their own mirror.**

The entire family grew suspicious. From quitting the career job, to not utilizing the master's in business degree to pursue a position in the corporate world, they questioned everything. I encouraged my brother to return to college, helped him with course work, and taught him how to study for exams. Now instead of trusting the guidance, he started doubting it and me. Aside from their personal rivalry, my sisters relied on me as a person who would always be there in times of need, and never turn my back on them. I no longer was dependable, and in their perception, they saw flaws. Perhaps on a deeper level my change in direction shook them. They feared the unwavering sister was not going to be there anymore. In general, my father did not hold great esteem for women. In contrast, he held a rare respect for me. I took on extra responsibility without a complaint or expectation of anything in return. I was the image of what he thought a daughter and a woman should be. All these bubbles burst when I followed this part of the path and wrote this book.

The negativity intensified in my parents' house each and every day. I yearned to move out, but financial circumstances prevented this. Sometimes our wants and desires are not conducive to what we truly need. Letting time run its course, and staying open, yields the best results. The right time and opportunity to move out presented itself, despite the fact conditions worsened.

Life can be like a tug of war, where a person's being is the center of the rope being pulled into a state of light or darkness. When you are completely in a place of light you feel your best, blissful, radiant. When you fall into the dark, you feel your worst, disharmonious, heavy. Typically, we reside in between degrees of these two states. Even though we may be propelled back and forth, there is a way to shorten and/or end this tug of war. Then there comes a time, where we must drop the rope all together.

Many times, we reject or deny the lessons we need, instead of allowing ourselves to learn them. Usually, these are the hardest and most significant ones, which our soul agreed upon before entering this body. This resistance in combination with our fears is what activates our demons. Our human nature is to steer clear of any discomfort, mind, body, or spirit. They appear in order to force us through the passageways of realization, where illusions of the mind diminish, and power of the soul thrives. When we do not persevere, they hold us back from fulfillment, purpose, and permanent peace.

Whether they are figurative or literal demons, we need to stop running, turn around, and face what needs to be faced. Just like procrastination, it remains in the back of your mind and weighs on you more than you realize. When we finally stop ignoring and do it, we get relief, no matter if what we were avoiding is good, bad, or indifferent. It is better to undertake the challenge than to suppress what will always be there and which will eventually catch up to you, one way or another. The benefits we reap are greater than the difficulties. **It is in the action of confronting our demons and moving past the obstacles, that sets us free and gives way to transformation.** In comparison to biological evolution, the soul's evolution follows the same theory. **In the advancement of the soul, our true essence becomes more resilient, expanded, and adaptive.** We gain strength, and inevitably suffer less. Do not give up. Keep pushing forward. It will pass. You have the tools, you are equipped to triumph.

Two of the main golden keys of life are freedom and true happiness. There are methods and practices to help you obtain them. Through centuries, they are tried, tested, and true. It is a PROCESS, but I have witnessed the success, in myself, and many others.

I discovered utilizing Reiki, meditation, music, and being in nature greatly assisted during times of darkness, healing, and development. Reiki is one method you can use to help quiet the storm within, and navigate through the turbulence we sometimes experience in life. **We collect 'material,' or energetic debris, that does not serve our highest good and throws our entire being into an imbalanced state.** Reiki slowly begins by utilizing the natural universal energy surrounding us and within us, to bring us into our natural state of optimal health and well-being.

Many of us have heard of meditation, there are quite a few misconceptions. It is not necessarily an involved or in-depth practice. **Overall, meditation is a simple art. It is a method of clearing and calming the mind.** This is achieved through mindfulness, intentionally being aware of your thoughts and how you apply them. As we are trying to still the mind, thoughts can appear. Just like watching clouds in the sky, you do not try to grasp them. You simply let them float by. You do not cling to thoughts, you let them dissolve. The energy exerted trying to hold thoughts back, results in giving those same thoughts more power.

Quieting the mind is like getting a full night's sleep, it rejuvenates the conscious and subconcious system. Meditation comes in many forms, where the action itself is meditative; from simple chores, tasks, driving, to sitting still and focused. Ultimately, the main goal of meditating is to remain in a state of peace, no matter what your external circumstances are. What this really means, is keeping a flowing connection between the mind and soul, at all times. When in dark places, it will prove to be invaluable.

Another way to reach a meditative state is through music. There is literally something within sound that resonates with our entire system. **Binaural beats create a frequency that works with the brain, placing it in a state of relaxation**. Other sounds emitted from instruments mimic our origin, our nature. The Native American and African drums reproduce the sound of our mother's heart beat in the womb. **Listening to certain rhythms and types of music enable calming of the most chaotic minds and nurturing of the connection to our authentic self.** Lyrics can express our feelings into words. **There is a universal mechanism that moves through music, a divine chord.**

Being in nature produces similar connectivity as music does. The same elements found in the universe, are found in us. Our physical bodies are made up of stardust. Different living greenery is not only therapeutic on a physical level such as reducing stress hormones and heart rate, but restorative to our entire well-being. It clears the mind and centers us. It is not an accident that trees produce the oxygen for breath which is the very essence of life, and we in turn produce the carbon dioxide they need to thrive. Nature sustains us, while fabricated material deprives us. The natural environment is where we feel most ourselves and free, it is part of divine creation.

These practices assisted me through the most difficult times. Implementing mantras alleviated the mental strain. Walking in nature lessoned the anxiety and dread. Receiving Reiki provided a reprieve from the suffering. The length and tribulations of this book were a full shock to my system. There was one wing broken from it all. Without Maya's support, I do not know if I could have picked myself up or made it through.

Maya said, "Stay underneath my wings, until you regain yours."

The Legacy of the Soul

As humans we seek the comfort in still waters. Yet, rapid currents push us off course, or so we think. The mind sails through uncharted territories, we try to control the destination, and at times try to return to those comfortable but stagnant waters. Our boat gets rocked about and we feel flighty with this plan. Letting go is the solution. All water connects somewhere, we are at just one small point in time. Let the soul be free to roam and set sail into the unknown. We may need to adjust our sails on occasion. Embrace the freedom, travel lightly, releasing expectations. You are being guided to your destiny when traveling in tune with the soul and beyond. Sometimes we stand in our own way, instead of trusting the process, in all its glory. Everything has its reason, purpose, or lesson. So let it be so, as it will anyway. Enjoy the journey.

I ended up crossing paths with a large cluster of individuals I have come to call "soul-connects." You are probably familiar with the term soul mates, this is only part of the foundation of what I discovered existed. It deepened my knowledge about the essence of soul connections. There are three forms of soul-connects: soul friends, soul mates, and twin souls. When you encounter one of these three connections, what transpires is a reunion of the souls and a spiritual attraction occurs. Now, being spiritually attracted to someone is not necessarily the same as sexual attraction. They are very different aspects.

Let us begin with a soul friend, which is the most ruling relationship of these three. You experience a familiarity, a deep comfort. The majority of the time you share overlapping interest, in addition to naturally exposing your true self. Regarding soul mates, these encompass the same characteristics of the soul friend. However, there is one defining difference between them; soul mates can be taken to a sexually intimate level. Taking the soul connection to a physical level can clash and complicate everything. Soul friends and soul mates can be looked at as embroidery on your quilt, threading together within your divine plan.

The final and third tier are twin souls. I approach this delicately as it is a very sensitive matter. Universally, from the beginning of time, twin souls were one sphere that split into two separate spheres. We can picture our souls as one egg-shaped compound of light, which divided into two halves. Separated, these individual cells stand complete and whole, though derived from the same makeup. This is the twin soul composition. They reflect a soul mate connection, having an immediate soul recognition and a sense of profound contentment.

However, a few elements set it apart. The level of intensity and pull of twin souls surpasses the majority of soul connections. Twin souls mirror the good, the bad, and the ugly. Even the pieces of themselves they have yet to discover. The reflections seen are not identical. Rather, they show and reveal areas we need to look at. This alignment is one of the most powerful you will share with another human being, but it does not mean you should lose yourself to it.

In this dynamic, generally there are five phases with twin soul connections: 1. Bonding/ Fusion, 2. State of Euphoria, 3. Conflict, 4. Division of the Bond/ Separation, and 5. Evolution/ Returning to Origin. With this connection, you want to do right by the other person, you want to gratify their needs, and/or you want to give generously as much as you can. If one begins sacrificing more, adapting, changing true self, the scales are tipped and the union becomes unbalanced. We must not forget about our own well-being. The idea of twin soul relationships is romanticized, but actually, the mirroring effect can cause one of the most challenging experiences in your life. Treasure your twin soul, value the experience, while honoring the destiny of the relationship in whatever state it is meant to exist.

When we share any of these types of potent connections, we almost automatically confuse or want to take it to a sexual place. More times than not, soul-connects are not meant to be physically entangled. The beginning is the heat of it, let the flame simmer down. With time, it will unfold if a sexual exchange is right. If that line is crossed, the resulting internal mess can take us under. The wisest decision is to accept the benefits of your souls coming together and being touched, not altering the makeup with physical intimacy.

Even when there is a soul connection present, we must not forget there is still a reality to consider. The mind of the other individual may conflict with their soul. Developed traits, maturity stage, past experiences, and unreached growth are things that create difficulties in allowing a thriving relationship. You cannot expect yourself to change their reality or mind. It is hard enough to change ourselves, let alone someone else.

The elevated feelings these soul connections give us, can also throw us off center. The emotional attachment can inhibit our decision-making. The magic enters when both sides are independently aligned with their own souls. That is the goal. Respecting everything in the melting pot, and allowing room for growth within soul-connects is essential. Do not give your power away to these relationships. What you truly feel is the deep desire to connect with your own soul, as we usually go through life mostly disconnected from it. The one you are really seeking is yourself. Accept the benefits of your soul being touched, and use discretion.

The soul evolution traveled from soul connections to dreams. Over several years, I encountered and learned there are special types of dreams that are deeply interactive, reaching a physical level. I came to call them "experience dreams." These active dreams involve intense life happenings which make you feel you lived it in realistic waking time. There is a significance in these dreams. Dreams can be a world to heal, experience, and explore. We can utilize them for revelations about ourselves, to release old wounds, reestablish internal power, and liberate thoughts of the mind.

At times, dreams have a particular magic to them such as prophetic, or higher awareness dreams, where your soul witnesses something your mind has not. Ultimately, they are transmitting projections of the subconscious mind and the soul's knowledge. In the dream world, the dominant conscious mind takes a step back, while your subconscious mind comes to the forefront. In the dream state, one may make new discoveries and receive inspired ideas. The massive spread of Christianity occurred due in part to a king's dream. A well-known genius formulated one of the most famous scientific theories in history, all from a dream that involved the stars. A famous musician of the century, composed an entire melody for a hit song through a dream.

The reality synched with the soul's evolution. I took the risk to leave my parents' house and moved into a small efficiency. The neighborhood was in many ways impoverished. Individuals, both very young and older, sold their bodies on the corner. I witnessed the destructive hold that drugs had over peoples' lives. The first night moving in, my car was broken into. Instinctively, I always lock the doors, yet somehow that night was different. It was done without damage or vandalization of the vehicle. There was a gold necklace hidden in the car which was going to pay for the next month's rent. A bag full of very sentimental items were stolen from the trunk. In all of this, they left two pairs of visible expensive tennis shoes behind. It was a test.

The financial risks taken and time invested for this book, propelled me to make sacrifices in order to survive. With a few hundred dollars in the bank left, I took a job cleaning peoples' homes and businesses. There were times when I felt defeated as I was on my hands and knees scrubbing toilets. Other times, I was not just cleaning, but cleansing the entire spaces energy. Throughout, I reminded myself this was temporary, it served a purpose for the time being, and it would pass. The key was to not look back and not to look too far ahead. Stay in the present moment. Life can change in the blink of an eye. Unexpected things happen, even miracles.

During this time period, I volunteered at Maya's holistic center and boutique. It started off providing extra help around the shop in relief for her mother who was unwell. I also took my first Reiki certification class to become a practitioner, with Maya as the instructor. Attempting to build a Reiki clientele base of my own with very little success, kept me at the cleaning company longer than I anticipated. However, almost a year into it, the right time to leave arrived. I was not prepared financially, nor had a steady flow of clients. The inner knowing trumped reality once again.

I continued the search for a job that would pay the bills, yet still allow time to help with the holistic center. With Maya's mother's health declining greatly, I took over her boutique shifts. In addition, on the days it was closed for business, I helped care for her and offered support for Maya. In the wake of her mother passing, I became more involved in the operations of the business. Maya randomly came across a job posting and with a feeling, forwarded the information. Ironically, the former co-worker who guided me to Maya, also personally knew and was a student of the company's owner. I got the job. This came at a crucial time when I was one month away from being destitute. Although walking a fine line between making and not making it, the opportunity came right before I fell. The monetary hardship lasted four long years and ended with the newly acquired job.

Parallel to this, Maya faced a difficult decision. Her current landlord wanted to move their headquarters into the center's current space and gave only a few months notice to leave the premises. She contemplated whether to just let go of what the family began, start a private practice in a smaller space, or search for another grander place to evolve in. After searching for weeks on her own and calling out, asking for a clear sign, an opportunity came about. There was a historic church that was abandoned, needed renovating, and extensive work. We went to see it and immediately the choice was clear. It was the sanctuary from her dream. Underneath the rubble, it was a beautiful place waiting to shine again. With love, time, and hard work, we knew it could become the right place to grow and help many people heal and discover their truth.

Determined to assist Maya in taking this huge leap, the commitment I made to the hiring company had to change. The agreed upon hours and days needed to be reduced and the job responsibilities required complete resorting. I risked the owner retracting the position. I held my breath and made the required call, expressing what I could, and could not do moving forward. The owner hesitantly accepted the terms. With a group of volunteers, we renovated the entire church building and the sanctuary of dreams came alive.

These contents embody the extreme spectrum of experiences with darkness and light. I met Maya and ultimately, she was my saving grace from the soul demons. They took my humanity, my vulnerability and twisted it into torment. I would not have made it to the end without her. Maya did not turn her back or run away, even when some of the pain was projected on her. She was the lighthouse for this book and my soul.

Staying connected to your soul is a source of power. It is the divine process of essentially discovering your true core. It is your gateway to truth. By peeling back the layers, you align with your purpose and mission. You feel whole, you gain insight, and experience life on a rich and more vibrant tone. When you are detached or living in the lower or ego self, you are deprived of all these things. Your soul is more powerful than you can comprehend. Your soul is a brilliant infinite jewel. Your soul is always present, an unwavering companion in this lifetime and many more. Its intelligence transcends anything and everything.

When connecting to the soul, being in the present moment amplifies the voltage. Your existence is more profound, along with deeper connections and relationships in all forms. Ruminating about the past or worrying about the future fades. You are awake, mindful, and grounded in your human feelings.

There is a sacred completeness in experiencing life fully, in all its presentations—even the ones we despise. It is being grounded in every aspect of life and self without detaching and trying to escape. As long as we are disconnecting from the moments we do not like, we are further away from being able to change them. It sounds counter-intuitive, but until we fully accept what is happening, we cannot move forward. By simple acceptance of where we are, we embody peace.

Frightening as it may be, letting yourself feel is beneficial. It does not mean agreeing to be in that place forever. It just means acknowledgment of being in that moment, right then and there. Yes, this is hard, but it does pass. Study yourself, know yourself, and trust yourself. Certain people are your torches. It is okay to entrust and let them light the way for a short while. It is not that we cannot trust others, it is that we cannot trust them as much as ourselves.

Life is like a puzzle. We are not incomplete, but rather, finding the pieces of who we are and fitting them into place. There is something bigger at work, a divine order to things, though many times reality demeans it. Whether we are aware or not, it is our deepest desire to be closer to divinity. Following the inner knowing, listening to your soul actualizes this. You can choose to deny and run away from your soul, but the voids within will only get bigger.

When our mind stays connected and balanced with our soul, we are then living life instead of just enduring it. Return to the times when your gut instinct was right. This evidence will reassure your mind.

Conversation between the Soul and the Mind...

The Soul asked the Mind, "Why do you torment me?"

The Mind responded, *"I have no awareness of your time or of your needs. I only feel what I am allowed to feel. I cannot expand my knowledge of divinity. I can only work around what has been defined in my logic."*

The Soul could not see any other way. It figured maybe to win the battle for truth is to instill another view in the Mind. Determined by their everlasting connection, the Soul began to cry. The Mind did not understand what was taking place, but understood that the Soul needed it.

The Mind ventured to ask, *"What is the matter, Soul? What has taken place in these last moments?"*

The Soul responded, "You cannot understand. You can only bring me turmoil. You lack even the sense to help me. You can only see what is allowed. To me you are weak, limited by yourself."

The Mind felt slight agitation and recoiled, *"You are stating very powerful words and treading on my territory. How can you call me weak? I am the one who can survive this reality of life. I am the one who can absorb knowledge of this world and use it to benefit us. I am the one under pressure to complete work, meet deadlines, and comprehend the guidelines I must follow to accomplish things."*

The Soul replied, "Exactly! You follow only what is given to you. You have no freedom. You only feel obligations. You only work to tame. You only do what is necessary. Have you ever asked yourself why can I not do more? Why can I not spread my wings and let the wind carry me?"

The Mind laughed at the Soul. *"That only leads a person to disappointment. How do you expect me to allow that to happen?"*

The Soul was happy. It achieved the purpose of allowing the Mind to admit what it clings onto.

"So," the Soul confirmed, "You do feel more than you said."

The Mind was confused.

The Soul further explained, "You finally admitted what is the underlying truth of your process. Disappointment is what limits you. All of your other components did not have that feeling included, but in the end, they are all linked to it. Your fear of disappointment is a pity. How can a person grow without taking risks in life? How can a person refuse wondrous opportunities to expand? To just restrict the self due to fear? Let me tell you something that will ultimately benefit the both of us."

Inhaling, the Soul exhaled, "Let us breathe in. Let us inspire each other to dream endlessly of truth. Let us free ourselves from the chains of this reality. Because we are eternally connected, we only grow together or apart. There is a truth instilled in every person. No matter what the reality offers, the truth of an individual will never die, be blinded from the light, or permanently submit to the harshness of reality. It can only be temporarily suppressed."

The Mind finally understood. It thought to itself, *"How could I not have seen this?"*

The Soul knew it was time. "Now you have understood. Join with me to bring this truth to life. Let us guide the person to their destiny."

The Mind agreed, but warned the Soul, *"I will follow the truth, but I cannot promise you that my makeup will not return to its original programming of fear."*

Exit

Whenever you open this book, you enter a doorway. A passageway to the truth of this world. The content is a mirror created for you. Reflect on your soul, reflect on your dreams, and reflect on that calling from within.

From the time the writing began, I was pushed into deep murky waters. Sometimes, drowning. The harder I tried to return to the surface and swim back to the comfort of the shore, the stronger the tides came crashing. In the end, I realized, as you will, we must let go and learn how to float.

I stumbled upon the message this world is in need of soul resurrection. The mind reigns, while the soul barely filters through this dense atmosphere. Many observations of people, places, and things acknowledged it. Yet, my soul convinced my mind to venture beyond this reality.

Here are two scenarios to contemplate:

    If you were to step into a car tomorrow, and a tragic accident happens that takes your life, ask yourself these questions: Who you are, at this point in time, is this how you would want to depart? What would you have changed?

    Let us pretend, we fast forward five years from now, and this future version of yourself is standing next to you. If you remained exactly the same, how would you see that? What do you think your future self would tell you to do, or change right now?

Now, take those answers and mindset, and live them. We all make mistakes. So what. What good does shame, guilt, or suffering do?

We evolve through stages, and that is exactly what occurred in creating this, leading to its greatest potential. I invite you to return to these testaments. This ending is just the beginning. From one soul to another, we will meet again.

"The hero of my tale, whom I love with all the power of my soul, whom I have tried to portray in all his beauty, who has been, is, and will be beautiful, is Truth." Tolstoy, Sevastopol.